ETHICS IN CRISIS

ETHICS *in* CRISIS

VERNON J. *Joseph* BOURKE

Professor of Philosophy
St. Louis University

THE BRUCE PUBLISHING COMPANY
MILWAUKEE

TO THE MEMORY OF
A FORMER TEACHER
MONSIGNOR GERALD B. PHELAN

ACKNOWLEDGMENTS

The author and publisher are grateful to those who have granted permission to reprint published materials: to the American Catholic Philosophical Association, for permission to reprint "Ethics and Multanimity" (*Proceedings,* 1963), "Foundations of Justice" (*Proceedings,* 1962), and "Wisdom as a Practical Virtue" (*Proceedings,* 1952); to Casa Editrice G. C. Sansoni, Firenze, for "Freedom as a Moral Virtue" from *Atti del XII Congresso Internazionale di Filosofia,* Vol. III, copyright 1960; to The Catholic University of America Press, for "Natural Law and the Contemporary Mind," from *Teaching Thomism Today,* edited by G. F. McLean, copyright 1963; to Dirrecion General de Publicaciones, Univ. de Mexico, for "Man in the Space Age," from *Memorias del XIII Congreso Internacional de Filosofia,* Vol. IV, copyright 1963; to Marquette University Press, for "Moral Problems Related to Censoring the Media of Mass Communications" from *Problems of Communication in a Pluralistic Society,* copyright 1956, and "Metaethics and Thomism," from *An Etienne Gilson Tribute,* edited by C. J. O'Neil, copyright 1959; to the National Council of Catholic Men, for "Natural Law and Human Rights," from *The Natural Law: A Return to God,* 1953; to The New American Library, Inc., and William Birmingham, for "Ethics and Contraception" from *What Modern Catholics Think About Birth Control,* edited by William Birmingham, copyright 1964; to Société Internationale pour l'Etude de la Philosophie Médiévale, for "Human Tendencies, Will, and Freedom" from *L'Homme et son destin* (Actes du premier Congrés International de Philosophie Médiévale, copyright 1958 (Editions Nauwelaerts, Louvain; Béatrice-Nauwelaerts, Paris, 1960); to the University of Buffalo Publications in Philosophy for "Material Possessions and Thomistic Ethics" from *Philosophic Thought in France and the United States,* edited by

Marvin Farber, copyright 1950; to the University of Notre Dame, *Natural Law Forum* for "Two Approaches to Natural Law" from *Natural Law Forum*, Vol. 1 (1958) and "Natural Law, Thomism, and Professor Nielsen" from *Natural Law Forum*, Vol. V (1960), copyright 1956, 1960.

FOREWORD

Forty years ago I started the study of philosophy at St. Michael's College in the University of Toronto. My first years of teaching at St. Louis University were devoted chiefly to speculative philosophy and its history, particularly in the Middle Ages. It was only about twenty years ago that I began to see that ethics was a subject badly neglected by American Catholic philosophers. Nearly all universities and colleges required some sort of courses in moral philosophy, it is true, but there was little Catholic writing in the field of ethics, and what there was seemed very largely second-rate.

My textbook (1951) developed from a feeling of frustration that grew out of long years of teaching ethics from various unsatisfactory manuals. It was a conscious effort to present the moral views of St. Thomas Aquinas in a form that would be somewhat adapted to the American scene in the twentieth century. In the ensuing years several ethics textbooks of a high quality have been written for use in Catholic schools. I like to think that I have been responsible, in a small way, for some of this increase in interest in ethics on the part of American Catholic scholars. Certainly I have tried to encourage graduate students to deal with problems in this field. Some of my students have published valuable studies in ethics.

Only recently I realized that most of my short studies written during the past fifteen years have actually centered on problems in ethics. Many of these have been published in out-of-the-way journals and in the proceedings of various associations, some of them in Europe. Other short pieces were in the form of unpublished lectures given at various places in this country and Canada. It has also been my good fortune to have served, since its inception in 1956, on the editorial board of the *Natural Law Forum,* published annually by the Notre Dame Law School. In this connection, I have had valuable contacts with professors of legal philosophy and jurisprudence from many of the great law schools in the United States. My interest in natural law (always somewhat cautious and critical) has grown much in this association. It has brought me a good deal of professional satisfaction to note how, during the years since World War II, many new national constitutions and systems of law (notably in West Germany, Italy, and Japan) have made some use of natural-law thinking. Indeed, it has caused me no little amazement to learn recently that some of the commissions entrusted with the preparation of new constitutions and legal bases for the emerging nations of Africa have used as reference works on natural law not only the well-known writings of Heinrich Rommen but also my *Ethics!*

With the foregoing in mind, I have been encouraged to bring together into one volume a selection of these articles on various topics in ethics. On the whole, they have not been altered for this edition. Some slight revisions were made where sentences contained material of merely topical or current interest. Perhaps it is useful to let people see that my views can change over the years as they have on the question of censorship. The notes have been brought up to date for the longer essays. That is why bibliographical references, in some cases, postdate the articles which they document.

Apart from the publishers whose kind permission to reprint are acknowledged elsewhere, the various editors and secretaries of learned societies who have helped to prepare many items for the press are entitled to my sincere gratitude.

VERNON J. BOURKE

CONTENTS

INTRODUCTION

Situationism: A Crisis in Ethics

There are cycles in the life of ethics, as there are in most other human activities, and we have now reached a crest of resentment for rules, laws, and normative judgments. Societal attitudes toward human behavior parallel this phenomenon (and doubtless somewhat condition ethical opinions) by their permissiveness. Particularly in the sphere of sexual morality, academic and even ecclesiastical writers now attempt theoretical and practical justifications of conduct which would have met with disapproval a generation ago. Ethics has reached a point of crisis, when many of the experts admit that their judgments are no more valid than the opinions of the man in the street.

A clear example of this development is found in an article in *Commonweal*.[1] The writer, an Episcopalian, severely criticizes the inflexible legalism of both Catholic and Protestant moral teaching and argues that there can be no absolute judgments in ethics. As he expresses the thesis of situation ethics: "nothing is inherently good or evil, except love (personal concern) and its opposite, indifference or actual malice. Anything else, no matter what it is, may be good or evil, right or wrong, according to the situation." Fletcher illustrates by discussing certain sexual problems but he insists that "Christian situationism" would take a similar view of truth-telling, business problems, national and international moral difficulties. Sexual promiscuity is not approved in general by situationists, but they claim that there could be cases (that of

[1] Joseph Fletcher, "Love Is the Only Measure," *Commonweal*, January 14, 1966, pp. 427–432; with a reply by Herbert McCabe, O.P., pp. 432–440. Fletcher is professor of Christian ethics in the Episcopal Theological School at Cambridge, Massachusetts, and the author of *Morals in Medicine* (1954) and *Situation Ethics* (1966).

the woman who seduces an enemy spy in order to entrap him and thus help her country) in which extramarital intercourse would be good. In no area do laws of conduct impose unqualified duties. This, Fletcher claims, is the ethic of Jesus, of St. Augustine ("Love with care and then what you will, do"), of Martin Luther, and of all broad-minded Christians.

The Anglican Bishop of Woolwich, John Robinson, holds similar views.[2] Christ's moral teaching was in no sense "legislative," prescribing universally right or wrong courses of action. Instead, "the Christian ethic was a radical 'ethic of the situation,' with nothing prescribed — except love."[3] If anything, Bishop Robinson takes a more permissive view of sexual behavior than Dr. Fletcher, insisting that there can be no "hard and fast Christian rule about sexual experience before marriage, since there is nothing intrinsically evil except lack of love."

There are many antecedents for situation ethics. St. Augustine did write, "Love, and do what you wish."[4] Of course, Augustine was talking about the love of God; in the immediately preceding section he quoted the portion of St. John's text that he was commenting on,[5] and plainly indicated that he was exhorting his readers to the love of God (dilectio Dei). Every reader of Augustine knows that he was a strong supporter of the teaching that some kinds of human actions are good and others evil. Indeed, two sentences prior to the famous quotation ("Love, and do what you wish") Augustine pointed out that "many things can be done which have a good species, yet do not stem from the root of love."[6] It is generally recognized that Augustine took a very positive stand on the immutability of God's law. He spoke of the "law of God which, ever abiding fixed and unshaken with Him, is tran-

2 Christian Morals Today (Philadelphia: Westminster Press, 1964); see also God, Sex, and War (Philadelphia: Westminster Press, 1965), in which D. M. MacKinnon, H. E. Root, Hugh Montefiore, and John Burnaby explore the topics on which Robinson has written.

3 See Ved Mehta's profile of Bishop Robinson, "The New Theologian," New Yorker, November 13, 20, and 27, 1965.

4 "Dilige, et quod vis fac." In Joannis Epistolam ad Parthos, tract. VII, 4, 8; PL 35, 2033. (The Latin text has no "with care" in it.)

5 1 Jn 4:9, "In hoc manifestata est dilectio Dei in nobis."

6 "Nam multa fieri possunt quae speciem habent bonam, et non procedunt de radice caritatis." In Joan. Epist. loc. cit.

scribed, so to speak, on the souls of the wise."[7] Augustine is one
of the greatest patristic sources for the theory of an immutable
eternal law.[8]

The most influential figure in the immediate background of
situationism, Dietrich Bonhoeffer, died in a Nazi prison camp in
1945. A Lutheran theologian with liberal views, Bonhoeffer was
involved in plotting the assassination of Hitler and was eventually
executed. Prior to his death he started a book on ethics in which
he argued that one is permitted to do any act (such as tyranni-
cide), provided the demands of the immediate situation justify it.[9]
Nearly all advocates of the "New Morality" appeal to Bonhoeffer
as a sort of martyr whose death has sanctified their position.

Catholic attention was directed to this "morality of the situation" by Pope Pius XII in 1952. Two papal addresses condemned
situation ethics in that year, and the immediate result was a flurry
of articles in Catholic journals explaining the theory and dealing
with its history.[10] Eberhard Grisebach had published a book in
1928 entitled *Gegenwart: eine kritische Ethik*. This work introduced the basic themes and terminology of *Situationsethik* in
Germany. Another German book on marriage was published in
1948 by Ernst Michel; it attempted to justify contraception, extramarital relations, and divorce by situational arguments dealing
with the difficulties encountered in family life. Ten years earlier
(1937), the Catholic writer, Heribert Doms, had offered a reap-
praisal of the purpose of matrimony in which the primary end
was taken to be personal union in the sex act, and two secondary
ends were proposed as fulfillment of the personalities of the spouses

---

[7] *De ordine*, II, 8, 25; the English is from the version by R. P. Russell, *Fathers
of the Church Series*, Vol. I, p. 301.

[8] Cf. A. Schubert, *Augustins Lex-aeterna-Lehre nach Inhalt und Quellen*
(BGPM 24.2) (Münster: Aschendorff, 1924).

[9] Two works of Bonhoeffer are now available in English paperbacks: *Letters
and Papers from Prison* and *Ethics* (finished by his friend Pastor Bethge), both
published (New York: Macmillan, 1965). See Mehta's third article, *New Yorker*,
November 27, 1965, for a striking evaluation of Bonhoeffer's present influence
in ethics and theology.

[10] "*De conscientia Christiana in juvenibus recte efformanda*" (radio address by
Pius XII, Vatican City, March 23, 1952); "Allocution to the World Federation of
Catholic Young Women" (in French, April 18, 1952); both printed in *Periodica*,
XLI (June–September, 1952) and in English in *Irish Ecclesiastical Record*,
LXXVII (August, 1962), pp. 137–142.

and the procreation of children.[11] Dom's book was not written in the context of situationism but it was a challenge to some of the same traditional views that were later attacked by situation ethicians.[12] Doubtless there has always been a segment of Catholic opinion reacting against legalism and the stress on absolute obligations in the moral area. In one form this movement makes the love of God and neighbor supplant rules, norms, and commands.[13]

However, situation ethics has a much broader background than these Catholic and German publications. It is actually an expression of a growing relativism in ethics and nominalism in metaphysics. Fletcher is quite aware of these aspects of his position. He contrasts the "legalists or absolutizers" with the "situationists or relativists." He points to Thomistic morality as an intrinsicism and to situationism as an extrinsicism in the tradition of William of Ockham. What this means in simple terms is that Fletcher thinks that all moral judgments consist in predicating good or bad of human actions, not because of any inherent character of the agent or of his action but solely by virtue of the surrounding conditions in which a given action is performed.

Central to such moral relativism is the denial of all reality to "natures."[14] This is not the place to debate again the problem of universals but it is well to recall that this is not merely a medieval problem. In practice, it does make a difference if you think that all human beings really share certain specifically common characteristics, or if you think that all humans are individually unique and that their class name, "human," is applied by extrinsic attribution. In the first point of view, human nature is universal and has certain intrinsic tendencies, finalities, rights, and duties; nat-

---

[11] *Vom Sinn und Zweck der Ehe* (Breslau: Ostdeutsche Verlagsanstalt, 1935); translated as *The Meaning of Marriage* by George Sayer (New York: Sheed & Ward, 1939).

[12] Cf. Antonino Poppi, "La morale di situazione. Presentazione e analisi dello sue fonti," *Miscellanea Franciscana*, 57 (1957), 3–63; condensed in English as "The Background of Situation Ethics" by F. J. Hunnefeld, *Philosophy Today*, IV (1957), pp. 266–277.

[13] A key work of this type is: Gérard Gilleman, *Le Primat de la charité en théologie morale* (Paris: Desclée de Brouwer, 1952); *The Primacy of Charity in Moral Theology* (Westminster, Md.: Newman Press, 1959). On the same theme: Albert Plé, "Thou Shalt Love," *Cross and Crown*, IV (1952), pp. 266–272.

[14] This point was well developed in Joseph Fuchs, "Situationsethik in theologischer Sicht," *Scholastik*, 27 (1952), pp. 161–183.

ural moral laws are simply the expression of these built-in properties. The second point of view makes nonsense of natural laws
of morality: it denies that common human nature in which they
might be grounded. On this nominalist assumption, moral rules
may be formulated but they are statistical, nonnormative, and
purely instrumental in value.

To review all the different movements in contemporary thought
which challenge the notion of "human nature" and consequently
of natural law would be a useless exercise. Instead, let us take a
brief look at existentialism, a kind of philosophy which has a
broad popular appeal because its exponents use novels and plays
to express their views. Existentialism is a rebellion against rationalism and the claim that there are fixed essences in reality.[15]
Despite the ever present concern of the existential thinker for the
practical life of man, few formal treatises on morality or ethics
have been produced by this movement. The leading German
existentialists have not written on ethics. In France, Georges
Gusdorf (*Traité de l'existence morale,* 1949) and Jean Nabert
(*Eléments pour une éthique,* 1962) would be possible examples.
Sartre's *Critique de la raison dialectique* (1960) was announced
as an ethical treatise but it is not that at all. Simone de Beauvoir's
Pour une morale de l'ambiguité (1947) deals with few of the usual
problems of ethics. The fact of the matter is that the broad thrust
of existentialist thinking is so relativistic that no general theory
of moral behavior is possible to it. Sartre is honest about this:
"There is no general morality — no general morality can tell me
what is to be done."[16] In effect, situationism is the ethics of existentialism.[17]

There are superficial resemblances between John Dewey's ethics
and situationism. He was very suspicious of any theory of un-

[15] As an example of this rejection of human nature, see J. Glenn Gray, "The
New Image of Man in Martin Heidegger's Philosophy" in *European Philosophy
Today,* edited by George L. Kline (Chicago: Quadrangle Books, 1965), pp. 31–58.
[16] *L'Existentialisme est un Humanisme* (Paris: Nagel, 1947), p. 47; see Walter
Kaufmann, *Existentialism from Dostoievsky to Sartre* (New York: Meridian, 1957),
p. 298, for a different English version. Sartre's *Saint Genêt, comédien et martyr*
(Paris: Gallimard, 1952), is a bitter diatribe against ethics.
[17] It is so treated in James V. McGlynn and Jules J. Toner, *Modern Ethical
Theories* (Milwaukee: Bruce, 1963); see Chapter VII: "Existentialism and
Situation Ethics," pp. 93–114.

changing natures and reacted against the rationalistic claims of
German idealism. The seventh chapter of *Reconstruction in Philosophy* (1920) surveyed the history of ethical theories and suggested
that most types of traditional ethics shared a belief in some sort
of authoritarian law based on the will of God or the acceptance
of an ordered cosmos. In place of this, Dewey taught that each
moral situation is to be approached as something unique, that its
practical meaning must be searched out in the concrete, that such
inquiry is a matter of personal reflection on the part of the individual agent.[18] Where Dewey would part company with recent
situationists is in his staunch support of the role of reflective
intelligence, social science data, and the values of democratic life,
in this moral inquiry. His common-sense adoption of a means-end
analysis, his conviction that there is a practical logic at work in
the ethical enterprise, his acceptance of certain instrumental ideals
(democracy, social welfare, the well-adjusted man) — all these set
John Dewey apart from extreme relativism. He was, however, just
as critical of absolutists and authoritarian legalism in ethics as
is any present-day situationist.

Whether situationism runs directly counter to the moral theory
associated with the name of Thomas Aquinas is worth asking.
Modern Thomistic ethics is usually classified as a natural-law
theory and regarded as supporting absolute and unchanging judgments on moral behavior.[19] Sartre, for instance, seems to see himself as engaged in some sort of crusade to free contemporary man
from the dogmatic absolutism of Catholic morality.[20] It is unfortunate that this mistaken notion of Thomism has even extended
into some Catholic circles. All that I can say is that before one
ventures to criticize an author one should read him. It was St.
Thomas who wrote:

[18] The key passage may be read in the paperback: *Reconstruction in Philosophy* (New York: Mentor, 1953), pp. 131–133.

[19] See T. E. Hill, *Contemporary Ethical Theories* (New York: Macmillan,
1950), pp. 248–256.

[20] In his chapter, "Sartre and Catholic Man," pp. 80–94, in *Jean-Paul Sartre:
The Existentialist Ethic* (Ann Arbor: University of Michigan Press, 1963), Nor-
man N. Greene perhaps overstates this opposition. Cf. Richard H. Beis, "Atheistic Existentialist Ethics: a Critique," *The Modern Schoolman*, XLII (1965),
pp. 153–177.

Any talk about general matters of morality is uncertain and variable. Still more uncertainty is found when we come down to the solution of particular cases. This study [ethics] does not fall either under art or easy exposition, because the reasons for individual actions are infinitely diversified. As a result, decision on particular cases is left to the good judgment of each person This means that one must prudently direct his attention to his own actions in order to consider what it is proper to do, at the present time, with all the particular circumstances kept in mind. It is the same as when a doctor faces a problem in medical practice, or when a pilot has a decision to make in steering a ship. Now, although this teaching may be uncertain on the universal level and not easy to explain in particular cases, yet we ought to study it so that we may offer some help to a person in the direction of his own actions.[21]

In the abstract it is possible to appraise certain broad types of activity and judge that they are suitable or unsuitable for a human being. Actions such as nourishing oneself, begetting offspring, helping other persons, and honestly communicating one's thoughts, are fitting for man. Other types of activity, such as harming oneself physically or mentally, hurting other persons, making lying promises, are not fitting. A Thomist would maintain that the discernment of these kinds of good or bad action is the work of right reasoning *(recta ratio)*. One of the key tests, *in the abstract,* on which such reasoning is based is this: Is this kind of action abusive of my person, or of the person of another human being? If it is, then it is an immoral kind of activity and, in general, should not be approved or done.

Such general rules are not to be confused with concrete, personal decisions about one's own moral problems. I may know quite clearly that it is wrong to steal, yet I may not be sure whether I am morally permitted to take this watermelon from this field under present circumstances. What the situationist does not seem to understand is the tremendous difference between a general ethical judgment ("stealing is immoral") and a wholly

[21] St. Thomas Aquinas, *Expositio in II Ethicorum,* lect. 2, n. 259; the translation by C. I. Litzinger, *Commentary on the Nicomachean Ethics* (Chicago: Regnery, 1964), Vol. I, p. 120, is not substantially different from mine. Some indications of the tentative and equivocal character of the original Aristotelian approach to the problems of ethics are provided in William E. May, "The Structure and Argument of the Nicomachean Ethics," *New Scholasticism,* XXXVI (1962), pp. 1–28.

individual decision concerning a personal problem ("I'll take this watermelon because I think I'm entitled to do so under these conditions"). Thomas Aquinas and most modern Thomists are in full agreement that one must take the whole moral situation of a proposed action into consideration when one freely decides to do or not to do something. Moral laws, rules, and norms of ethical judgment are not judgments on individual actions; they are but guidelines for the agent who wishes to make his own decisions as well as he can. St. Thomas did not think that law makes an act to be good or bad; rather, he taught that legal precepts result from the recognition that certain kinds of human activity are really appropriate to men under given conditions. The reader may judge for himself whether the following lines were written by a legalistic ethician:

> Thus, by opposition to the virtues, sins are differentiated into species according to various subject matters, for example, homicide, adultery, and theft. Nor should we say that they differ in species according to the difference of their precepts; on the contrary, the precepts are distinguished on the basis of the diversification of virtues and vices; there are legal precepts so that we may act in accord with virtue and avoid sins. Of course, if there were any sins that were such simply because they were legally prohibited, then it would be reasonable in their case for these sins to differ specifically according to a difference of their precepts.[22]

In his *Questions on Evil* St. Thomas developed a very thorough explanation of his understanding of the influence of concrete circumstances on the good or evil quality of moral activity.[23] This is, in a sense, a moral situationism which does not ask us to reject ethical laws because they fail to settle our problems automatically — but which does invite us to use the teachings of traditional ethics and the generalized experience of mankind as general directives which guide but do not determine the personal decisions that we make as moral agents. Before you decide whether

[22] St. Thomas Aquinas, *Quaestiones disputatae de malo.* II, art. 6 c. There is no complete English version of this work.

[23] *Op. cit.*, articles 5 to 8, in the second Question, constitute a treatise on the concrete conditions of human action, i.e., on moral circumstances; parts of this treatise are in English in *The Pocket Aquinas* (New York: Pocket Books, 1960), pp. 204–206.

you may take this watermelon, here and now, it is not enough to recall some law governing this kind of action. Nor is it enough to do some abstract speculating about the nature of man. Nor is it enough to focus attention on some ultimate end of human life. Practical moral decision requires a person to think of any proposed action *in its concrete context*: Who am I who may do this? What precise relation have I to other people involved? What sort of action is this in itself? What are the factors of time, place, and manner of operation which modify this proposed action? What are the predictable results to myself, to other individual persons, and to human society, of this proposed action? All such considerations are circumstantial, and situational if you wish, but they enter into the final constitution of the moral quality of any human activity.

General rules of behavior do not decide our moral problems for us. Natural law is but a set of partly known general rules. Natural law is not a blueprint for your life or mine. When I teach ethics, I can at best communicate to students some understanding of what is good or bad, in general, for human beings. I cannot, and should not, try to solve the individual and personal difficulties which come up in the lives of my students. This is what is not grasped by the advocate of situation ethics: relativity in the personal judgment of individual actions is far different from the problem of the validity of universal ethical judgments. Such misunderstanding would not be critical — except for the fact that through it many people today are becoming convinced that we can now throw out all guidelines for human conduct.

ETHICS IN CRISIS

I. ETHICS IN PROFILE

1. Metaethics and Thomism*

In recent English works it has become rather common to distinguish three levels of practical discourse: moral, ethical, and metaethical.[1] In such a division moral sentences express a man's personal attitude toward certain problems in his own life — or they may express the moral code of a given people or culture. Using Maritain's language, one might say that such a view of moral discourse is practico-practical. It is not necessarily philosophical; its basis may be accepted without much reflection.

Ethical discourse is philosophical and reflective. In ethics one solves none of one's own moral problems. Linguistically, the ethician makes statements about moral discourse. One could attempt to distinguish the moral from the ethical by saying that the moral is first-intention discourse, while the ethical is in a second-intention relation to the moral. This is neat but not adequate. These old-fashioned logical terms narrow the thing down to thinking, to cognitive experience alone, even to that special sort of cognition which is conceptualization. Both morality and ethics seem to have wider horizons than this.

If a man says, "I ought to pay my taxes today," or if he feels that "Joe shouldn't have pushed Fred off the cliff," he is on a moral level. Besides knowledge, his discourse implies a certain attitude, some affective commitment on his part.

If another man says, "The statement, 'I ought to pay my taxes today,' is the expression of a duty"— then this whole state-

* From: *An Etienne Gilson Tribute*, ed. C. J. O'Neil (Milwaukee: Marquette University Press, 1959).
[1] Cf., for instance: Paul Edwards, *The Logic of Moral Discourse* (Glencoe, Ill., 1955), pp. 19–42.

ment belongs in ethical discourse. Just as the economist, *qua* economist, makes no investments, so the ethician, as such, solves no concrete moral problems.

At this point the Thomist may be thinking that this is nothing new, that it is the traditional distinction between prudential reasoning and moral (ethical) science. There is some similarity but the likeness is not complete. For one thing, prudence suggests right reasoning and, of course, man's moral discourse is often wrong. It is useful to have some name for that generic process by which we work out our own moral problems; it is not formally ethical but it may be called moral. Elsewhere,[2] I have tried to establish a terminology to take care of a similar distinction between moral reasoning to a conclusion in which one *knows* what is to be done, and the moral reasoning which ends in an *action* which terminates the process. The former process is the *cognitive* moral syllogism; the latter is the *operative* moral syllogism. However this does not entirely take care of the difficulty. Ethics is not identifiable with any group of conclusions to the cognitive moral syllogism. Ethics moves on a different level toward generalized conclusions, while the moral syllogism (in both types) terminates in a particular conclusion. This emphasizes a point which Thomists always must face if they endeavor to understand their contemporaries in philosophy. Thomistic ethics implies a whole theory of knowledge and reality which either is not known, or is consciously rejected, by most other philosophies today. Contemporary ethics is usually nominalistic. Generalized statements are used but not as descriptive of real universals. Indeed, any philosophy nowadays which stresses the reality of essences or universals is liable to be labelled "platonism."[3] So, the distinction between moral and ethical discourse cannot be identical with the division between prudential reasoning and practical science.

In any case, the foregoing suggests the possibility of a third level of practical discourse, that of *metaethics*. There is a tendency now to initiate a horde of *meta*-disciplines. A few years ago, metaphysics was in disrepute; recently it has been imitated, nominally at least,

2 *Ethics* (New York, 1951), pp. 225–229.
3 Cf. Morton White, *Toward Reunion in Philosophy* (Cambridge, Mass: Harvard University Press, 1956), pp. 9–17, 55–56, 121–125.

by other so-called ultimate studies, *meta*-logics, *meta*-mathematics, *meta*-linguistics and so on. In a nutshell, metaethics is concerned with statements about ethics. The present article would be an example of metaethical procedure. As conducted by language analysts (who have introduced the term) metaethics is not a system of morality. The individual philosopher who works in metaethics may be a utilitarian, a hedonist, a pragmatist, possibly even a deontologist. His moral commitment, or lack thereof, may show only in the examples which he discusses. Metaethics, then, examines the groundwork and methods used in *any* type of ethics.

There is even a possibility that metaethics could be associated with Thomistic ethics. It is to the consideration of this possibility that the present paper is directed. Is there room and need for an overview of the ethics of Thomism, analogous to the sort of thing that analysists do in metaethics? I am going to suggest that there is. It matters little whether we use the name, metaethics. What is important is that we become aware of the difference between writing and thinking *about* ethics, and working out ethical problems. It is quite possible that many things discussed in metaethics have no place, for instance, in a course or textbook for undergraduate students of ethics. It is also possible that advanced research in ethics and the training of teachers of the subject require some concentrated attention to the problems of metaethics.

Let us consider, first of all, the way in which treatises of Thomistic ethics start. There is usually a chapter or so devoted to the kind of study that ethics is. Granted that it always develops that Thomistic ethics is a demonstrative science, and that its degree of precision is less than that of some other parts of philosophy or science, what are we doing in this introduction? The prolegomena to ethics are often lengthy excursions into matters involving logic, epistemology, and general theory of reality. Are these introductory notes ethics? They remind one of the program notes to a symphony concert or the effort of a painter to give his views on painting. The program notes are not music, nor is the aesthetic or technical explanation art. Likewise, to decide whether ethics is a demonstrative science is partly a logical matter. There is a theory of proof, originating in Aristotle's *Posterior Analytics*, which most Thomists use. Do they first do some ethical reasoning and then reflect on this process to see the character of what they have done? Or do they make an initial option for this sort of syllogistic and then go on to apply it to human problematics? Whatever the answer may be, it would seem a good thing to be aware of the importance of examining this initial step. A Thomist does not need to be told about the effects of a small error in the beginning.

But the problem of the character of ethical procedure is not merely a logical one. Some people see that it is also metaphysical. Yet the presuppositions of the ethician are not extensively and thoroughly treated in the usual book of Thomistic metaphysics.

The predicate "good" has been the subject of much discussion in twentieth-century ethics. Thomistic metaphysics may have a wonderful explanation of it. But where is this explanation in a modern monograph? Suppose we observe Joe helping Fred and we judge or assert that Joe's action is good. Do we mean that Joe's act is a participant in the transcendental good?[4] If so, then any act that Joe does is good. Surely we mean more than this: we are asserting that Joe's act is *morally* good, that it is distinguishable from other possible acts which could be of contrary character, morally bad. Viewed as a class, morally good acts are considered to resemble each other in a manner that is not typical of morally bad acts. Is there, then, a universal which is moral goodness? What would be the metaphysical status of such a universal? Is it some special kind of relation between the action and some real term of reference? If so, what is this term of the moral relation? Is it human nature (individually or specifically)? Is it some law? Is it some supreme being? These and like questions arise from ethics but it is doubtful that they can be wholly answered by ethics.

Similar questions are asked about the contrary moral category, evil. The quick handling of evil in the ordinary treatise of Thomistic metaphysics, saying that it is simply a privation of good, has alienated many thinkers who are impressed by other things in Thomism. If we think concretely of a bad action (as the Russian novelists do), we may come to realize that it occurs quite as posi-

4 Elizabeth Salmon, *The Good in Existential Metaphysics* (Milwaukee: Marquette University Press, 1953), pp. 64–73, adverts to the problem of the relation between transcendental good and moral good.

tively as any good one.[5] On this score, the evil act participates in transcendental good. (It is well known that some texts of St. Thomas, springing from the tradition of Pseudo-Dionysius, suggest the opposite: that the more evil an action is the less goodness and reality it has. There must be something wrong here; the logical conclusion would be that the greatest sins have the least reality! This may be good platonism, for evil does not really belong in a platonic world, but it is not good thinking.) Evil action also implies a relation to a moral scheme of reference — just as important as the relation of the good act, with just as many, or more, real consequences. Indeed there are more possibilities of evil action than of good. Where are these problems treated in metaphysics? Often they are not. Yet it is on issues such as these that a moral philosophy will find acceptance or rejection.

It is not hard to find more work for metaethics. The Thomistic ethician seems to assume that ethics is a purely cognitive discipline. He is aware that prudence has its appetitive parts (this is quite evident in St. Thomas' analysis of the three acts of prudence[6]), but he is inclined to see ethics as simply another kind of knowledge. This it may be. Some readers of Aristotle's *Nicomachean Ethics* understand ethics in this remote and almost speculative way. It is a question whether Thomistic ethics, however, should be regarded as merely a demonstrative science. Perhaps it is also a wisdom. Consideration of the end of human life is basic and formal to the ethics of Aquinas. This end is a principle for all ethical procedure; moreover, this end is God, the First Cause of all. A discipline of such a character comes very close to satisfying the Aristotelico-Thomistic definition of a wisdom.

Ethics is extremely sensitive to the personal attitudes and affective-appetitive dispositions of those who work at it. This sensitivity may be observed at many points in the development of Thomistic ethics but nowhere more definitely than in the discussion of the end of human life. Thomists say that the end is a formal

---

[5] Cf. G. Klubertanz, "The Empiricism of Thomistic Ethics," *Proceedings of American Catholic Philosophical Association*, XXXI (1957), pp. 22–23.

[6] Integral parts such as docility, promptness, decisiveness, and caution suggest affective or appetitive dispositions. For an interesting parallel view of prudence cf. Bernard Baruch, *My Own Story* (New York, 1957), Chap. VII.

principle in practical science.[7] Now one way of determining the
ultimate end of man is metaphysical. One studies the nature and
capabilities of men and concludes (in the Thomist tradition) that
there is a specific nature in all men, with a built-in finality directed
to an eventual culmination of human energies in a continued act
of knowing and loving the perfect Being. Let us agree (of course
many contemporary philosophers will not) that this reasoning is
valid. Is the finality of human nature simply that of the intellect?
Is the work of the ethician completed when he comes to an intellectual grasp of this relation of man to his end?

It is possible that the role of *right appetite* extends beyond prudential reasoning and into the area of ethics. This rectification of
human tendencies has a long history in medieval thought. It
shows very clearly in the position of St. Anselm of Canterbury. For
him, man is inclined toward goods of a lower order by the *affectio
ad commoditatem*, to higher goods by the *affectio justitiae*.[8] Pres-
cinding from the precise distinction here involved, we can see that
this teaching (with its origin in St. Augustine) recognizes basic appetitive dispositions toward the good for man. Later, St. Bonaventure represents a tradition in which synderesis disposes the will of
man to favor the moral good and to repel moral evil. This is an
inborn disposition, an aspect of right appetite. Thomas Aquinas
made synderesis a habit of the practical intellect but retained the
notion of a natural rightness of the appetite in man.[9] Maritain is
one of the few modern Thomists who have seen that this appetitive
rectification may have some repercussions in ethics.

Today there is a type of positivism which asserts that ethical
statements are noncognitive or emotive. Such a position denies
truth value to ethical judgments or utterances. Noncognitivists
claim that ethical statements cannot be true, for they are neither
tautologous (analytic), nor are they simply empirical (reducible
to sense data). Years ago, the Cambridge school tended to deny

[7] A whole study could be written on the origin and validity of this axiom: such
a study would belong in metaethics.
[8] St. Anselm, *De concordantia*, PL, 158, 536; cf. J. R. Sheets, "Justice in the
Moral Thought of St. Anselm," *The Modern Schoolman*, XXV (1948), pp. 132–139.
[9] *S.T.*, I-II, q. 57, a. 5, ad 3m: "The truth of the practical intellect depends on
conformity with right appetite." Cf. *In decem libros Ethicorum expositio* IV, lect.
4, n. 1174.

that ethical sentences could have any meaning. But it could hardly be maintained that such utterances are mere nonsense, so today they are said to have noncognitive or emotive meaning. Ethical sentences are hortatory, approbative, emotive, and persuasive in value. This concession seems to have disturbed those Thomists who have bothered to read Ayer and his friends.

However, it may be that the noncognitivists are partly right. They may have put their finger on something important. Ethical conclusions are not of the same character as those of mathematics or physics. For one thing, the ethician aspires to some practical influence on human conduct. To live well it is not necessary to know mathematics, nor is it necessary to have a formal knowledge of ethics. Yet some of the things which ethicians discuss must be faced by every man who is concerned about his own conduct. Moreover, Thomists say that ethical judgments are normative. This implies that such propositions cannot be regarded as merely abstract or speculative truths. Doubtless there is something wrong with denying all cognitive meaning to ethical sentences; this does not mean that we should ignore the affective-appetitive character of these utterances. If I say that four equals two plus two, I need not be much concerned if another man says, "So what!" But if I say that murder is bad, I may well be worried if another man says, "So what!" Thomists are perhaps too little interested in what might be called the "public relations" aspects of their ethics. They have been satisfied to erect neat "systems" but have not been much concerned with convincing their contemporaries that ethics can have consequences.

There are other reasons for regarding ethics as more than a cognitive discipline. Readers of Gilson know how he has emphasized, in the past two decades, the impossibility of young people's mastering metaphysics and a purely philosophical ethics.[10] One of his reasons goes back to Aristotle's *Nicomachean Ethics.* There we are told that the appetites of youngsters are in a turmoil, making it most difficult for them to think about profound and ultimate matters. (I prescind from the truth or falsity of Aristotle's dictum.)

[10] "Thomas Aquinas and Our Colleagues," in *A Gilson Reader,* ed. A. C. Pegis (New York: Doubleday, 1957), pp. 290–292.

The point is that Aristotle, Aquinas, and Gilson would all be classified as cognitivists in ethics — but they have all been aware of the immediate effects of appetitive dispositions and attitudes on the work of the ethician.

Such considerations bring us to recognize a certain validity in the efforts of continental ethicians to discover the relations between the *Sein* and the *Sollen,* of British thinkers to determine the meaning of the predicate, *good,* and of American ethicians to relate facts to values. The statement, "Fred is in this room," admits of empirical verification and is factual. That "Fred ought to be here," is not so obviously a factual claim. Indeed it does not express a simple fact but a very complicated judgment.

It must be admitted that Thomist ethicians often handle value judgments as if they were nothing but truths of fact. Some writers give the impression that moral values can be seen as existing realities.[11] Reflection suggests, however, that ethical statements are not as directly and immediately verifiable as factual assertions. Whatever *recta ratio* means in the thought of St. Thomas Aquinas, it is not as simple as factual experience. It involves an elaborate process of reasoning from what is given in human experience to conclusions which may be "intuited" finally, but only after an extremely complicated series of inferences. To suggest that all that an ethician has to do is to go around intuiting real values is a parody on the thought of Thomas Aquinas. Mathematical conclusions, such as the numerical value of pi, are not verifiable on inspection, or by simple sensory experience. And ethical propositions appear to be much more intricate than those of mathematics. Surely there is room for much more work here, work for the metaethician.

Very important in a demonstrative discipline are the principles, the starting points which give direction to the demonstration. We know that Thomists consider that man's practical intellect is equipped with a special habit (synderesis) enabling it to understand the starting point of all practical discourse. The formula for

11 "It is this concept of intuition, by which moral values are apprehended as objective realities, which is a distinctive feature of Thomistic moral philosophy." Gerard Esser, S.V.D., "Intuition in Thomistic Moral Philosophy," *Proceedings of the American Catholic Philosophical Association,* XXXI (1957), p. 176.

the first practical principle, so known, is: *Good should be done; evil should be avoided.*[12] It is odd that few other types of ethics advert to, or make any use of, such a first proposition. In a way, Kant seems to offer an alternative in his famous categorical imperative. Yet the Kantian maxim: *Act so that your individual action may become a universal rule of action,* is in no way equivalent to the principle of synderesis. Kant's rule endeavors to offer a way in which one can tell what acts are good. St. Thomas' rule does not; it tells you to do them when they are good, not to do them when they are evil. This indicates the futility of trying to make a rationalistic deduction of specific moral duties from the principle of synderesis.

We cannot take the "Good should be done" rule and proceed as if we were Kantian formalists. It is not an *a priori* judgment intuited before we have any sense experience. That it is known in the first stages of moral and ethical reasoning is accepted by all Thomists. However, some writers consider it to be intuited (and so, apparently, analytic), while others take it as an induction from sensory experience (and so, synthetic).[13] Many things remain to be examined here, both as to the original grasping of such a practical principle and to the eventual application of it to special problems.

There is, of course, a rather widespread impression that Thomistic ethics (in spite of its air of rational procedure and its claim of starting with sense experience) is actually a theological approbative theory.[14] Thomists are thus taken to be people who *believe* in the precepts of the Decalogue and the Sermon on the Mount, and who erect a purported system of ethics on these items of faith. There are many examples of such a religious ethic in the writings of Protestant and Jewish scholars of our day.

This is a point which requires careful metaethical considera-

12 *Questiones disputatae: De veritate,* q. 16, a. 1 and 2; S.T., I-II, q. 94, a. 2.

13 Father Esser, "Intuition in," *op. cit.,* pp. 168–175, offers an explanation closely related to A. C. Ewing's intuitionism; P. Hoenen, *Reality and Judgment according to St. Thomas* (Chicago: Regnery, 1952), pp. 164–182, has developed a theory of first principles arising from sense data.

14 For the terminology: T. E. Hill, *Contemporary Ethical Theories* (New York, 1950), pp. 97–113. Hill does not put Thomism in this classification; cf. *infra,* note 20.

tion. Does a Catholic ethician approach his problems with the same attitude that we find in ethicians without a strong religious commitment? Here we touch on a larger controversy which has engaged the attention of Gilson during much of his mature life. It is the question of the status of a Christian philosophy.[15] The difficulty is especially acute in reference to ethics. Is the Catholic committed in such a way that he cannot bring an open mind to ethical discussions? If we answer affirmatively, then how can he be classified unless as a theological approbative ethician? If we answer negatively, we must admit that leading Thomists (Gilson and Maritain, for example) and the apparent weight of papal pronouncements are against this negative. Frankness would seem a virtue in approaching this problem, for one should not assume the mantle of the philosopher while breaking the rules of the craft.

Maritain has made his position clear.[16] He thinks that the Christian ethician is consciously subordinating his ethics to theological principles. So too, Gilson's general support of the Christian philosophy theme seems to imply a similar decision regarding the Christian ethician.[17] However, both Maritain and Gilson distinguish the Christian philosopher from the Catholic theologian. And many Catholic thinkers do not accept the notion that their philosophy is subordinated to theology. They think that they are entitled to be called philosophers. They think that they are doing what Aristotle, or G. E. Moore, or C. L. Stevenson would regard as ethics. It is another unresolved question for metaethics.

The relation of Thomistic ethics to other disciplines treating human conduct needs to be studied.[18] Should the ethician try to learn something from the social sciences, from philosophies of law, from aesthetics, from the various branches of psychology? A nega-

[15] For a recent history of the controversy: Maurice Nédoncelle, *Is There a Christian Philosophy* (New York: Hawthorn, 1960).

[16] Bernard Wall (trans.), *Science and Wisdom* (New York: Scribner's, 1940), pp. 70–220.

[17] Both the *Christian Philosophy of St. Thomas Aquinas* (New York: Random House, 1956), and the *History of Christian Philosophy in the Middle Ages* (New York: Random House, 1956), treat the point in their opening pages.

[18] Cf. Herbert Johnston, "The Social and the Moral Sciences," *Catholic Educational Review*, LV (1957), nos. 7–9; offprinted in 37 pages.

tive answer would seem hasty, even obscurantist. Much information about man's conduct is offered as matters of fact or interpretation in these studies. Both Catholics and non-Catholics work in these related fields; surely their efforts are not wholly to be ignored. Of course, it is a mistake to assume that data from these disciplines are all factual, or on the same level of facticity, or of equal reliability. If a social scientist reports that 8 percent of the people in a certain state commit suicide each year, this is a first-level fact and verifiable. On the other hand, if he reports that the members of a certain tribe do, or do not, believe in a supreme being, this is not so obviously a fact. One would have to know how this information was obtained, how queries were worded, what the scientist's understanding of the term, supreme being, was. Such a report does not seem to me to record a first-order fact. Surveys of moral opinions, attitudes, and theories are often less than factual. The use of statistical techniques gives such reports the appearance of scientific data. But the gathering of the crude information, before statistical analysis, is open to much variation in precision and reliability. The ethician need not grant the same importance to second-order statistical "facts" that he would to a more immediately verifiable report. Still further removed from facticity are those generalizations and hypotheses, in the social sciences, which are called "laws" of human behavior. They are often found to be but the personal opinions of the scientist, or hangovers from long-forgotten theories which have unconsciously guided the scientist to conclusions of extremely doubtful status.[19]

What, then, is the Thomistic ethician to do with the evidence of these sciences? He can hardly incorporate it whole hog into his subject. Apart from the various degrees of facticity noted above, he will find definite conflicts between various schools of sociology, psychology, and so on. Discrimination must be exercised. Comparisons must be made. A whole new group of problems thus arises in making an appraisal of the information from these "soft" sciences. This is a task for which the ordinary ethician is ill-equipped. The

[19] Cf. Alexander Macbeath, *Experiments in Living* (London, 1952), pp. 19–21, for an amplification of this theme.

comparative study of the ethical import of the various sciences of human behavior appears as another area for the attention of the metaethician.

Legal theories provide a special difficulty. Jurisprudence has been studied for thousands of years. Various cultures, philosophies, political organizations, and ethnic groups give rise to diverse notions on the origin and nature of the laws which govern man. Thomism, for instance, is often identified with natural-law ethics.[20] But natural law means one thing to the Stoics, another thing to Thomas Aquinas, and still another to Hobbes or Rousseau. With divergent notions on the nature of reality and knowledge come different meanings for law and nature. How is the ethician, *qua* ethician, to settle the great problems which extend beyond the horizons of practical philosophy? By working at ethics, does he equip himself to accept or reject realism? Can he, by ethical procedures, discover the most reliable analysis of human nature?[21] The study of the history and meaning of legal views, and their relevance to ethics, is beyond the scope of ordinary ethics.

Thomistic ethics is a very complex position. This makes it hard to classify in a history of ethics. It is a teleological ethics. The problem of the goal, or end, of human life, led to many theories in ancient times. Following Varro, St. Augustine enumerated 288 opinions regarding the nature of man's ultimate end.[22] It may be that Thomism coincides with one of these teleological views. There is still some argument as to which one. However, in contemporary ethics teleological classification means little. Present-day philosophy has very little use for final causes. It is advisable to consider other bases for the classification of ethics.

Histories of modern ethics divide theories on the basis of their explanation of moral judgment. Hedonism, utilitarianism, deontologism, and so on, can be distinguished in this way. Should the critical factor in deciding whether to do a moral action, or not,

[20] Hill, *op. cit.*, pp. 248–253, so classifies the ethics of Thomism, giving Gilson and Maritain, among others, as examples of natural law ethicians.
[21] Thomistic ethicians divide man's higher psychic functions into two kinds: cognitive and appetitive. British ethics sticks to the threefold division of associationistic psychology: cognition, affection, and conation. The difference is very important in a theory of moral values.
[22] *City of God*, XIX, 1.

be the amount or quality of the pleasure associated with its accomplishment, or the contribution which the act makes to the public welfare, or the conformity of the act to duty as grasped by the moral agent? There are many other theories of moral judgment. Where does Thomistic ethics stand here? In stressing happiness and the personal rewards for good living, Thomism appears to some to be a eudaimonism. In its emphasis on justice, charity, and the consequences of human action, Thomistic ethics resembles social utilitarianism. And while it does not regard moral duty in the formally Kantian way, still Thomism stresses the obligatory force of conscience. Sometimes it appears that Thomists wish to embrace all the better known criteria of moral judgment and to call them their own. This does not make it easy to situate such an ethics.

A historian of philosophy might say that, at least, Thomistic ethics is an intellectualism, as opposed to a voluntarism. We have seen earlier that this is not clearly so. The notion of right appetite, the influence of moral habits, take the ethics of modern Thomism beyond the limits of moral intellectualism. Similar problems come up if we attempt to consider it a formal or a material ethics. Indeed, some of the discussions now conducted by noncognitive ethicians have a familiar ring to Thomists. There are affinities between the procedure of emotive ethicians and the old studies of voluntariness, moral predication, and the relation of technical to nontechnical language.

It is, then, hard to place Thomism in contemporary ethical classifications. Oddly, it appears to resemble evolutionary ethics in its stress on finality. Yet evolutionism looks to a nonexistent goal, while Thomistic ethics sees man's happiness as the approach to an already existing Being. This whole problem of classification is a metaethical one.

We have seen that the term, metaethics, has been coined as a name for thinking and talking about the sort of problems which arise, not *in* ethics, but *about* ethics. One of these problems has to do with the kind of study that ethics is. Another centers in the meaning of good, when used as an ethical predicate. This leads to difficulties about the status of moral evil. The respective roles of cognition and affective appetition in ethical procedure provide another such problem. The fact-value relation requires more study. More thinking and writing might be done on the starting point of Thomistic ethics. The relation of ethics to theology and the social disciplines constitutes a vast area of supraethical problematics. Last, we have noted some of the difficulties which occur in classifying Thomistic ethics. To these and similar matters metaethics is directed.

2. Ethics and Multanimity

Of recent years there has been a growing tendency, in American Catholic colleges and universities, to substitute courses in moral theology for the courses in ethics.[1] I do not feel that this is a step in the right direction and I should like to explain why I take this position.

The whole problem of the relation between theology and philosophy is, of course, tremendously complicated and I cannot attempt to deal with it in a short essay. However, a few things may be said about it before we turn our attention to the status of ethics in Catholic schools today.

First of all, there *is* some difference between working as a theologian and working as a philosopher. The theologian has a certain acquired skill (the intellectual habit of theological knowledge) in reasoning from appropriate premises to theological conclusions. His starting points, or principles, include information taken from divine revelation, from the teaching tradition of the Church (I am thinking here of the Catholic theologian), from other theologians, and so on. By and large, these beginnings seem to be what is most distinctive of the theological *habitus*. There is also a special "light of reason" which is distinctive of the theologian. It is typical of theology to explain things from the top downward: to explain earthly beings and events in terms of supramundane causes. This is simply to say that theology is theocentric: God is the focal point of theological argument. Of course, a theologian also has access to other types of knowledge which he may use in his work, to ordinary natural experience of life and reality, to the facts of history, to the various data and theories of natural science,

[1] Spellman-Aquinas Medalist's address to the American Catholic Philosophical Association (Boston, 1963), *Proceedings*, XXXVII (1963), pp. 19–32.

and to diverse philosophical arguments and theories. It is unlikely
that he will be an expert in all these fields. During the first thousand years of Christianity, some use was made by theologians of
Platonic and Neoplatonic philosophy but, apart from the teaching
on the categories, practically no theological use was made of
Aristotelian philosophy. In the second millennium of Catholic
theology, Aristotelianism came into widespread use.

In the classical sense of the word, philosophy started and became rather highly developed many centuries before there were
any Catholic theologians. Plato and Aristotle knew nothing of
Christianity, yet they are still commonly regarded as competent
practitioners of the philosopher's craft. In this classic meaning,
philosophy is also an acquired habit of the human intellect but
it is different from the habit of theology. I do not need to remind
you that the first philosophers took their start from man's natural
experiences and endeavored to reason to certain conclusions about
the ultimate nature of reality and the qualities of a good human
life. The premises of the original philosophers did not include
divine revelation. That the religious culture of the Greeks may
have somewhat influenced Plato and Aristotle, sometimes negatively
and sometimes positively, may certainly be admitted, but the pre-
Christian Greek philosophers were not theologians in the present
sense of the term.

During the Middle Ages, many thinkers worked both in the
area of theology and in that of philosophy. This was true not only
of Christians but also of Mohammedans and some Jews. St. Thomas
Aquinas was a professional theologian who knew a good deal
about philosophy. His career shows that it is possible for one
and the same person to combine, to some extent, the habit of
theological thinking with the habit of philosophical knowledge.
At times this combination made difficulties for Thomas Aquinas.
Whatever disagreement he had, around 1270, with John Peckham
and the Franciscan school, and also with Robert Kilwardby within
his own order, the basis of the controversy was a diversity of
philosophies and not of essential points of Christian belief. When
Etienne Tempier, the bishop of Paris, condemned certain teachings, in 1270 and 1277, which have been thought to include some

of the views of Thomas Aquinas, the underlying positions thus censored were philosophical ones (the question of the analysis of human understanding, of the intellectual determination of acts of volition, of the unity of substantial forms, and so on). Tempier's action, whether right or wrong, was an act of ecclesiastical discipline taken as a result of the Bishop's concern for the purity of Christian doctrine but it carried over into the area of philosophical discussion.

It is most instructive, in this connection, to recall the propositions condemned in 1277 by Robert Kilwardby, then archbishop of Canterbury. There were thirty theses: four in grammar, ten in logic, and the remaining sixteen in natural philosophy. Typical examples of the teaching forbidden at Oxford by Kilwardby are:

> that there is no active potency in matter; that when the intellective soul is introduced [into the embryo] the sensitive and vegetative souls are corrupted; that Aristotle had not discovered that the intellective soul endures after death; that the vegetative, sensitive and intellective souls are one simple form; that the living and the dead body is body in the equivocal sense, and that the dead body, as dead body, is body in a secondary sense; that matter and form are not essentially distinct; and that the intellective soul is united with prime matter in such a way that the corruption of this union leaves only prime matter.[2]

Remember that these are things which Kilwardby said could *not* be taught. The condemnation ends with the warning that any master who knowingly teaches these errors at Oxford University is thereby deposed from his office, and any bachelor who does the same may not be promoted to the magistrate and must be expelled from the university. This is philosophizing by episcopal edict. None of these so-called errors listed by Kilwardby is an essential point of Catholic doctrine. As the contemporary Archbishop of Corinth objected: "he condemned no catholic truth but rather many philosophical truths."[3] In effect, Kilwardby forbade the teaching of certain Thomistic views in the philosophy of nature.

---

[2] "Isti sunt errores condemnati a fratre R. Kilwardebi, archiepiscopo Cantuariensi . . . ," Documentum XXXIX, in *Fontes Vitae S. Thomae Aquinatis*, cura M.-H. Laurent, O.P., Saint-Maximin: *Revue Thomiste* (1937), fasc. VI, pp. 615–617.

[3] Cf. *ibid.*, p. 617, for the report by William of Ockham on Archbishop Pierre de Conflans' objection.

To my knowledge, this prohibition of Thomism at Oxford has not
been formally rescinded (as was the Paris prohibition in 1323[4]) and
so it may still technically be forbidden to teach Thomistic natural
philosophy in the archdiocese of Canterbury!

I mention this interesting example of the confusion of two different disciplines not to cause trouble for Catholic philosophers in
England, for we may take it that Kilwardby's edict has fallen into
desuetude, but to show what may happen when a person tries to
philosophize by nonphilosophic means. Kilwardby's attempt to
establish philosophical conclusions by his authority as a bishop
is a lesson in futility. Indeed, St. Thomas thought that the appeal
to authority has little place, even in the teaching of theology. In
a much-quoted statement in his fourth *Quodlibetal Question*, St.
Thomas said:

> The purpose of the magistral disputation in the schools is not
> to remove error but to instruct the listeners, so that they may
> be brought to understand the truth that is intended as an end.
> In this case, the argument should be based on reasons which in-
> vestigate the root of the truth, and which explain how the
> statement is true. Otherwise, if a master determines a question
> by means of bare authorities, the listener may become certain
> that the point is so but he will get no scientific knowledge or
> understanding — and he will go away empty-handed.[5]

I am fully aware that the "bare authorities" mentioned by St.
Thomas mean texts quoted from standard theological writers.
The point is that he was fully aware of the impropriety of using
methods of demonstration in a given science, whether theological
or philosophical, that do not belong to that discipline. Elsewhere
he points out how ridiculous it would be for a person engaged in
a learned discussion to attempt to prove his point by taking an
oath to that effect.[6] It is similarly unfitting to try to prove a philosophical conclusion by nonphilosophical means.

Now there have been many changes in both theology and philosophy since the thirteenth century. The fourteenth century saw the
development of an incipient skepticism concerning the demonstra-

---

[4] Cf. Documentum LV, in *Fontes*, VI, pp. 666–669.

[5] St. Thomas Aquinas, *Quaestiones Quodlibetales*, IV, q. 9, 18 c.

[6] *S.T.*, II-II, q. 89, a. 1 c: "derisibile enim videretur si quis in disputatione
alicujus scientiae vellet propositum per iuramentum probare."

tive character of both disciplines. William of Ockham cast doubt
on the character of theology as a demonstrative science. His main
point seems to have been that theological premises lack that
rigorous evidence which was demanded of the starting points of
demonstration in strict Aristotelian logic.[7] Moreover, Ockham is
a clear example of a theologian who continued to use philosophy
for his own purposes but who felt that philosophy has very little
truth in it. As Guelluy says, "the work of the Venerable Inceptor
appears to be that of a theologian who recognizes some value
in the work of the philosophers, but a value that is only very
relative."[8] In general, Ockham emphasized the imperfection and
uncertainty of human knowledge and doubted the capacity of the
human mind to discover what is true.[9]

Such views propounded by Christian thinkers in the fourteenth
century (and there were many others who were equally skeptical;
Ockham was not alone) had their influence on later Catholic
theology and on the course of modern philosophy. Something of
St. Thomas' optimistic confidence in the value of both disciplines
was lost. It is not difficult to see that something of the spirit of
the fourteenth century still stalks philosophy today.

During the past thirty years a few Catholic thinkers have again
begun to emphasize the inadequacy of philosophy. Unfortunately
these voices have been those of some of the leading scholars in the
field. With more and more urgency, they have suggested that both
in metaphysics and in ethics Catholic students ought to be taught
with an eye to what they already accept on faith. What is needed,
they say, is a subject which will be called Christian philosophy:
some sort of amalgam of faith and reason.

Ethics is to be "Christian Ethics": a sort of practical moral
science which will borrow some principles from theology so that
it may offer surer guidance to Catholic students. This is not to be

[7] Cf. R. Guelluy, *Philosophie et Théologie chez Guillaume d'Ockham*
(Louvain-Paris: Nauwelaerts et Vrin, 1947). Guelluy concludes (p. 364): "en
niant que notre théologie soit une science, il ne rejette pas la possibilité
d'enchaîner des syllogismes corrects, mais seulement celle d'arriver à des juge-
ments sur la verité du dogme, qui ne soient pas des actes de foi."

[8] *Ibid.*, p. 369.

[9] *Ibid.*, pp. 375–376: "on ne peut nier que le système d'Ockham conduisait
normalement à la mise en doute du principe de causalité et à un agnosticisme
assez radical."

moral theology but an ethics that is subalternated to theology, in the sense that engineering, for instance, is indebted to pure mathematics for some of the information which the engineer uses without himself establishing, discovering, or even thoroughly understanding it. A purely philosophical ethics is not to be attempted because such a subject would be an abstraction, out of touch with the existential condition of man. Philosophy by itself knows nothing of the fall of man or original sin; philosophy lacks an adequate knowledge of the ultimate end of man. So the thing to do, for those who teach moral science, is to utilize the sure foundations of Christian belief concerning man's origin and destiny. According to this program, we must philosophize within the faith.

My reaction to this proposal is that it is a good way to ensure that Catholic philosophers will live within their own ghetto. It cuts off intellectual communication with the life and course of philosophy in general. Surely one cannot think that this proposal is in keeping with the spirit of Thomas Aquinas who read the philosophic works of pagans, Jews, and Mohammedans and was ready to meet Aristotle, Maimonides, and Averroës on their own grounds.

At the same time that this proposal to modify the character of ethics has developed, some curriculum planners and administrators have picked up the idea that there is something wrong with philosophy and they have used this judgment to change the status of speculative and practical philosophy in Catholic colleges and universities in the United States. In some institutions, only the non-Catholic students are offered the opportunity to study philosophy. There has always been some latent suspicion of philosophy on the part of some Catholic academicians. Now that a few philosophical spokesmen have intimated that a purely natural philosophy is not all that it should be, other voices are heard saying: "We always knew that there was nothing to philosophy; let us replace it with something else." In the area of moral science, the suggestion is to teach moral theology as a substitute for ethics.

Since St. Thomas can hardly be accused of not granting theology its proper role in Christian education, a brief look at what he has said on this matter, in the very first article of the *Summa of*

Theology, should be helpful.[10] The question that Aquinas asks is: whether it is necessary to have another discipline besides the philosophical ones. Note what is implied: philosophy exists but has theology a right to exist as a study? Of course theology is a legitimate study, St. Thomas replies. The first sentence of his answer puts the thing very clearly: "it was necessary for human salvation that there be a teaching in accord with divine revelation, apart from the philosophical disciplines which are studied by human reason." He proceeds to explain that man is ordered to God as an end exceeding the grasp of reason, that man needs to know his end in order to direct his intentions and actions to God, and that divine revelation was necessary to provide this knowledge to all men. Let us note his next words precisely:

> For the truth about God as investigated by human reason comes to man in few cases, and after a long time, and mixed with many errors: yet the entire salvation of man, which is in God, depends on a knowledge of this truth.

These lines have lately been used to cast doubt on the whole enterprise of philosophy. Isn't St. Thomas saying here that philosophy is a failure, that it needs theology to give it the truth? I think not.

What St. Thomas is saying is precisely this: (1) only a minority of people are capable of doing original work in philosophy; (2) it takes a long time for philosophers to discover the truth about God; (3) what truth they do discover is imperfect and mixed with errors. This does not mean that Aquinas thought that philosophy was to be abandoned or converted into some hybrid discipline. Indeed, after writing these lines, St. Thomas devoted some of the best years of his life in that very active period in the late 1260's and early 1270's to profound and lengthy explanations of the philosophical works of Aristotle. St. Thomas Aquinas was not selling philosophy down the river; nor was he saying that philosophers should work in the light of divine revelation. He knew full well that philosophy is not theology. He presented a perfectly reasonable argument for his own professional work: most men are unable to study philosophy; all men need to know something

[10] *S.T.,* I, q. 1, a. 1; Ottawa edition, Vol. I, 2 a-b.

about God in order to be saved; so another sort of instruction must be provided for them, one which is different from philosophy and which he calls *sacra doctrina*. (Incidentally, I think it would be preferable today to call the professional instruction that is used in the training of priests by some other name than that which is used to designate the religious instruction of lay students in Catholic schools. Priests should study and know theology; non-professionals should study Christian doctrine. But that is apart from my subject.)

The other point that St. Thomas makes in his first article is directly pertinent here. He insists that philosophy is a generically distinct study from theology. In a recent issue of *The New Scholasticism*,[11] there is a brief notice of a little book by Wilhelm Keilbach which says: "The book subscribes to the fairly recent definition of philosophy as the science of all things in their ultimate causes by the light of unaided reason." Well, I don't know what "fairly recent" means, here, but I think this definition is roughly the same as the meaning that Aquinas gives to philosophy in his first article. The second objection points out that philosophy treats "of all beings . . . even of God," and adds that one part of philosophy is called *theologia*; hence no other teaching than philosophy is needed. Clearly St. Thomas has to reply to this rather sharp difficulty. Here is his complete answer:

> A different cognitive principle (*diversa ratio cognoscibilis*) produces a differentiation among the sciences. For, the astronomer and the natural philosopher may demonstrate the same conclusion: for instance, that the earth is spherical. But the astronomer does it by a mathematical method, by one that abstracts from matter, while the natural philosopher does it by means of a consideration based on matter. Hence, nothing prevents treatment of the same things by philosophy, according as they are knowable by the light of natural reason, and by another science, inasmuch as they are known by the light of divine revelation. Hence, the theology that belongs under sacred doctrine differs generically (*differt secundum genus*) from that theology which is offered as a part of philosophy.[12]

This makes sense, I think. St. Thomas has the difficulty well

[11] Vol. XXXVI (1962), p. 412.
[12] *S.T.*, I, q. 1, a. 1, ad 2: the translation is from *The Pocket Aquinas* (New York, 1960), pp. 298–299, where the full context may be read.

under control. Philosophy is one discipline; sacred theology is a generically different one. There is no question that philosophy is a legitimate enterprise; nor does St. Thomas suggest that it needs to be redone under the wing of theology. That would destroy their generic distinction as knowledges and would result in confusion.

It is true, in the next article,[13] St. Thomas proceeds to explain how one kind of knowledge may depend on a higher knowledge for some of its principles, as optics does on geometry and musical theory on arithmetic. Does he then say that we should have a Christian philosophy that is subordinated to Christian theology? Not at all. In fact, St. Thomas never talks about Christian philosophy. What he does say is that *sacra doctrina* is subordinated to the kind of knowledge that God and the blessed in heaven possess. He could have said that philosophy should be put under theology had he thought so (the whole problem of their interrelations was obviously in his mind in the first article), but St. Thomas has said nothing about philosophy as subordinated to any other discipline.

What about ethics, then? Its purpose is not to teach all men what they must know in order to be saved. Ethics aims at a reflective examination of what is good or bad in human activity here on earth, in the light of ordinary human experience and reasoning. Such knowledge is practical and useful, even though ethics cannot solve all the problems of human life. Neither ethics nor moral theology is a substitute for personal prudence. Natural goodness has a meaning — if not, why insist on the importance of natural moral law? Moral theology brings a new dimension to the study of morality but it presupposes that its students possess a good knowledge of natural morality. The best way for them to achieve this is through the study of ethics. Recall that it was a commission of Dominican scholars (including St. Thomas and St. Albert) who decided that students in the Order of Preachers should study liberal arts, mainly philosophy, before beginning their study of theology.[14]

Let me remind you of two things about Aristotle's ethics in the thirteenth century. The first is that we know of no ecclesiastical

[13] *S.T.*, I, q. 1, a. 2 c; Ottawa edition, Vol. I, 3 a.

[14] For the provisions of the General Chapter of Valenciennes, June, 1259, cf. *Fontes*, VI, pp. 559–562.

prohibition of the teaching of the *Nicomachean Ethics* during this whole century.[15] Oddly enough, Christian scholars and authorities seemed to feel that there was no need to censor or restrict the academic use of this admittedly pagan treatise on the good life. The second point is not easy to establish and I shall not try to document it here. I simply refer you to the historical research by Dom O. Lottin on the psychological and moral teachings of the twelfth and thirteenth centuries.[16] The point is this: as Catholic moral theology developed in these centuries into a well-organized discipline, it borrowed much of its method, fundamental data, arguments, and even some conclusions from the *Nicomachean Ethics* of Aristotle.[17] There is no question, historically, as to which science is the debtor. Aristotle's ethics owes nothing to Christian moral theology but the Latin theologians who produced the various treatises in moral theology are continually indebted to the *Nicomachean Ethics*. Much of the psychology used by moral theologians is adapted from Aristotle. The powers of the human soul, the theory of habits and virtues and vices, the remarkable analysis of the voluntary, the teleological ordering of man to his ultimate end — this whole fabric was lifted from Aristotle. If you doubt this, read St. Augustine (who did know Aristotle's *Ethics*) and compare his discussions of moral questions with those of the moral theologians of the thirteenth century.

In view of these historical facts, it is odd to find people today speaking and writing as if moral theology were an entirely independent phenomenon from ethics. When Greek ethics was absorbed into Christian moral teaching, it was indeed modified and raised to a higher level of perfection. The resultant Christian ethics is moral theology.

However, moral theology could not have borrowed from ethics in the thirteenth century if there had not been at that time an already constituted discipline of moral philosophy. The question now arises: Does moral theology need ethics today? I think it does.

15 Cf. Martin Grabmann, *I divieti ecclesiastici di Aristotile sotto Innocenzo III e Gregorio IX* (Roma: Saler, 1941).

16 *Psychologie et morale aux XIIme et XIIIme siècles* (Louvain-Gembloux: J. Duculot, 1942–1954), 5 vols.

17 For a few indications of St. Thomas' debt, cf.: V. J. Bourke, *St. Thomas and the Greek Moralists* (Milwaukee: Marquette University Press, 1947).

I think some Catholic philosophers should recognize their duty as scholars to work in the field of philosophical ethics. That is the main thought that I should like to leave with you.

Both philosophy and theology are habits which can be acquired by human intellects. Unless they are understood by living men in each generation, philosophy and theology not only make no progress: they die. There is no science or knowledge in books. Understanding is the function and possession of living intellects only. What Aristotle or Thomas Aquinas understood is of no benefit to you, unless you also understand it. Let us have but one generation of Catholic scholarship that is ignorant of the resources of ethics and we will have suffered an irreparable loss in learning, in the Church and in the world.

But cannot moral theologians be the people who will know ethics and keep it going? I think not. If the ethician works on the level of ordinary human experience as interpreted by unaided reason, and if the moral theologian uses divine revelation in the light of his faith, then it is quite unlikely that one and the same man can do both jobs. I grant that some genius may occasionally come along who can shift gears from the level of ethics to that of moral theology and then revert, when necessary, to the method of ethics. I have to grant this, because St. Thomas did it. Read the third book of the *Summa contra Gentiles,* where he professes to treat morality from the point of view of divine law. Notice how many of his arguments and solutions to moral problems are nothing more than restatements of passages in the *Ethics* and *Politics* of Aristotle. Take a look, for instance, at his arguments for monogamy[18] and note how much is Aristotle and how much is from Christian sources.

However, St. Thomas is also a striking example of the inherent difficulty that one and the same thinker has when he tries to be both an ethician and a moral theologian. Some of his ablest interpreters are baffled by his performance. What weight should we give to his *Exposition of the Nicomachean Ethics?* Is this the moral thought of Thomas Aquinas? If it is not, as some seem to think,

---

[18] *Summa contra Gentiles,* III, 124; this is St. Thomas' last treatise on matrimony, because the material on this topic in the *Supplement* to the *Summa Theologiae* was taken from the earlier *Scriptum in IV Libros Sententiarum.*

then he spent a long time making this commentary — and not thinking.

Finally, let us take a quick look at the other key word in my topic — *multanimity*. This term is borrowed from Crane Brinton,[19] simply to avoid repetition of the expression, "pluralistic society." It reduces to the same thing: we live in a world in which thinking men do not agree, and in which such disagreement is regarded as very valuable. This point requires emphasis because most Catholic thinkers are atypical in this cultural attitude.

Now in such a state of affairs, I feel that there should be some able Catholics who will think and write as philosophers and not as theologians in disguise. There is no necessity to conceal the fact of their religious commitment but, if they devote themselves to philosophy, Catholics should do so in all intellectual honesty, using the methods and knowledge open to any philosopher and upholding the acknowledged professional standards of the field. This is particularly so in ethics.

Communication and discussion with ethicians of various points of view is advisable and almost mandatory. The professional philosopher should be willing to present his views to other professionals and in turn to listen to their views. Frankly, it is difficult for priests and nuns to be accepted on this basis. Thinkers who do not share their Catholic beliefs are impressed by the special personal status of a priest or a religious. It is hard for the Protestant or Jew to see how you can be a spokesman for religion on Sunday and a philosopher on Monday. I say this in all candor and sympathy because I have worked most of my mature life with priests and I know how the clergy are received at general professional meetings. They are treated with courtesy as men apart from the common run, marked by their obvious religious commitment. I speak this plainly because there seems to be a rather general Catholic notion that lay persons should not teach ethics. On the contrary, they are the people who should teach practical philosophy, not exclusively but in most cases. Let us divest ourselves of the mistaken notion that there is some religious aura to ethics; there is not.

[19] *A History of Western Morals* (New York: Harcourt, Brace, 1959), p. 467.

This is why I would close with a twofold plea. I would ask some able young Catholic philosophers who are laymen to devote more of their time to ethics. This is a part of philosophy for which the lay person is especially suited by virtue of his status in life. The problems of the lay students in our colleges are more closely allied to those of their lay instructors than to those of a priest or nun. There is no suggestion here that only lay persons should teach ethics. I am simply stating the obvious: the lay philosopher has a closer involvement in the wide range of ethical problems than has his religious colleague. The field of ethics is difficult and the risk of misunderstanding and reproof is great. Yet in a world such as ours the contribution that needs to be made to the philosophical study of ethics is obvious. Moral theologians usually have an audience limited to their own coreligionists. Ethicians should address mankind at large. A few years ago Father George Klubertanz remarked that very few articles on ethical topics are published by American Catholic philosophers.[20] We are still not doing enough in the field of practical philosophy.

This brings me to my final plea, addressed to persons in academic, administrative, and ecclesiastical authority. I would ask for a little more tolerance and charity for the efforts of Catholic philosophers. Remember that very few philosophers have become heretics. Remember that the philosopher is not worth his salt if he does not occasionally try something new and different. Remember that the ethician cannot find what to say about abortion in the twentieth century by looking up this term in an index to St. Thomas Aquinas. Ethicians who are Catholics are not official spokesmen of their Church. They should be offered constructive criticism and advice, of course, but also a certain amount of sympathetic understanding, for they have chosen to pioneer on unfamiliar paths.

If my two pleas do not receive some favorable response, then I fear that ethics as an academic discipline in Catholic colleges may have to go the way of the dodo bird. And I would venture to predict that, if this happens, the next candidate for deterioration if not extinction will be moral theology.

[20] "The Empiricism of Thomistic Ethics," *Proceedings of the American Catholic Philosophical Association*, XXXI (1957), pp. 1–24.

3. *Facts and Ethical Judgment*

My purpose is to examine the relation of ethical judgment to the facts of an ethical problem.[1] I do not propose to study the thought of Thomas Aquinas on this question, nor the precise views of any other writer in the long history of ethical theories, but simply to offer my present notions on this topic. My treatment will entail mentioning certain standard and well-known approaches to the question, of course, but I am not now interested in the history of the problem.

Let us take the following as an example to which we shall refer at times in the course of the discussion. A man *(A)* is standing on a dock with a life preserver at his feet, watching another man *(B)* drowning in a lake. Riding by in a train, I observe the situation but am unable to stop the train and save the drowning man. However, I make a judgment on it: "*A* ought to throw that life preserver to *B*." (Let us stipulate that the facts are as stated and that there are no other observable facts that greatly alter the case.)

Our problem is to discover a basis for my ought-judgment. Note that this judgment may be expressed in several alternative ways: *A* "owes it" to *B* to throw him the life preserver; the circumstances "require" this of *A*; *A* "*must*" (is "*obliged*" to, "should") do this; it "would be better" for *A* to do it, and so on. I might even shout: "Throw that life preserver to *B!*" These are not necessarily identical expressions but they have roughly the same meaning. From a linguistic point of view, there is in this example a transition from a set of indicative statements describing observable facts to a final response expressed in another mood, subjunctive, optative, or even imperative.

One of the first thoughts that will come to the minds of many people is that *A* ought to do this, because there is some sort of law

[1] Paper delivered at the Colloquium on Thomism and Contemporary Philosophy, St. Louis University, June 12–15, 1956.

governing this case. Many would say that God's law prohibiting murder covers the situation. In a society in which all member persons believe in the same God, and in the same divine laws, this theological answer may be quite adequate. However, I do not think that my ought-judgment simply means that, if *A* believes in God, then he is obliged by God's law to throw in the life preserver. I think that *A* should do it even if he is a nonbeliever.

Much the same may be said to the person who asserts that the obligation expressed in my ought-judgment stems from state law. My ethical judgment may, or may not, coincide with that of a legal expert who reasons within the framework of a given system of positive law. The ethician may presume at times to judge the ethical value of a state law — but obviously only if his ethics is grounded in something other than the law of his political community.

There is also the so-called natural-law approach to our question. Such a theory claims that certain types of human actions are good, when they are reasonably in keeping with the nature of the human agent and with the real character of the context in which his action is performed. This natural-law theory presupposes a view of knowledge and reality in which *nature* is understood somewhat in the sense of a real universal. (Of course, there is another kind of natural-law theory which says that the moral law is whatever God wills it to be; that is a different story.) When it is said that a certain kind of action is forbidden by the natural moral law, what is meant is that this type of action (say, murder) is incompatible with the rational nature of mankind in general. More than this, it means that murder is rationally definable as unfitting in the circumstances surrounding such a killing. "Thou shalt not murder" is not equivalent to "Thou shalt not kill"; it is more nearly equivalent to "Thou shalt not kill another human being, of thine own authority, voluntarily, and with malicious intent."

There have been natural-law ethicians who have claimed that they reach their knowledge of moral laws by intuition; others say that they use an induction from past experiences; others claim to deduce the moral law from some initially grasped principle; still others try to calculate the consequences of a certain type of action in reference to the interest of the individual person or of society. Advocates of natural law have belonged to many schools of ethics. Natural-law thinking is not an adequate ethical position. It demands reinforcement from some more basic philosophical position. We must look elsewhere for a more complete answer to the is-ought problem.

Let us turn, next, to the suggestion that my ethical judgment arises from my *intuition* that a given action is good or right. Ethical intuitionism has had a long and varied history. Perhaps most types of classical ethical theory have made some use of the intuitionist approach to our problem. In our day we think of it as chiefly a British theory but many German ethicians combine some kind of intuitionism with axiological ethics. I admit to a certain hesitating fondness for ethical intuitionism. Yet the position is open to serious objections.

The British type of ethical intuitionist claims that he directly perceives that a certain human action is morally good or evil. He adds that it is quite impossible to define this predicate "good" in terms of anything else. In other versions of ethical intuitionism, the concrete "ought" in a given situation is held to be intuited and not to require further justification. As far as the directness and immediacy of the intuition are concerned, this conscious grasping of an ethical value is compared to the seeing that something is yellow. Yet the intuitionist does not assert that ethical goodness, or oughtness, is a simple sensory quality.[2] Faced by criticism from a nonintuitionist, the ethical intuitionist cannot debate the issue. He bases his theory on a private experience. He can only express pity for the moral color blindness of his critic.

This brings us close to the heart of the problem. It seems to me that ethical intuitionism confuses two different orders of judgment concerning moral actions. In one order we have the moral agent making his own decisions about his own moral actions. On this level, the individual good or evil in a concrete state of affairs may be grasped in a peculiarly private and incommunicable manner by the person who is immediately involved. This does not seem to me

[2] Cf. the opening pages of G. E. Moore, *Principia Ethica* (London: Cambridge University Press, 1903), for the now classic statement of this theory. Cf. Mary Warnock, *Ethics Since 1900* (London: Oxford University Press, 1960), pp. 16–78.

to be the level of *ethical* judgment; it is in what Thomists call the prudential order. One cannot teach that sort of thing; one lives it. On the other hand, there is the level of judgment that is concerned with making a somewhat universal decision, applicable to more than one agent, in more than one situation. It appears that the first sort of judgment is moral, while the second is ethical. Moral conceptions may be ultimately indefinable but ethical notions and judgments should be open to discussion, definition, and reasonable inspection by other competent people. What I am saying is that personal morality is private but ethical thinking is open to public debate. The ethician should be able to give his "reasons" for his views.[3] Otherwise he cannot teach his subject or criticize competing positions.

It is interesting to reflect on the epistemological and psychological background of British intuitionism. Two levels of human cognition were generally distinguished throughout ancient, medieval, and early modern philosophy. What the Greeks called *nous* and *aisthesis,* Francis Bacon and John Locke called understanding and sensation. However, these distinct levels of cognition were already becoming fused, at the time of the transition from late medieval to modern thought. One branch of Scholastic philosophy contributed to this loss of distinction between intellection and sensation: this was Ockhamism. For good or for ill, William of Ockham obscured this distinction by denying all reality to universal meanings. He retained the two-level language, only by means of the feeble explanation that understanding is merely a deeper cognitive penetration into the same individual object that is already grasped in sensory perception. It is but one step, then, to Hobbes' claim that understanding is nothing but the "addition and substraction" of sense images. Eventually the term "understanding" will almost entirely disappear from British philosophical terminology. This is rather obvious in the famous Oxford translation of Aristotle. The *nous* of the treatise *On Soul* is translated as "reason" — yet W. D. Ross and his associates knew perfectly well that *nous*

---

[3] There is some affinity between my position here and the "good reasons" ethics of S. E. Toulmin, P. Nowell-Smith, and R. M. Hare. For bibliography on this movement. Cf. Paul Edwards and Arthur Pap, *A Modern Introduction to Philosophy* (New York: Free Press, 1965), p. 367.

does not mean the same as *logos*. Where "reason" is utterly impossible in this translation, *nous* is rendered as "mind," or even "insight."[4]

When the influence of the Austrian theory of values appeared in contemporary British philosophy, the English had to speak of the cognition of meanings, intelligibilities, objects of understanding. These are clearly not sense properties. Franz Brentano and his followers were modified realists and gave a certain ontological status to universals. *Gegenstandtheorie* demanded something more than the function of sensory perception. English philosophers who were interested in values had to find some term to name the cognitive awareness of axiological objects, without compromising their commitment to nominalism. They turned to the noun "mind" which has no verbal forms; etymologically it means "memory" (Anglo-Saxon, *gemynd*). It was necessary to introduce some verb with the same lack of philosophical ancestry — and thus someone hit on the verb, "to intuit." For decades the British could not even decide whether to spell it with, or without, a final "e." Roget did not even list it as a verb; nor does the *Standard Imperial Dictionary,* which is the British equivalent of a small *Webster.* In any case, intuitionism in ethics acquired a much different meaning from that given to it in the eighteenth century.[5]

The difficulty that I see in intuitionism, whether British or Continental, lies in its refusal to face up to the universality of values. If ethical values are not merely subjective attitudes, if they are knowable in a public way as ideals of action or judgment, then I think that they must be universals. That is to say, in judging that *A*'s proposed action is good, or ought to be done, I am thinking in terms of a goodness or oughtness generally applicable to any man in circumstances of the same type as those faced by *A*. And this stands for more than a logical test of generalization; values are not mere formulas, they have some objective character.

---

[4] See Ross's exposition of Aristotle's "active and passive reason," in *Aristotle* (London: Methuen, 1923), pp. 148–153.

[5] Richard Price, *A Review of the Principal Questions in Morals* (1758), defined intuition as "the mind's survey of its ideas, and the relations between them, and the notice it takes of what is or is not true and false, consistent and inconsistent, possible and impossible in the natures of things." L. A. Selby-Bigge, *British Moralists* (Indianapolis: Bobbs Merrill, 1964), no. 668.

This is precisely what a man like G. E. Moore could not bring himself to say. He cannot say that he intuits the universal goodness in terms of which he judges this act to be good, but only that he intuits this action as good.

Because of widespread dissatisfaction with British intuitionism and its failure to offer anything more than *ad hominem* reasons for the ought-judgment, we find a quite different theory in some recent ethical writings. This is the position of emotivism. A generation ago British logical positivists were saying that imperatives, ejaculations, wishes, and expressions of emotions did not submit to logical analysis. It was rather hastily concluded that such utterances are nonsense. On second thought, some writers decided that these expressions, while without descriptive meaning, might be said to have emotive meaning.[6] A man who listens to a musical performance and then enthusiastically shouts, "Bravo!" may not be describing anything but he is clearly conveying his attitude of approval. If, alternatively, he says with evident sincerity, "That was good," his utterance has much the same emotive meaning.

Now there is in emotive ethics an obvious desire for clarity. Some very dense and obscure passages have been written in the name of ethics. A good deal may come close to sheer nonsense. Definiteness in thought and speech is quite necessary for the philosopher. It is a good thing to have to face the question: "Precisely what do you mean?" In the short history of the movement, emotivism has done a useful service in forcing contemporary ethicians to stand up to this sort of questioning. Yet I do not admire the purely emotive position, in which it would be taken for granted that a new logic of moral discourse is all that ethics needs.[7] Ethics is more than a practical logic. It is quite possible to seek too much clarity in areas where the realities are not entirely clear. In more tradi-

[6] C. L. Stevenson, "The Emotive Meaning of Ethical Terms," *Mind*, XLVI (1937); reprinted in O. A. Johnson, *Ethics* (New York: Holt, Rinehart and Winston, 1965), pp. 429–445. The theory is more fully developed in Stevenson's *Ethics and Language* (New Haven: Yale University Press, 1944). Cf. A. Stroll, *The Emotive Theory of Ethics* (Berkeley, Calif.: University of California Press, 1954).

[7] It is difficult to find representatives of a pure emotivism; most advocates modify their position by adopting features from utilitarianism or naturalism. Cf. Paul Edwards, *The Logic of Moral Discourse* (Glencoe, Ill.: Free Press, 1955), pp. 139–223.

tional language, the emotive ethicians appear to expect the same precision in practical reasoning that they find in theoretical reasoning. The major concern of the emotive school is, of course, meta-ethics. This is equivalent to what used to be a standard introductory chapter in the older textbooks: "Is Ethics a Science; If So, of What Kind?"

Some criticism of the emotive approach to the ought-judgment centers on an apparent confusion between the moral philosopher and the moral agent.[8] When the emotivist says, "I approve of, or have a pro attitude toward, throwing in life preservers in situations like this: do you likewise," his added imperative has much the same force as my statement that A ought to throw in the life preserver. Starting with first-person discourse and the analysis thereof, the emotivist suddenly turns to third-person assertions, or even to the imperative mood. Logic is hardly enough to justify this sort of transition. The problem is, precisely, to discover whether there is any justification for moving from factual description (which may be first or third person) to another mood, the subjunctive or the imperative. To find an adequate solution many emotivists have partly embraced some other approach: naturalism, modified utilitarianism, subjectivism, or something else.

Still another answer to our question is offered in American naturalistic ethics. The naturalistic ethician thinks that the observable facts of an ethical problem may be gathered and interpreted by much the same methods that are employed in any other science. After all, when we wonder what ought to be done with a problem in chemistry, the thing only requires that we make sure of our facts and then follow scientific methods for working to our conclusion. The ethical naturalist is well aware of the difference between the complexity of facts in moral problems and the comparative simplicity of data in the physical sciences. Yet he sees no need to abandon here, in the area of human problematics, a methodology that has proved successful elsewhere.[9]

---

[8] Cf. John M. Hems, "Reflecting on Morals," *Philosophy*, XXXI (1956), pp. 99–116.

[9] For a not unappreciative survey: Jude Dougherty, "Recent Developments in Naturalistic Ethics," *Proceedings of the American Catholic Philosophical Association*, XXXIII (1959), pp. 97–108.

It is when stated in naturalistic terms, however, that the difficulties of our problem stand out most clearly. How can purely descriptive knowledge of facts entail a corresponding oughtness? If five persons out of every thousand commit suicide in a year, does this mean that they ought to do this? Perhaps there is some parallelism with the working out of other types of problems. If you wish to draw a straight line, you *ought* to use a straightedged ruler. So too, if you wish to live a good life, you *ought* to throw life preservers to people who are drowning. Yet the two "oughts" do not seem to have the same character; the need to draw straight lines is technical, while the need to live a good life springs from the whole context of human life. If naturalism could find some workable way of ranking facts, with corresponding ranks for the oughts that are related to these facts, more credit could be given to the theory. But I notice a tendency in many naturalistic ethicians to avoid such ranking as nonscientific.[10]

What attracts me to naturalism is its obvious interest in the actual data of human activity — an attitude built on reaction to the apriorism of idealistic and tender-minded ethics. Not so attractive in the naturalistic theory is the dogmatic assumption that "nature" must be self-explanatory, and that nature is the closed system of scientifically observable and verifiable phenomena. Such a meaning of nature excludes not only the supernatural but also the spiritual. Or, to use terms without immediate religious reference, contemporary naturalists seem to me to exclude certain elements of mental and personal experience which can only be ignored by a tremendous effort in the way of abstraction from certain obvious facts of human experience.

The supreme aim of naturalistic philosophy is cognitive: to know the facts as they are. These facts are taken as completely objective. To be subjective is to be biased, narrow-minded, and judgmental. Yet how is it possible to reduce an ought-judgment to the purely cognitive order? Ought-judgments often give rise to imperatives. If I say in reference to our example, "Throw in that life preserver!"— what naturalistic account can be given for this command?

[10] A scientific discussion of many types of oughtness is offered in H. L. Hollingsworth, *Psychology and Ethics, A Study of the Sense of Obligation* (New York: Ronald Press, 1949).

Still vigorously defended, and often combined with some of the foregoing ethical positions, is the old theory of utilitarianism. Man's controllable actions do have consequences, both to himself and to human society. On this theory I shall say very little. Any worthwhile ethics must be utilitarian in this simple sense. Opposition to utilitarianism stems chiefly from a very narrow interpretation of Kant, in which approval is given only to those acts done out of the sheer sense of duty or the pure love of the good-in-itself.[11] The autonomous-will theory deliberately ignores one whole facet of human experience: from birth until death we are constantly stimulated to effort and activity by our desires for rewards and our fears of punishments. These consequences of human action are real. To act as if they were fictions may appear at first glance as very high-minded; actually, it is narrow-minded.

To advocate the inclusion of consideration of the social and personal consequences in a valid ethical theory is not to ignore entirely the defects of utilitarianism as it has developed in the history of ethics. Presupposed in the theory is the assumption that one knows in advance what promotes the personal and the social good. Usually social utilitarians take what is generally accepted in their own society as morally good. Hedonists employ a calculus of personal pleasures and pains which never reaches a terminal solution. On a utilitarian basis, how could I decide that A should throw in the life preserver? Do I know that A's personal or social advantage requires such an action?

In spite of the sketchiness of this survey of ethical positions, it enables us to see why value theory developed. I have mentioned efforts to rank various actions and moral attitudes in degrees of importance. Value theory is a new name for an old quest for standards of judgment. Value is a useful term under which to group what is appealing, interesting, or prized, in any state of affairs. It is amusing to hear people ridicule the description of opium in terms of its dormitive qualities and then quite seriously speak of the moral value of a human action. Both are verbalisms of some

[11] For an interesting critique of the "good-will" theory, cf. Henri de Lubac, "Can a Will Be Essentially Good?" in B. V. Schwarz (ed.), *The Human Person and the World of Values* (New York: Fordham University Press, 1960), pp. 121–131.

methodic utility. What is significant is what we do with these words after we have decided to use them. In contemporary axiology, values run the whole gamut from identification with immediately observable realities, through the nether world of "objects" which are neither things nor properties of things, to the presentations of the private worlds of subjective consciousness. It is impossible for me to take any position regarding value theory in general, for it can represent almost any ethical position. Instead, I should like to comment briefly on one type of axiology which may have some promise.

Values may be viewed in terms of certain relations inherent in the observed facts of a moral state of affairs. Taken in a very neutral sense, empirical facts imply nothing other than mere facts. To reach an *ought* from a given set of facts, it is necessary to look into the factual situation for certain needs, tendencies, or connectives, among the facts. These are relations. In many kinds of classical ethics, moral relations are understood in terms of teleology. Finality in Thomism (the notion that all men are ordered to an ultimate end, and that human actions are subject to ethical approval or disapproval because of their conformity or nonconformity to this teleological ordering) is a relational concept. Such moral relations must be understood in a realistic sense.

Real relations and ultimate ends became unfashionable in most types of modern philosophy. Eventually, values were introduced (in Austria, by people with some background in scholastic Aristotelianism) to fill a certain void in philosophical discourse. Such value theory tends to take a middle course between extreme realism and subjective fictionalism. Values are fitted in between things and purely personal attitudes. In the area of economic value, the commercial worth of an article is identical neither with the existing thing that is produced, nor with the individual demand of the customer.[12] Economic articles are goods; they are concrete articles presumed to be good-for-something. Their value is determined by a reasonable appraisal of some relation between the customers and the economic articles (whether things or services). This appraisal

[12] W. D. Lamont, *The Value Judgment* (New York: Philosophical Library, 1955), attempts to ground a general theory of value on a study of economic valuation.

views economic value in an order which includes variable but real factors of time, place, and other pertinent circumstances.

Similarly, ethical values present themselves in their own order — no less complex than the economic order. It is a complexus of relations. There are various ways of approaching it. One way is to think of the relationship between a human agent and his purpose in life (this is the way of Thomistic teleology). Another way is to think of the actions of this agent as characterized by a value-quality; these actions are good-for-something, right-for-something (this is the way of axiology). Valuation seems to me to take us beyond discrete, empirical facts. It directs our thinking to this relationship which requires an objective. Rigorous development of value theory may lead to conclusions paralleling, or amplifying, the judgments of teleological ethics.

Yet the difficulties associated with the identification of ethical values are great. Many of the same hard questions that were formerly asked about universals may now be asked about values. Indeed, while value may sometimes be considered as a concrete aspect of a given thing or state of consciousness, it may also be viewed in itself and then it takes on something of the character of a universal. To say that we intuit such values is the source of further difficulty. Some Thomists regard this appeal to intuition (even to the intuition of nonnatural properties) as another way of saying that man is able to go beyond his initial sensory experience and *understand* certain intelligibilities which mediate between the knowing and appetitive person and the real objects which constitute his operational environment. This would again imply a theory of real relations.

There is an ethical position which interprets the ought-judgment in terms of the attainment of happiness. In one version, this is the view of those who think that what ought to be done is that which will perfect, or more fully realize, the self of the moral agent. I like this position, although I realize that it is not easy to discover in advance whether a given action or omission will contribute to the eventual perfection of human personality. Taken narrowly, the theory may appear but a systematization of selfishness. All I can say to this is that it should not be taken narrowly.

An ethician cannot afford to ignore the existence and demands of other selves; nor can he remain devoid of interest in the general welfare of his society.

One aspect of eudaimonism is little discussed by Thomists, even though they make considerable use of the theory. Are there any moral acts so bad, so out of keeping with the ultimate happiness of the agent, that one such action would completely ruin one's chances of achieving happiness? (This is the problem of Graham Greene's *Heart of the Matter*.) In my example: if *A* simply watches *B* drown, knowing full well that he should save him, can such a refusal prevent *A* from ever becoming happy? Is there anything that *A* can do to remedy his failure to save *B*? I am not asking whether God in His mercy may forgive *A*; that is a theological question. But I do wonder whether there is room in a purely philosophical ethics of self-perfectionism for the concept of mercy.

Looking back over this discussion of various views of the factual basis of ethical judgment, I could say (as Augustine did in reviewing his *City of God*): "I have raised more problems than I have answered." Three comments suggest themselves.

1. Each of the foregoing ethical positions, taken by itself as exclusive of the others, seems to me to be but a partial view of the basis of ethical judgment.

2. Each of the foregoing positions can be useful in the attempt to understand the basis for ethical judgment.

3. Adequately to account for the ought-judgment, one would have to consider all these approaches to the problem.

Thomistic ethics is not to be identified with any of these positions taken exclusively; rather, it has some affinities with all of them. In surveys of contemporary ethics, modern Thomism is usually classified as a natural-law theory. I do not think anyone in the thirteenth century woud have so classified Aquinas' moral thinking. More perceptive historians may see that Thomism is actually a kind of realistic self-perfectionism. In point of fact, few philosophers relish the idea of being pigeonholed within a limited school or system of thought. While Thomism is in some sense a school of ethics, its proponents represent a wide variety of views.

As I see this problem of the ought-judgment, several things must

be done to explain its ground. First of all, an ethician cannot be
satisfied with a mere repetition or gathering of the observable facts
of the human situation. He must offer some interpretation of these
facts. This requirement entails a willingness to make some generalized judgments. These will be in the pattern: "Any person in
A's position ought to throw in the life preserver." This requirement distinguishes ethics from morals; the moral judgment is not
general, it is my personal decision in facing my own problems of
right and wrong action.

Second, I take it that the formal rule governing ethical reasoning is the synderesis principle: "Good ought to be done; evil ought
to be avoided." This is not a rule directly governing moral judgment or action. There are no human actions which consist in doing
the good-in-general or avoiding moral evil-in-general. Viewed
theoretically, the synderesis principle is a logical tautology: the
good *is* what ought to be done; the not-good *is* what ought to be
avoided. Actually, this is a formula of the principle of identity,
as applied to activities. In the practical order of thought, however, this principle is not tautological. It is not the same thing to
know what to do and to do it. You do not know what to do if
you simply know the good-in-general, or some universal value,
such as justice or peace. You know what to do when you inspect a
morally challenging state of affairs and make a personal decision
in the light of your present knowledge of the pertinent facts, of
your previous experience and convictions regarding similar problems, and of your ability to think through to the foreseeable consequences of a proposed action. This sort of decision is a moral
judgment, not an ethical judgment. Ethics is not immediately
applicable to action, just as the theoretical part of any science is
not immediately applicable to laboratory procedure. Ethics deals
with certain generalizations made by a thinker who is at one remove from the real problems of morality. The ethician may judge
that life preservers ought to be thrown under conditions similar
to those described in the example; he may even say that it is his
opinion that *A* ought to throw in the life preserver here and now.
This is a very different proposition from: "I ought to throw it in
now."

This does not imply that specific ethical judgments are to be *deduced* from a first principle, such as the good-should-be-done rule. In Kantian language, the formal character of the ethical ought-judgment depends on an understanding of the synderesis principle, but the material content of ought-judgments can only come from experience of the facts of life. Formally you could express any sort of nonsense in the pattern of the synderesis principle. You could say that this circle ought to be squared. The test of an ethical judgment is not simply formal. Ethical judgments must be grounded in actual experience of moral facts, and in those generalized "facts" which constitute an understanding of the relation of the moral agent to the real context of his action.

The word "fact" is quite ambiguous. My primary inclination is to limit the term to present events that are observable and verifiable by a number of observers. This strict usage would exclude historical facts, purely psychological events of consciousness, and generalizations about strict facts. However, I realize that ethical usage tends to accept all these as instances of facts. It might be well to distinguish more clearly the different levels and degrees of immediacy of facts. The point on which I would insist is that most facts of ethical importance come rather directly from ordinary sense experience. (In this observation, I am at one with the naturalist in ethics.) The proposition that all men die, for instance, may be taken as a generalized fact based on ordinary experience. This proposition is important in ethical knowledge. It is a fact, only by extension of the empirical meaning of fact; indeed, I should prefer to call it a truth.

As far as ethics is concerned, the facts known through scientific reports (physical or social) are not of a different character from those acquired through ordinary sense perception. I take it to be a well-reported fact of common experience that something exploded over Hiroshima in the 1940's, killing and maiming many Japanese. I do not regard as a fact the theory that this bomb was made of particles arranged like little billiard balls, according to the pictures in current physics books. This is an effort of contemporary scientists to convey something which they partly understand but have never seen. I do not think that such scientific explanations are of primary importance in ethics. Certain facts (e.g., that some rocks are radioactive, in other words they stimulate Geiger counters) are now known through scientific instruments and are not known without such instruments. This kind of scientific fact can be ethically significant.

Very few such scientific facts are found in the deliverances of social scientists. Statistical reports seem to be somewhat removed from the factual. If someone questions a few thousand Americans about their belief in God and then comes up with the report that over 90 percent of Americans believe in God, this statistic appears to me to have little factual character. Belief in God is too much of a variable to be treated univocally. You might just as well claim that the so-called average family of one and three-quarters children is a fact. It takes only a little reflection (as Berkeley would say in his most pontifical manner) to see that there has never been a family of one and three-quarters children. A great deal remains to be done to investigate the relevancy of social science data to ethical judgment.[13]

A recent survey of psychoanalytic views of the human person has a good deal to say about the ethical importance of "facts" achieved through psychoanalytic methods.[14] I could find only two things offered as facts in the whole book. These two are: (a) the claim that abnormal conduct can have a meaning in terms of some past event in a patient's life; (b) that unresolved conflicts at an unconscious level are pathogenic.[15] These appear to be opinions that have been entertained by others than the psychoanalytic fraternity. They may be true opinions: I don't know. They appear to be conclusions of a highly subjective character. What Kinsey regarded as eccentric conduct — say celibacy — a Catholic social scientist may consider to have positive value.

Scientific opinion need not be taken as factual information

[13] See some suggestions on anthropology and ethics in Charles Fay, "Natural Moral Law in the Light of Cultural Relativism," *Anthropological Quarterly,* 34 (1961), pp. 177–191; see also Margaret Mead, "Some Anthropological Considerations concerning Natural Law," *Natural Law Forum,* VI (1961), pp. 51–64.

[14] Joseph Nuttin, *Psychanalyse et conception spiritualiste de l'homme* (Louvain-Paris: Vrin, 1950); translated as *Psychoanalysis and Personality* by George Lamb (New York: Sheed & Ward, 1953).

[15] *Op. cit.,* p. 88 in the French text.

for the ethician. Court cases often present the ludicrous spectacle of "scientific" witnesses flatly contradicting each other in the name of facts of science. (Fortunately, ethicians are rarely called as expert witnesses.) Instructive is the well-known case of the Switched Babies.[16] Two babies were born in a Chicago hospital on June 30, 1930, and taken home nine days later. The Watkins took baby *A* and the Bambergers baby *B*. On the back of baby *A* the Watkins found the Bamberger name tape; the Bambergers found a Watkins name tape in their wastebasket. The families decided to investigate. The nurses had no helpful information. The appearances of the babies were similar. Eight scientists were called in to decide whether the babies were in their proper homes. A dermatologist examined birthmarks and found that they had no evidential value. One fingerprint expert decided that the babies were properly located; a second fingerprint man said that the prints gave no definite indications of relationship. A neurologist found that baby *A* resembled Mrs. Watkins in its reflexes and suggested that the babies should stay in their original homes. An anatomist took head measurements and decided that the babies were in the wrong homes. A blood analyst found that baby *B* had identical blood with the Watkins and decreed that the babies should be exchanged. At the end, the committee of eight experts voted five to three to exchange the babies — and they were duly switched.

What ought to have been done in this affair was certainly a moral problem. Those babies are now mature persons. They may still be wandering around Chicago, trying to figure out whether they are Watkins or Bamberger. I do not suggest that an ethician could have made a better decision: that is not his job. He could have warned the experts that opinions are not facts. The fact which initiated the investigation and which seems to have predetermined its outcome was not a scientific one: the name tapes were in the wrong homes. In most ethical problems, and in all moral ones, one empirical fact is worth a good many scientific opinions.

[16] E. A. Burtt, *Right Thinking* (New York: Harper and Bros., 1946), pp. 466–467, gives more details on this case.

Four points stand out in general summary: (1) Ethical judgment goes beyond the descriptive knowledge of the facts of a practical problem. (2) Most practical facts are contributed by ordinary observation; some by physical science; few by social science. (3) What is added to the facts in ethical judgment is a philosophical interpretation, variously and partially approached in different ethical theories but centering in a core of ethical agreement on many basic issues. (4) Ethical judgments are by no means infallible; nor do they automatically solve the problems of moral discourse, for the latter are of a different order from the problems of ethics.

4. *Freedom as a Moral Value**

Human freedom is not adequately defined as the absence of external restraint. There is a great deal more to man's liberty than is suggested in this inadequate statement. One fruitful approach to the understanding of what it means to be free lies in value theory. It is proposed, here, to begin with certain views concerning the nominal character of freedom, then to suggest a relational theory of values, and finally to mention some applications of this axiology to the notion of freedom.

To speak simply of freedom, as if it were an entity, is to reify an abstract ideal. British language analysis has done a service to philosophy in pointing this out: even name-words (nouns) do not always name things. Freedom is not a thing. In reality, men are free in some of their activities. A man is free when he is able to exercise some degree of self-determination and of spontaneous activity. To be free has two aspects: (1) the agent is not subject to complete control from without (this is the *negative* phase); and (2) the agent is possessed of the internal power to act in some way which he decides upon for himself (this is the *positive* phase). I think that both aspects are requisite to the free man. Of the two, the positive aspect is primary and basic. This is clear from the fact that the absence of external restraint is of no significance without the positive presence of the inner ability to act as a self-determining agent.

It is advisable, also, to distinguish personal from social freedom. Both are human but they are not of equal status. Personal liberty is fundamental. A person may live and function (though not well)

* This paper was delivered at the Twelfth International Congress of Philosophy (Venice, 1958), and was printed in *Atti del XII Congresso Internazionale di Filosofia* (Firenze: Sansoni Editore, 1960), Tome III, pp. 61–66.

apart from society; you cannot have a human society apart from persons. Robinson Crusoe before meeting Friday is personally free. Obviously he is subject to no social restraints; he may fall victim to certain physical compulsions but, as long as he lives, he is positively free to perform certain actions. Societal freedom is characteristic of an organized group of persons. The nominal, or dictionary, meaning of freedom in reference to a society also includes negative and positive notes: the social group must not be wholly restrained from without, and it must be possessed of the inner capacity for self-determination.

Both personal and societal freedom are compatible with various degrees of restraint and of inner capacity. A complete absence of external influence is rarely found. A prisoner is free to walk in his cell but not outdoors: he is still free to walk. Heart trouble may preclude his walking more than a few feet at a time: he is still free to walk. Moreover, restraints of one type may make possible new freedoms of another type. Thus a rule against driving to the left may be regarded initially as a constraint on the automobile driver but it actually facilitates the free flow of traffic in two directions on a highway. Similarly, free speech is made possible by the acceptance of certain rules of signification; without such regulation human speech would be gibberish. Freedom to vote is only valuable where restraint is placed on the number of times one may vote; otherwise voting becomes nonsense.

In general, value may be located in reference to the subject-object relation. Some people think that value is entirely in the cognitive or affective consciousness of the person who prizes something. Others regard value as rather objective and thingish, as a sort of quality inhering in a real or imaginary object. Still others identify value with a certain kind of relation which embraces both prizing subject and prized object. Thus baldly stated, it would seem that the third position has all the advantages of the first two, without their exclusiveness. It is possible that some values are almost entirely subjective, that others are predominantly objective. The relational account of value (which should not be confused with the view that all values are relative) is taken as conducive to optimum clarification of the problems of axiology.

It should be admitted that general theories of value (for example, Perry's view that value is "any object of any interest") usually find acceptance because of an inherent vagueness which offends no one but which, by the same token, provides little basis for discrimination. If a theory of value is kept so general that it permits one to judge that all things, real or imaginary, are valuable under some possible circumstances, it exceeds in imprecision the scholastic theory of transcendentals. The philosopher will find it more satisfactory to limit his conception of value to that relationship between subject and object in which interest in some optimum condition arises.

Moral value I would take to be a specific type of worth —to be distinguished from aesthetic, commercial, biological, and other such varieties of value. Thinking of man as a real agent, able to control some of his actions and interactions involving his environment, we can observe certain characteristics which modify these human actions. They are judged to be good or bad, right or wrong, worthy of praise or blame. Such judgments are moral and the acts to which they are applied are moral because they can be evaluated in terms of a certain relationship between man's behavior and the real frame of reference in which man acts. This real context of human action includes man himself and all those external realities making up his environment. Moral ideals are arrived at in a variety of ways. Some kinds of ethics stress contributions to societal welfare (social utilitarianism); others emphasize the individual perfection of the personal agent (eudaimonism, hedonism, deontologism, self-realization). It is probable that all such approaches to the clarification or establishment of moral ideals are somewhat inadequate, when taken in isolation from other views. That is to say, the theory of social utilitarianism is partly valid: some human acts *are* morally approvable because they contribute to the welfare of human society. But this is not the only basis on which man's acts have moral value. Other human actions are morally worthy because they contribute to the happiness or perfection of the individual person. Thus moral value is not simply an arbitrary quality of the subjective consciousness of the human agent, nor is such value a nonsubjective quality of the real environment within which man operates. Rather, moral value is a relational characteristic discerned in the suitability (or unsuitability) of a given action or omission of man, when such an event is viewed in terms of man's place in the rest of reality.

Moral value, then, is not a simple physical or sensible quality. It does no service to moral philosophy to claim that any honest observer can "see" the value of a human action as good or bad. Crude intuitionism negates the possibility of discussion, of comparative analysis, and of further philosophical investigation of moral value. While I would insist that morality cannot wholly be translated into other types of value, this does not mean that it is impossible for the moral philosopher to throw some light on its constitution by means of a patient study of the kind of agent that man is, and of the intelligible pattern of his relations with other things. That religious ideals play an important role in establishing the moral views of a given agent or ethical position is obvious. If all men had the same religious attitudes, then this universal commitment would doubtless enter into the philosophical study of moral value. But contemporary men are not in religious agreement; hence, a purely philosophical account of moral value must be sought among these facts, concepts, and understandable relations which are available to any open-minded observer of man's condition. Whether it is possible thus to develop an adequate theory of moral behavior without introducing religious standards is now much disputed. Some serious Catholic thinkers (such as Jacques Maritain) say that an adequate natural ethics is not possible. The history of disagreement among moral philosophers may seem to bear out this gloomy prospect. However, even if a perfect ethical position be an unattainable ideal, this need be no cause for discouragement or abandonment of the search for partial clarification of the values which characterize man's free activity. Few (if any) sciences can lay claim to perfection of development. Philosophical theories of moral value may still make an important contribution to human life, even if they are far from perfect.

The consideration of freedom offers a very promising approach to the discussion of moral value. Unlike some other moral themes, such as the meaning of good, right, or duty, meditation on what it means to be free requires us to acknowledge the complex structure of the moral relation. It is easily possible, for instance, to make the mistake of deciding that the judgments, "This act is good" and "This paper is white," are of much the same kind. The predicates, *good* and *white,* may seem to be attributed in much the same way. One might conclude that goodness is merely an experienced quality, incapable of further analysis. Such a misconception is not likely in reference to the judgment, "This man is free." As we have seen, freedom has both an intrasubjective and an extrasubjective aspect. Present emphasis on "absence of external restraint" as the meaning of freedom renders it more obvious that freedom has some reference to the possible influence of extrahuman factors. A free man is such because of his internal condition but he also must enjoy a special relationship with the world about him. He must not be wholly impeded in the performance of certain actions and in the assumption of certain personal attitudes.

Inwardly the free person is also marked by a rather complex structuring which bears on the character of moral value. Various psychologists will acount for this in different ways. The more useful and enlightening psychological considerations do not take personal freedom as a mystery completely beyond analysis. Let me illustrate my point by reference to a classic position, that of Aristotle. He observed the dual character of human choice, hesitating between calling *proairesis* an intellective appetition or an appetitive intellection. Let us not be misled by any modern antipathy to Aristotelian terminology or to faculty psychology. With Aristotle an important insight enters the stream of human speculation on freedom: there is something cognitive about the act of free decision, and there is something affective in it too. Neglect of either feature tremendously limits our view of man's freedom.

Further light on human and personal freedom is thrown by Aristotle's analysis of voluntariness. That a man may *partly approve* of a certain event in which he is involved, and at the same time *partly disapprove* of it, was clearly seen by Aristotle. Indeed these mixed attitudes are not unusual in the moral life; a person's attitudes toward his external actions, and toward many of his emotional responses, are frequently complex. One pays taxes

willingly and yet not willingly. He accepts an honor gladly, yet
with some awareness of its disadvantages. He comes to Venice
because he wants to, but he dislikes the expense involved. To all
such actions he is voluntary and self-determining, yet his voluntariness is far from perfect approval; there is some involuntariness
present. Now, voluntariness is not identical with personal freedom
but they are closely related conditions of the person. Their parallelism indicates the complexity of both.

Some contemporary "attitude" theories of value tend to over-
simplify these complex conditions of freedom. Even linguistic
analysis is apt to pass over the polyvalence of liberty. One does
not usually assume a simple pro attitude toward a human event;
one is *for* it to some extent, *against* it from another point of view.
Indeed it is this very ambivalence of human attitudes that enables
the agent to take an independent stand on moral issues and thus
to assert his freedom.

The free man finds himself the center of a mixed assembly of
known facts, abstractions, ideals, values, and relations. His very
freedom is a fact, yet not identical with any of the simple, sensibly
observable facts of a given moral problem. His freedom may
function also as an abstraction and an ideal. Certainly it is a moral
value; to be free is to experience the very ground of all other moral
values. In its most general sense, personal freedom is a certain
relation: the free agent stands in a definite reference to his sur-
roundings and to the various components of his consciousness.

Social freedom introduces greater complexity into this relation.
The free society adds to the constituent freedoms of its members
a new complexus of interpersonal relations. A well-organized group
of persons presupposes self-determination within the group and
some nonrestriction from outside the group. The moral value of
societal freedom is analogous to that of the person but is constituted of additional facts, ideals, and relations.

Both personal and social freedom involve many factors and
aspects of moral value which merit further analysis. It is difficult
to understand how anyone could maintain that they are but simple
objects of moral intuition.

II. *THE ETHICAL AGENT*

5. *Human Tendencies, Will, and Freedom**

In our contemporary world, freedom is a much-prized value. Indeed human liberty is now exalted to the point at which it is no longer submitted to philosophical analysis but is rather regarded as an absolute. This present-day assumption, that man's freedom is self-evident and obvious, is nowhere more apparent than in the recent studies occasioned by the Columbia University discussions of freedom and the right to knowledge. With the excep- of a small number of works (notably the publications issued from Louvain and St. John's University[1]), most of these investigations took it for granted that everyone knows what freedom is — and that the real problems center in the use of this master value.

The great thinkers of the Middle Ages did not make this gratuitous assumption: their efforts to analyze and understand the character of human liberty extended over many centuries. Although many modern political philosophers would smile at the suggestion that the roots of our contemporary concepts of the rights and liberties of the human person are to be discovered in the Middle Ages, this will be precisely the claim of the present paper. To understand the extent and character of man's freedoms today, we must rediscover our heritage from medieval thought.

FINALITY OF MAN INTERNAL AND EXTERNAL

That human nature and human functions are end-directed is not disputed in medieval philosophy. One great source of this

---

* From: *L'Homme et son Destin* (Louvain: Nauwelaerts; Paris: Béatrice-Nauwelaerts, 1960), pp. 71–84.

[1] L. De Raeymaeker, *et al., Truth and Freedom* (Louvain: Nauwelaerts; Pittsburgh: Duquesne University Press, 1954); and *Concept of Freedom,* ed. C. W. Grindel (Chicago: Regnery, 1955).

teleological position is the Christian belief that man's life is but a journey to a destination in another world. The other source is Greek philosophy, especially Aristotle with his insistence on final causality in physics and metaphysics and on the identity of the end and the good in practical philosophy. Although one may argue about the manner in which the finality proposition is known or established,[2] it is an historical fact that patristic and medieval thinkers practically always view human action in relation to certain goals.

However, this does not mean that all is clear in medieval notions of finality. One basic ambiguity is inherited, perhaps, from Aristotle. All motion or change is a progressive actuation of potency toward some end. When Aristotle describes the ontogenetic development of the animal, he seems to picture the end of this process as an ideal stage of maturity within the agent. The tadpole has not yet reached this stage but, when it becomes a mature frog, in full possession and use of all its powers, it then reaches its biological end. The final cause, here, is not some already existing being. Before it is attained, the end for the biological individual is a certain nonexistent status of self-perfection. Let us call this biological self-perfectionism *internal finality*.

On the other hand, when Aristotle explains the movement of the heavenly bodies, he pictures them as being moved by certain intelligences which know and desire an already existing being. These intelligences are eternally stimulated by this other being, so that they move themselves and their spheres. This stimulation is not in the order of efficient but of final causality. The end that they contemplate and desire is outside themselves and will never be within them. Let us call this astronomical version *external finality*.

Now then, which kind of finality did Aristotle find in the life and operations of man? It would seem that he tried to use both and was not fully aware that this effort could be the source of difficulties. If we take the *Nicomachean Ethics* (particularly Book X) as a morality of self-perfectionism, we are opting for internal finality. If we read the work as the writer of the *Eudemian Ethics*

[2] Cf. G. P. Klubertanz, S.J., *St. Thomas' Treatment of the Axiom,* "Omne agens agit propter finem," in *An Etienne Gilson Tribute,* ed. C. J. O'Neil (Milwaukee: Marquette University Press, 1959), pp. 101–117.

did (and as most medieval commentators, including Thomas Aquinas, did), we stress the notion that ultimate human happiness consists in an approach by man to the contemplation of an already existing and nonhuman being. In some sense, this perfect being is the goal of man's finest activity — but this is an end which is external to human nature.

It is not that these two conceptions of finality are entirely incompatible. Obviously, the Aristotelian man, in approaching his external end, perfects himself and thus approaches his internal end. Yet there remains some ambiguity. It is not merely an Aristotelian difficulty: the leading medieval philosophers take different positions on the relative importance of internal and external finality.

TENDENCIES AND HUMAN APPETITION

Man's whole nature and all his operations may then be viewed as tending toward some end, or ends. We may speak, as did many thinkers in the Middle Ages, of cognitive or even entitative finality. However, it is in the order of appetition that human finality is most apparent. That is why it is proposed, in what follows, to consider several key theories of human appetition in patristic and medieval thought. Clearly this short treatment cannot be offered as a complete history of medieval analyses of the appetitive side of human nature. Actually there are comparatively few pioneer studies in this area of medieval speculation. I am not unaware of various essays on theories of love in medieval writings, or of certain investigations of the determinism-voluntarism theme, or of various investigations of the end of man in medieval thought. Particular mention should be made of the remarkable studies conducted by Dom Odon Lottin on the psychological and moral theories of this period. However, it is rather evident that, in comparison with what has been written on the medieval theories of cognition, of the general nature of reality, even of logic and aesthetics, the amount of work devoted to human appetition by medievalists is indeed meager.

For this reason, what is said here is very tentative and modest in scope. It is offered as a set of suggestions for research which still

remains to be done. Each theory will be associated with the name
of a major personality in the period — not to intimate that he is
the first or only man to treat human appetition in this way but
rather for mnemonic purposes.

Although Augustine is not a medieval philosopher, his psychology is influential throughout the period; so that is reason enough
for starting with him. The Augustinian man is a union of body
and soul, and in this union the soul predominates in all ways.
This human soul is the immediate principle of all its operations:
there are no distinct potencies or faculties of the soul in Augustinian psychology. As knowing, the human soul is *mens;* as con-
taining, or present to, all objects of past, present, future, or of
eternity, this same soul is *memoria;* and as inclining, desiring,
loving, this soul is *voluntas.* This is the famous trinitarian analysis,
inspired by the biblical teaching that man is made to the image
of God.[3] It is important to stress the point that mind, memory,
and will are not potencies of the soul. Augustine is aware of some
distinction of psychological functions but he identifies the whole
soul, as dynamic and active, with the will of man.

There is no other appetite than will in the Augustinian man.
All human tendencies, from the highest to the lowest, stem from
the soul-as-will: *voluntas est animi motus, cogente nullo, ad aliquid
vel non amittendum, vel adipiscendum.*[4] So, we find but one single
appetite in man. There are no appetitive sense powers in Augus-
tinism, neither concupiscible nor irascible appetite as separate
potencies.

Of course, Augustine knew full well that man can entertain
diverse desires and loves. Love is but will taken in a stronger
sense.[5] The same will may be attracted to God at one moment, and
to sensual pleasures at another. Augustine calls love the "foot"
of the soul: with it man can take a step toward God, in a move-

[3] *De Trinitate,* Books IX-XV. Cf. M. Schmaus, *Die psychologische Trinitätslehre
des hl. Augustinus* (Münster i. W.: Aschendorff, 1927).

[4] *De duabus animabus,* 10, 14.

[5] *De Trinitate,* XV, 21, 41, speaks of "voluntatem nostram vel amorem seu
dilectionem quae valentior est voluntas."

ment of charity; and with this same "foot" man may step down to the goods of concupiscence.[6] As will tends toward God, it is charity and spiritual love; as it inclines perversely toward lesser goods, it is called cupidity or libido. Diversification of this one appetite is provided, then, by the local terminus, or end, of its respective movements. This introduces the *pondus* theory, a famous teaching which reappears in the writings of Albert and Bonaventure but of which there is scarcely a mention in Thomas Aquinas. Augustine borrowed from ancient physics the notion that different kinds of bodies have different "weights" impelling them to seek their proper places. He suggested that the soul also has its "weights" inclining it toward diverse objectives.[7]

Two things deserve to be noted concerning the *pondus* theory. First, while it is obviously a teleological explanation, one cannot be certain whether it is a theory of internal or of external finality. The distinction of tendencies by reason of a diversity of termini suggests an externality of the end. Yet weight, in ancient physics, was not considered the external pull of one body on another. It is quite probable that Augustine thought of *pondus* as a directional principle internal to the agent. His frequent insistence on the sole responsibility of the will for its actions falls in line with an internal finality interpretation.[8]

A second look at the *pondus* theory indicates an underlying ambiguity. God is called the proper weight of man's soul.[9] The two great "loves" of the soul are distinguished by their termini, by whether man turns to God or away from Him.[10] It is difficult to avoid seeing something of external finality here. In any case, Augustine's acceptance of external finality did not imply a necessitarian determination of man's will from without. He always maintained that willing is, in some sense, quite free. A lower,

---

[6] "Pes animae rectae intelligitur amor; qui cum pravus est vocatur cupiditas aut libido; cum autem rectus, dilectio vel caritas. Amore enim movetur tanquam ad locum quo tendit." *Ennar. in Pss.* 9, 15.

[7] *De civitate Dei*, XI, 28: "Nam velut amores corporum momenta sunt ponderum. . . . Ita enim corpus pondere, sicut animus amore, fertur quocumque fertur." Cf. *De musica*, VI, 11, 19; *Conf.*, XIII, 9, 10; *Epist.*, 55, 10, 18; *Epist.*, 157, 2, 9; *Ennar. in Ps.*, 29, 2, 10.

[8] Consider his discussion of the theft of the pears: *Conf.*, II, 4–9.

[9] *Conf.*, XIII, 9, 10.

[10] *De civitate Dei*, V, 11; XI, 28.

ordinary freedom (that of *liberum arbitrium*) implies the ability spontaneously to choose a lesser or a greater good. A higher freedom (*libertas*) involves no alternatives and consists simply in the love of the greatest good, God.[11]

THE PLURAL-APPETITE THEORY: ST. JOHN DAMASCENE

Among the Greek patristic writers we find descriptions of what appear to be several human appetites. This plural view is transmitted through John Damascene. Part of his great theological work was translated in the mid-twelfth century by Burgundio of Pisa, as *De Fide Orthodoxa*,[12] thus offering a plural analysis of appetition to Latin scholars. Two theological controversies occasioned detailed studies of the functions of willing: (1) heretical teachings concerning the operations of will in Christ met with opposition; and (2) another heresy developed discussion of the place of the divine will in the work of creation.[13]

John Damascene's pluralization of human appetites extends in two directions. As in Aristotle's psychology, rational appetition is distinguished from irrational appetition. Damascene thus seems to be the immediate source for medieval theories of the concupiscible and irascible appetites. These two appetites are deemed capable of "obeying" reason, and thus of participating in the moral and religious life of man.[14] Moreover, on the rational level Damascene speaks of willing under two different names: *thelesis* and *boulesis*.[15] The relation of these is not entirely clear in Damascene's account. *Boulesis* names an appetition for a definite end, even for what is rationally impossible such as earthly immortality. It seems to correspond to what we call *wishing* in English. Aristotle

---

[11] Cf. E. Gilson, *Introduction à l'étude de saint Augustin* (Paris: Vrin, 1949), p. 204.

[12] Damascene's *Fons Scientiae* is in PG 94, 790–1225; Burgundio's Latin is newly edited: *De Fide Orthodoxa*, Burgundionis versio, ed. E. M. Buytaert (St. Bonaventure, N. Y.: Franciscan Institute Publ., 1955).

[13] H. A. Wolfson, in his *Philosophy of the Church Fathers* (Cambridge, Mass.: Harvard University Press, 1956), Vol. I, pp. 464–486, surveys some of the philosophical influences of these heresies. Cf. also: O. Lottin, "La psychologie de J. Damascène," *Revue Thomiste*, XXXVI (1931), pp. 631–661.

[14] *De Fide Orthodoxa*, II, 30; ed. Buytaert, p. 123.

[15] *De Fide Orth.*, II, 22; PG 94, 944; ed. Buytaert, p. 118.

had so used the term *boulesis*. On the other hand, *thelesis* is not found in Aristotle but is the Greek Christian name for will.[16] Choice of means is called, with Aristotle, *proairesis*. Plainly, Damascene does not equate *boulesis* and *proairesis*.

Now this psychology of appetition is a compilation of materials from Nemesius,[17] Maximus, Clement of Alexandria, and Gregory Nazianzen.[18] The thing which stands out in this treatment of man's appetitive tendencies is the pluralization of powers. One cannot say that Damascene recorded a theory of really distinct faculties of appetition — but Thomas Aquinas will later teach that there are three psychic appetites in man, and will cite Damascene as the authority for his view.[19]

THE TWO "AFFECTIONES" THEORY: ST. ANSELM

Augustine's *City of God* had made famous the distinction of two human "loves": the love of God and that of earthly things. St. Anselm of Canterbury gave this dualism a new orientation: there is only one will in man but it can be modified by two special tendencies (*affectiones* or *aptitudines*). One of these dispositions is the *affectio ad volendum commoditaten,* a willful inclination toward personal happiness and satisfaction in man's life on earth.[20] The *commodum* is a good of the same order as the individual will. The other added disposition of will is the *affectio ad volendum*

[16] Whether Damascene merely meant (as Gilson says, *History of Christian Philosophy in the Middle Ages* [New York: Random House, 1955], p. 601) that *boulesis* is to *thelesis* as volition is to will, is not clear. Cf. F. Adelmann, *The Rational Appetite in the "De Fide Orthodoxa" of St. John Damascene*, St. Louis University dissertation, 1955; M.-D. Chenu, *Introduction à l'étude de s. Thomas d'Aquin* (Montréal-Paris: Vrin, 1950), p. 96, notes how translation of both *thelesis* and *boulesis* by *voluntas* led to ambiguity.

[17] Cf. B. Domanski, *Die Psychologie des Nemesius* (Münster, 1900), (BGPM, III, pp. 5–210).

[18] Cf. Wolfson, *op. cit.,* p. 465; Gilson, *History of Christian Philosophy . . . ,* p. 601.

[19] St. Thomas cites Gregory Nazianzen and John Damascene to this effect, in his *Sed contra, Summa Theologiae,* I, a. 81, a. 2.

[20] "Per affectionem quidem quae est ad commoditatem, semper homo vult beatitudinem et beatus esse. . . . Propter commoditatem autem vult aliquid ut cum vult arare vel laborare ut habeat unde tueatur vitam et salutem quae commoda judicat esse." *De concordantia praescientiae Dei cum libero arbitrio,* c. 11; PL 158, 536.

rectitudinem, an inclination to desire something simply because it is right and just.[21]

Anselm calls this higher "justice" natural, because it characterized the will of Adam before the Fall, but present-day theological terminology would, without question, label it supernatural. Moreover, Anselm's *affectiones* theory introduces the whole matter of personal motivation for moral action. One man wills to do his daily work, say as a farmer, because he can make a living at it. A second man does the same work simply because it is the right thing to do. (Much later in the history of philosophy, Immanuel Kant will take up this problem of the pure motive.)

Now Anselm refused to consider the first man a truly good and free man. He could not grant that liberty consists in the freedom to do whatever one wishes, even to sin.[22] Instead, he insisted that true liberty stems from the *affectio ad rectitudinem,* from the will disposed toward the purely right and good. Thus he developed his famous definition of *liberum arbitrium* as the *potestas servandi rectitudinem propter justitiam.*[23]

We are here at one of the high points in medieval thinking on appetitive freedom. Man is eminently free, not when he is choosing between alternatives, or rejecting a greater for a lesser good, but when all his choices are made for the highest motive, for the greatest good. This position on *libertas* is a development of something already implicit in Augustine's psychology of will. It is an extremely Christian view which endeavors to take man beyond the limitations of self-interest. It is a high-minded notion of liberty which has almost disappeared from the modern world.[24]

WILL AS NATURE AND AS REASON: ST. THOMAS AQUINAS

Whatever John Damascene meant by his distinction between

[21] "Per illam [affectionem] quae est ad volendum rectitudinem, rectitudinem vult, et rectus, id est justus, esse." *Ibid.* Cf. J. R. Sheets, "Justice in the Moral Thought of St. Anselm," *The Modern Schoolman,* XXV, (1948), pp. 132–139.

[22] "Potestas ergo peccandi, quae addita voluntati minuit ejus libertatem, et, si dematur, auget, nec libertas est, nec pars libertatis." *Dialog. de libero arbitrio,* PL 158, 491.

[23] *De concordantia,* c. 6; PL 158, 517.

[24] For a similar teaching in St. Bernard, cf. P. Delfgaauw, O.Cist. Réf., "La nature et les degrés de l'amour selon saint Bernard," in *Saint Bernard Théologien* (Roma: Editiones Cistercienses, 1953), pp. 233–244.

thelesis and *boulesis,* the theological masters of the thirteenth
century developed it into a doctrine of new importance. We find
this teaching very plainly in Aquinas, though we could discover
it also in the Franciscan *Summa Fratris Alexandri* and in Roger
Bacon, St. Bonaventure, and St. Albert.[25] St. Thomas expounds
Damascene in this way: "The will of man is twofold, namely the
natural will, which is called *thelesis,* and the rational will, which
is called *boulesis.*"[26] His further explanation points out that his
theological contemporaries call the first will *voluntas ut natura,*
and the second *voluntas ut ratio.* Thomas also explains that these
are distinguished as *acts*: *thelesis* being a will-act "insofar as
it bears on something which is willed in itself," and *boulesis* being
another will-act "insofar as it bears on something which is willed
only by reason of its connection with something else."[27] This
changes Damascene's *boulesis* (which had been the wishing of an
end, or of a thing for its own sake) into the willing of means to an
end. There is no question that, in this late work (*S. T.,* Pars Ter-
tia), Aquinas is speaking of two different *acts* of will; he uses
actus voluntatis in reference to each. By one sort of act, man naturally inclines toward an end; by another sort of act, man rationally and as a result of deliberation (*consilium*) tends toward
a known means to an end. As Thomas says: "These two wills are
not diversified according to a power, but only according to a difference in their acts."[28]

Many efforts have been made to explain this *natural* inclination,
or movement, of will to end in St. Thomas' teaching. We can,
at least, notice here that it is not called natural in contrast to a
supernatural movement, but in distinction from a deliberated act
of will. The problem here is not identical with that of Anselm's
two *affectiones;* nor is it quite the same as that of the natural-
supernatural discussions in later Scholastic theology.

An excellent recent study[29] stresses the parallelism between the

[25] See the historical annotations to St. Thomas, *S.T.,* II-II, q. 18, a. 3 (Ottawa
ed., 1944, t. IV, 2546, b26).
[26] *Ibid.,* obj. 1.
[27] *Ibid.,* in corpore.
[28] *Ibid.,* ad primum.
[29] G. Verbeke, "Le développement de la vie volitive d'après saint Thomas,"
Revue Philosophique de Louvain, 56 (1958), pp. 5–34.

life of the will and that of the intellect in the teaching of Aquinas. It is suggested that this *vouloir premier,* which is natural, is an inclination toward the good-in-general and also toward man's ultimate end.[30] Yet, as natural, it is a necessary tendency. If this *voluntas ut natura* is a necessary act, and if it is the source of all other acts of willing, how can Thomism avoid the stigma of determinism?

One effort to get out of such difficulties relies on a distinction between the exercise of the will-act and its specification.[31] Thus, no exercised act of will would be necessary but some acts may be necessarily specified and others freely specified. Does this mean that, before man's will ever performs any action, it is specified by nature (and more ultimately by God) so that from its first exercised act onward it actually desires man's ultimate end? Thomists usually refuse to say this but speak instead of a virtual or habitual desire for this final end.

St. Thomas' treatment of the natural desire for the vision of God is well known.[32] There are many problems arising from this theory. Is the natural desire under discussion a tendency of man's will or of his intellect — or is there any difference here? Is this *desiderium* an appetite, an inclination, or a fully exercised act? If it is a tendency naturally common to all men, why is there so little awareness of it among twentieth-century philosophers and psychologists? Where does freedom enter St. Thomas' analysis of the acts of willing?

Such difficulties do not present themselves when we consider the good-in-general as the object of the *voluntas ut natura.* This transcendental good excludes no being and is thus quite unspecified. It is when we restrict the object of natural willing to man's ultimate end that we face difficulty, for there are other beings than God, and other goods than the highest good. St. Bonaventure knew this and bluntly rejected the position that all men have a natural and necessary tendency toward the vision of God. Here is what Bonaventure says:

[30] *Ibid.,* pp. 19–20.

[31] *Ibid.,* p. 25.

[32] *Summa contra Gentiles,* III, cap. 49–63; see the *Introduction* to my translation: St. Thomas Aquinas, *On the Truth of the Catholic Faith,* Book III, Part I (New York: Doubleday, 1956). Cf. also: V. Cauchy, *Désir naturel et béatitude chez saint Thomas* (Montréal: Editions Fides, 1958).

When therefore it is said that every will tends toward happiness, this is understood of happiness considered in its universality, in which appetite all men, as Augustine says, communicate; but so far as happiness is taken in a limited sense for that which consists in the vision of God, neither is it sought by all or nor do all tend toward it.[33]

The difference between Bonaventure and Aquinas on this cardinal point lies in a different notion of what the human will is essentially. Duns Scotus is clear on the point. He speaks, at times, of a natural intellectual appetite in man. Yet, to avoid the difficulties which a theory of will gets into when will is first viewed as a natural, and so necessary appetite, Scotus puts will in a different genus from appetite. Under the strong influence of Augustine and Anselm, he situates will in the genus of *libertas*.[34] Thus he takes will as essentially free and, in this, he is true to the Franciscan school from Bonaventure onward.

Later Scholastic philosophers combined Scotus' and Thomas' divergent views of the human will. Present-day Thomism is not entirely clear on the point. Thomists often speak of free will (and demonstrate it *ad nauseam* to college students) but Thomas Aquinas talks about free choice, about free consent, but not about *libera voluntas*. The will is not free by nature for Aquinas; it becomes involved in certain free actions when it enters into a joint functioning with the deliberating intellect. We need today a thorough study of the role of *intentio* in St. Thomas' appetitive psychology: not only of the intending of man's ultimate end but also of the volitional tending toward limited, finite ends.

TWO SUPREME GOODS THEORY: MARSILIUS OF PADUA

It was perhaps inevitable that certain medieval thinkers should eventually challenge the claim that man's natural desire for happiness is necessarily and simply a desire for the future vision of God. Even in the thirteenth century, we find some philosophers (apparently in the Arts Faculty at Paris) suggesting that man may prop-

[33] Bonaventure, *In II Sententiarum,* d. 38, 1, 1, ad primum (ed. minor, Quaracchi, t. II, pp. 915–916).

[34] *Opus Oxoniense,* II, d. 25, 1, 16; cf. Gilson, *Jean Duns Scot* (Paris: Vrin, 1952), p. 579, for further texts and discussion.

erly look to happiness in a good life on earth.[35] These writers ask
why man must exclude one or the other of Augustine's two "loves":
why not aim at both? Why not say that there are two great goods
available to man, one in the eternal order, the other in the temporal order? From this question, it is but another step to the
opinion that man has two final ends, a theory not unknown to later
Scholasticism.

Marsilius of Padua, writing his *Defensor Pacis* in 1324,[36] is a
key figure in this development. His opening sentence speaks of
"the greatest good of man, sufficiency of life . . . ."[37] Marsilius'
whole political argument rests on the claim that the universal
human desire for happiness is (in Ciceronian terms) a natural
tendency toward the sufficient life. So Marsilius says:

> Let us therefore lay this down as the principle of all things
> which are to be demonstrated here, a principle naturally held,
> believed, and freely granted by all: that all men not deformed or
> otherwise impeded naturally desire a sufficient life, and avoid
> and flee what is harmful thereto.[38]

Of course, Marsilius considers a peaceful and full life on earth
to be the highest natural good for man. At the same time, he
grants that eternal life is man's highest end but he takes that
end to be the concern of theologians and not of practical philosophers.[39] He frankly teaches that there are two final ends for
man: one in the City of God, the other in the City of Man.[40]
In this he is simply echoing the anonymous commentator on the
Nicomachean Ethics who wrote in the thirteenth century: "Therefore there is a happiness either from a divine cause or from a
human cause. And I say that is both from a divine cause and a
human cause."[41]

[35] Cf. S. MacClintock, *Perversity and Error. Studies on the "Averroist" John
of Jandun* (Bloomington: Indiana University Press, 1956), pp. 71–80, 165–166.
[36] Much attention has been directed to Marsilius by the recent translation,
with a preliminary volume of doctrinal studies: *The Defender of Peace*, translated by A. Gewirth, 2 vols. (New York: Columbia University Press, 1951–1956).
[37] *Defensor Pacis*, Disc. I, cap. 1; tr. Gewirth, II, p. 3.
[38] *Defensor Pacis*, Disc. I, cap. 4; tr. Gewirth, II, p. 12.
[39] *Defensor Pacis*, Disc. I, 6, 2; tr. Gewirth, II, p. 21.
[40] Cf. Gewirth's discussion, *op. cit.*, Vol. I, pp. 37–39.
[41] Cf. R. A. Gauthier, "Trois commentaires 'averroistes' sur l'Éthique à
Nicomaque," in *Archives d'histoire doctrinale et littéraire du moyen âge*, XVI
(1948), p. 274.

What is happening in the fourteenth century is actually a continuation of a revolution in medieval thinking on human tendencies, appetites, and ends. Marsilius appears to revive something of the internal finality which we noticed in Aristotle's biological works.[42] Man's natural desire is transposed to a common will of the people for a not-yet-existing end, for a goal which does not influence the will by final causality but which is, instead, efficiently projected as an end by collective human desires. Already in the fourteenth century, the appeal of final causality and external ends is losing ground in philosophy. Thomas Aquinas' finalism comes to be regarded as a sort of rationalistic determinism.[43]

In the transitional period of late medieval thought, the freedom of man came to be more and more identified with an absence of external restraint. This notion has continued to dominate modern ethical and political thinking. In the earlier Middle Ages, human liberty denoted the presence of an intrahuman power of self-determination, and even (in the *libertas* of Anselm) the presence of a suprahuman ordination of man's will toward eternal justice and happiness. There is little doubt that this change in philosophic and religious outlook on the appetitive tendencies of man marks one of the dividing points between medieval and modern philosophy. The full implications of this change cannot be realized until students of the history of philosophy recover more of the riches of medieval efforts to analyze the appetitive functions of man.

[42] Cf. Gewirth, *op. cit.*, I, pp. 54–67. That Gewirth overstresses his case, is argued by P. Munz in a critical review; *Speculum*, XXXIII (1958), pp. 284–293.
[43] Apparently an opinion shared by Gewirth, *ibid.*

6. *Wisdom as a Practical Virtue*

In a discussion of the place of any intellectual habit in moral thinking it is important, I think, to distinguish two kinds of reasoning about moral matters.[1] First of all, there is the type of thinking done by the moral scientist (moral theologian or ethician). This sort of reasoning seems to have three special characteristics: it is hypothetical, universal, and terminally cognitive. By doing it well one tends to develop the habit of moral science. The second kind of moral reasoning is that of the moral agent (the person faced with the problem of making a decision about his own action in terms of ultimate happiness). This type of reasoning may be described as realistic, operative, and terminally singular. By doing it well man tends to acquire the habit of prudence.

Since both forms of practical reasoning may be reduced to uses of discursive reason entailing a pattern which is in some sense syllogistic, let us call the first type the *cognitive practical syllogism* and the second the *operative practical syllogism*.

Using this terminology, we find that the cognitive practical syllogism is hypothetical. This is not too good a name for what I mean but I can't think of a better one. What it signifies is that the problems faced by the moral scientist are "if" problems. Thus an ethics teacher with no money to spare may reason about the morality of taking interest on a loan. He may conscientiously ponder the problem but his attitude toward it cannot be exactly the same as that of man who has some money to invest and who

[1] Originally titled: "The Role of a Proposed Practical Intellectual Virtue of Wisdom," *Proceedings of the American Catholic Philosophical Association*, XXVI (1952), pp. 160–167.

must decide whether to use it in this way or not. This thinking of the moral scientist in the cognitive syllogism might be compared to that of the speculative philosopher using second intentions. The latter thinks about thoughts of things. Similarly, the moral scientist thinks about right reasoning on human actions. Because of this parallelism, I should agree to call moral science intentional, provided that term were not open to ambiguity. It may even be suggested that it would be better to use the term *speculative.* But to my mind that would be misleading, for moral science is concerned with practical knowledge but in a way which is once removed from *praxis,* from actual doing.

On the other hand, the moral agent confronted by a real problem reasons about the action, whether it is to be done or not, by himself. He does not think about the way to think of such an action; he thinks about the action. It is in this sense that I should call his reasoning realistic, as opposed to theoretical, or hypothetical, thinking of the first type.

But this is only one point of difference. The second distinguishing feature lies in the contrast between the universal and the singular. As science, the knowledge of the moral scientist must be somewhat universal in its conclusions. Consider the morality of the decision to bomb the Abbey of Monte Casino during World War II as an example. We could think of this problem very practically and concretely, and come up with a moral conclusion. What would be the nature of our reasoning on this matter? It would be not only hypothetical but also somewhat generalized. That is to say, our decision would be applicable to many similar problems. Otherwise it could not be representative of moral science. You might object that a moral scientist could judge that General "A" was either right or wrong in what he did, and this decision of the moral scientist would be wholly singular. But I do not consider that such a singular judgment, the kind of judgment that is made by a judge in a law court, to be part of the work of a moral scientist. To make a right judgment of another man's action is the function of a sort of social art which is akin to prudence, or jurisprudence in the classic sense.

Perhaps if we look at the other side of the thing it will become clearer. In the operative moral syllogism the reasoner tries to reach a conclusion which applies only to one case, to this personal problem of action. His final practical judgment is quite singular. It is so limited to one case that it applies properly to no other. The operative moral syllogism moves toward a resultant which is not universal. It would help if we could insist that this resultant, viewed as a purely singular cognitive judgment, be called moral conscience, and if we could insist further that the name "moral conscience" never be given to the universal conclusion which terminates the cognitive practical syllogism. But it is now practically impossible to establish such a precision in terminology.

To sum up this consideration of the second differentiating factor, let me say that the conclusions of moral science always have some plurality of possible applications, whereas the conclusions of the moral agent are each of unique application to one case only. That is why the former may become precepts of moral law, while the latter are never laws.

Finally, I would characterize the reasoning of the moral scientist as cognitive, where that of the moral agent is operative. Moral science finishes with a knowing function which is not, *in itself,* a moral action or operation. From this point of view we could say that moral science is speculative; but it is also practical. I think it can be very confusing to speak of the "speculativo-practical," or to use similar terminology. The prime point to be kept in mind is that the moral scientist is finished with his work when he reaches a conclusion as to how a certain kind of practical problem should be judged, while the moral agent is not finished until he judges, makes his choice, and does or omits the action.

This leaves us with a necessary clarification in our topic. The work of moral science is not the same as the work of prudence. The cognitive moral syllogism is not the same as the operative one. It seems to me that such a distinction is essential to a good consideration of the possible practical uses of the virtue of wisdom.

WISDOM AND THE MORAL SCIENTIST

I do think that some habit of wisdom must form part of the equipment of the moral scientist. More bluntly, I do not see how anyone can presume to teach or write ethics or moral theology without some imperfect grasp of speculative wisdom. Such a thinker must never lose sight of the ultimate end of human actions. His thinking gets its formal character from the constant reference of his subject matter to the final cause of man's life. This final cause is the highest, or ultimate, cause. The ancient view of wisdom, which we find in Greco-Roman philosophy, certainly seems to have regarded this habit as practical. We have only to think of the continued stress, in the Platonic dialogues, on the moral and political applicability of *sophia* and *phronesis* to see the patronage which this view has among classic philosophers. It is true that Aristotle shows some hesitancy on the point, in the sixth book of the *Nicomachean Ethics* (and this explains why St. Thomas is not too definite on the practical uses of wisdom), but viewing ancient thought as a whole, I think we can say that, from the period of the seven sages onward, there was never much question that a moralist needed the virtue of wisdom.

The same thing can be said of the *sapientia* doctrine of the Fathers of the Church. Ambrose, Augustine, and Damascene are typical; they do not hestitate to make wisdom operative. In fact, patristic writers have little interest in the distinction between the speculative and the practical. The Fathers place their emphasis rather on the superior and inferior uses of *ratio,* and this does not correspond at all to the speculative-practical division.

However, I should like simply to record my conviction that practical wisdom does have an important part to play in the work of the moral scientist.

WISDOM AND THE MORAL AGENT

The question which interests me is whether there is any value in thinking of wisdom as a practical virtue in the life of the average moral agent.

To begin, I think we should settle on a working meaning for the term *wisdom*. There is a tendency, in the text of St. Thomas,[2]

[2] *In III Sententiarum*, d. 35, q. 2, a. 1; q. 1, a. 2 et 3; *Summa contra Gentiles*, I, 1; *S.T.*, I, q. 1, a. 6; I-II, q. 57, a. 2, c. Cf. M. L. Martinez, R.S.C.J., *Recta Ratio According to St. Thomas Aquinas* (St. Louis University dissertation, 1950), pp. 179–184.

to shift in various contexts from one notion of wisdom to another. I do not mean the differences between mystical, theological, and metaphysical wisdom. These three seem to have this in common: the highest cause which the mystic, the theologian, and the metaphysician consult is God. All three habits are wisdom in the unqualified sense; they differ in the manner (*modus*) in which each habit is possessed, and in the perfection and scope of each habit. They do not differ in regard to the identity of the Being who is the first and highest cause.

It is another distinction of wisdoms to which St. Thomas directs our attention. This is the difference between wisdom in the unqualified sense (*sapientia simpliciter* may be mystical, theological, or metaphysical) and the wisdom which is restricted to a given genus. Thus we read: "that man is called wise in any genus who considers the highest cause of that genus."[3] To illustrate this, St. Thomas proceeds to give the well-known example of the wisdom of the architect, who knows the end of his work but not necessarily the end of human life.

To speak of that kind of qualified wisdom which has reference only to a highest cause within a certain genus would only confuse the issue for us. We can easily see that the business prudence exercised by a capable banker is certainly governed by a knowledge of the primary purpose of his work. Such a man could be said to possess banking wisdom, since he is skilled in thinking in terms of the highest cause within his field of work. But these habits of prudence and wisdom in the banker are not identical with their moral counterparts. To put it simply, the highest cause within the genus of banking activities is not God but something else. If the banker takes God into his considerations, he does this as a good man and not merely as a good banker. Let us exclude from our considerations, then, the reduced meaning of wisdom which would take it as a habit of thinking in terms of the highest cause within one genus.

So, when we ask our question, whether wisdom may play a part as a practical virtue in the life of the moral agent, we are really asking whether such an agent may profitably use the habit of

[3] *S.T.*, I, q. 1, a. 6, c.

thinking of his moral actions in relation to the highest cause in the moral order. With the question put in this way, I do not understand how we can fail to give it an affirmative answer. Some reference of voluntary action to the ultimate end would seem necessary to every good moral agent.

But let us see what this means. In a familiar section of the *Summa Theologiae*,[4] St. Thomas outlines the teaching of Aristotle on the five intellectual virtues and apparently adopts it as his own. The habits of the speculative intellect are wisdom, understanding of principles, and science; those of the practical intellect are art and prudence. Then Thomas asks whether all of these are necessary to a life of moral virtue. He answers that wisdom, science, and art are not so required, but that the understanding of principles and the habit of prudence are absolutely necessary for moral virtue.

We can understand what St. Thomas was thinking of here. There are many good people, even saints, who are uninstructed in demonstrative science, art, philosophy, even in theology. Probably most of the great Christian saints would come more or less in this category. However, it is clear that wisdom is deemed not necessary to moral virtue, when wisdom is taken in the strict Aristotelian sense of a purely speculative *habitus*. Even with the enlargement of the meanings of wisdom to include the theological, we would have to agree with St. Thomas that a saint need not possess this habit. It is not necessary to be a theologian in order to live a good human life.

But does this preclude the use of a more practical form of wisdom in moral life? In prudential reasoning, which is that of the generally good moral agent, we find various steps. Some Thomists endeavor to use the analysis of the elicited acts of intellect and will, which is found in the early questions of the *Prima Secundae*, to throw some light on the workings of prudence. There is some question as to whether this psychological analysis (in which the will-acts are wish, intention, consent, choice, use, and fruition) is applicable to the prudential series of reasoning. St. Thomas does not relate the virtue of prudence to these elicited acts. How-

[4] I–II, q. 58, c. 4, c.

ever, consideration of these steps in the moral act[5] does suggest
that voluntary action requires some directing of the proposed
action to an end, some deliberation on the act as a means, and an
intelligent decision as to whether the action is to be done or not.
Accompanying this intellectual process, there is a concomitant
series of will-functions.

Now, while it is not necessary actually to make reference to the
ultimate end in every act of moral deliberation, I think it is
necessary for good moral action that the agent have and use the
habit of reasoning in terms of man's ultimate end. Without this
habit, he cannot have *moral* prudence; he might have some sort
of secondary prudence, like that of the banker, but not right reason
concerning moral problems.

What is the habit of maintaining some reference to the ultimate
end, in the consideration of all moral problems? If we say that this
habit is simply prudence itself, we must be aware that we are then
attributing a sapiential function to prudence. It is possible that St.
Thomas felt that this aspect of practical wisdom is already included
in the integral parts of the virtue. One of these parts is providence,
or foresight (*providentia*), and it consists in the practical intellectual function of ordering present and future voluntary actions to
the end of human life.[6] Note that this integral part is not simply
for the consideration of actions in relation to a proximate end,
but rather *in finem humanae vitae*. Yet, so far as I know, when
St. Thomas does identify prudence with some kind of wisdom, he
qualifies the proposition by adding that prudence is not "universal
wisdom."[7] This is the way in which St. Thomas usually speaks
of the kind of wisdom which is restricted to a certain genus.
However, it may be that St. Thomas is merely reminding us that
prudence is not moral science, neither moral philosophy nor
moral theology.

In any case, if we grant that the sapiential part of prudence is
sufficient to take care of the need of any good moral agent to
refer his voluntary actions to his ultimate end, then we should

---

[5] Cf. V. J. Bourke, *Ethics* (New York: Macmillan, 1951), pp. 58–66.
[6] *S.T.*, II–II. q. 49, a. 6, c. et ad 2m.
[7] "Prudentia enim est quaedam sapientia, sed non universalis sapientia." *In
Epistolam ad Ephesios*, cap. 5, lect. 6.

remember that this is a minimal requirement of practical wisdom. There should be room in a more perfectly developed moral character for a distinct habit of practical wisdom. We know of the possibility of that special form of wisdom which is a Gift of the Holy Spirit. In a noteworthy answer to an objection[8] St. Thomas has indicated the difference between this nonspeculative type of wisdom and the purely intellectual habit of wisdom:

> It must be said that wisdom is taken in two ways, for judgment pertains to the man of wisdom and there are two ways of judging. It is possible, in one way, for a man to judge by way of inclination (*per modum inclinationis*) as is the case when the possessor of a habitus of virtue judges rightly concerning those things which are to be done in accord with virtue, insofar as he is inclined toward these acts; hence the statement in the tenth book of the *Ethics* [1176a17] that the virtuous man is the measure and rule of human acts. And it is possible, in another way, by way of cognition (*per modum cognitionis*) as is the case when someone who is instructed in moral science judges concerning acts of virtue, even if he does not possess the virtue. So, the first way of judging divine matters pertains to the wisdom which is a Gift of the Holy Spirit . . . and the second way of judging pertains to this subject [theology] inasmuch as it is acquired by study, even though its principles are taken from revelation.

Let us observe in this text the distinction between an affective wisdom which stems from moral virtue and a cognitive wisdom arising from science. Though St. Thomas gives the Gift of the Holy Spirit as the name of the affective wisdom, he also cites Aristotle as a philosophical author who has found a place for that wisdom which is imbedded in a life of virtue. Certainly Aristotle was not thinking of the Gift of the Holy Spirit.

In what way, then, may practical wisdom become a habit of the virtuous man? First, in the way already noted, that is, as an integral part of prudence. Second, it may be possible as a distinct practical virtue. If we consider the mature moral agent, we find that he will differ from the child in the adult's efforts, vague and informal though they be, to reflect upon his moral convictions. Initial opinions about moral behavior are acquired from family customs and admonitions, from instruction in school, from the

[8] *S.T.*, I, q. 1, a. 6, ad 3m.

example of early associates, and from religious education. We can hardly doubt that most people pass through periods of wonder, self-criticism, and practical philosophizing, even though they have no opportunities to develop a technical habit of moral science. Such people form personal and reflective views on human life and its purpose. I think we are justified in concluding that these adults make for themselves a philosophy of life which includes some acceptance of a Supreme Being and some inclination to adapt their lives to patterns of action which are considered right. Even the average college graduate who has studied a little philosophy can hardly be regarded as a moral scientist in the technical sense, yet he will usually have a habit of judging his moral problems in terms of some ultimate view of life. If such agents also have religious convictions they can usually assimilate their natural philosophical convictions to the ideals of their religious outlook. The resultant of such average moral thinking is not moral science in the strict sense, for such men are not ordinarily able to express their views to others in an orderly manner, nor could they teach what they feel to be right. But their reflective habit of mind is probably more than ordinary moral prudence. If anyone were to say to me that this is precisely what prudence is, then I should agree, with the qualification that it is a wise prudence. There may even be some value in singling out this possible habit of practical wisdom and emphasizing its termination in a vague knowledge but a clearer affective inclination to the Highest Good. At times St. Thomas seems to drop the rigid classifications of the Aristotelian virtues and to remember that there may be these imperfect practical virtues of the heart. In at least one discussion of moral conscience, he suggests that the judgment of conscience may be governed not only by the habits of synderesis and moral science but also by the habit of wisdom.[9]

It is worth noting that an effort has recently been made to identify and describe an integrating natural moral virtue which could unify and inform man's various natural virtues in the manner that charity informs the whole structure of supernatural character. Dom Lottin has suggested that this task be assigned to the

---

[9] *De veritate,* q. XVII, a. 1, ad 4m.

virtue of religion.[10] He has related this claim to the act of intention conjecturing that it may be precisely the habit of religion which could coordinate all of man's natural virtues in terms of the ultimate end. Dom Lottin puts his point before us with little hesitation: "Whatever it might be in the supernatural order, it is evident that in a purely natural order of things it would have belonged to the virtue of religion, in its full sense, to affirm that intention of gaining the last end through an orientation in this direction of the whole of human life."[11]

Now my reaction to this sort of suggestion is mixed. The virtue of religion, as described by St. Thomas, enables a man to perform well certain special actions whereby he acknowledges the obvious natural dependence of man upon God. True, this meaning of religion has nothing to do with revealed and supernatural religion. It is a natural virtue. But I find no real basis in the text of St. Thomas for the suggestion that religion might inform the natural virtues as charity does the supernatural habits. If we must talk about natural moral character, I would be more inclined to use practical wisdom as the dominating virtue in this sphere. But all this conjecturing arises from asking a question based on a contrary-to-fact supposition. The question is: If man were not supernaturalized, what would be the constituents of moral character? As a practical philosopher, one's only answer to such questions must be: But he is supernaturalized!

I have intended to suggest, then, that a discussion of practical wisdom requires a preliminary distinction between the work of moral science and the work of moral prudence. Second, I think that some sort of wisdom, perhaps both speculative and practical, is needed by the moral scientist. Third, I would grant that no habit of speculative wisdom is necessarily required in the good average moral agent. Finally, I think that there is a kind of practical wisdom, a wisdom of the heart, that wisdom which comes *per modum inclinationis,* which is at least a possible practical virtue in the life of the average moral agent.

<hr>

[10] Odon Lottin, *Principes de morale* (Louvain, 1947), pp. 251–252.

[11] *Ibid.,* p. 252. Lottin cites to the same effect: J. E. Van Roey, *De virtute charitatis. Quaestiones selectae* (Mechliniae, 1929), pp. 21–23.

7. *Moral Obligation: Absolute or Relative?**

We may take as a working definition the statement that moral obligation is some sort of necessity which is at times recognized by an agent when he faces a situation in which he finds himself free to decide to act or not to act, or free to choose one way of acting rather than other ways. By *necessity* in this statement we cannot mean physical necessity; if the agent is completely determined to one way of acting, then he has no choice and is not free. Rather, this moral necessity seems to be of the nature of an imperative which can be disobeyed, but only at the expense of some personal disquietude in the agent, some feeling of failure to meet the demands of a given situation, some indication of self-blame. These conscious disturbances in the moral agent who does not conform to his moral obligation seem to me to stem from a particular judgment of what should be done or omitted.

I am aware that there are many varieties of moral theory and consequently many differences in moral terminology. Some moral philosophers refuse to speak or think in terms of moral obligation. To circumvent these "idols of the theater" let me illustrate the consciousness of moral obligation by using a personal experience. A few years ago, I was driving my automobile to the meeting of a scientific academy and was accompanied by a friend who is a medical doctor. We had two hours in which to complete our trip and had no time to stop. On the way we passed another automobile which was wrecked, its occupants evidently hurt. We slowed down and saw that there were several other people who had stopped to help the injured. I decided quickly to drive on, for a stop would have made us late for our conference. Later, both my friend

* Paper delivered at the XIth International Congress of Philosophy (Brussels, 1953), printed in *Proceedings* (Amsterdam-Louvain, 1953), Vol. X, pp. 142–146.

the doctor and I admitted that we should have stopped, since we had no assurance that there was a medical man on the scene. We have spoken about this incident several times since and are both inclined to think that we failed to act properly in this situation. Now this is the typical situation in which moral obligation appears. I think we may take it that all mature human beings, irrespective of their philosophical differences, have felt or known such experiences.

Understanding obligation in this sense, we may then ask: What is the character of this sort of obligation? Is it relative or absolute? This is equivalent to asking whether I am certain that I should do, or omit, the concretely proposed action. If I am not certain, then I have no judgment of moral conscience. If I am certain, then I cannot act against the judgment of conscience without incurring some sort of conscious self-condemnation. It is possible for me to fail to conform to my conscience but, if I so fail, I know and feel that I have not done my best. There can be no question of relativity here; each judgment of conscience is applied to a unique set of circumstances. A moral judgment on the propriety of doing or omitting this action in this set of circumstances is absolutely binding on the agent involved. If it were not, we would have to say that the agent makes no morally certain judgment.

On the other hand, there are moral situations in which the agent cannot make an immediately certain judgment as to what he should do. These are the difficult situations. I think we may say that these difficult situations reduce to two types. There is first the situation in which the agent is perplexed because he has not enough knowledge to form a definite and subjectively certain practical judgment, yet he knows that there is time enough, before action is required, to acquire this knowledge. In this type of difficulty, an absolute obligation is present: the agent must get this possible knowledge and then make his decision as to what he ought to do. The eventual judgment is absolutely binding. The reason for saying that such subjectively certain practical judgments are absolutely binding is found in the very character of moral action. Man must be able to direct his moral actions by taking thought upon their goodness or evil. If he could not do this, there would be no personal awareness of responsibility for such actions. But granting the ability so to direct one's free actions is equivalent to the admission that each man is fully aware of moral obligation in connection with some of his proposed actions. To say that such obligation is always merely relative is to reject the possibility of finding clear directives for human action.

Second, there is the situation which demands immediate action, and in which the agent simply does not know what he ought to do. He has no time to consult others or to acquire new knowledge. It seems to me that this type of situation is not faced in classical theories of moral conscience. What we have here is a practical problem which this agent is unable to solve. Can we say that he is morally obligated to solve it rightly? Obviously not, for no rational solution is open to him. It is useless to talk about taking the safest course. If one line of action is "safer" than the other, and they are otherwise of equal moral value, then this is not an example of perplexity. It is plain that the judgment of conscience, in such a case, is that one should do the "safer" action. However, where the agent cannot reach a moral decision as to what he should do, the situation is not a moral problem. It should be mentioned in moral discussions, but only to be excluded. Whatever such an agent does will be done outside the sphere of moral action. He can make no rational choice because he cannot find reasons for acting in one way rather than in the other. (For instance, a man is hunting with a friend; the friend is seriously injured in a fall; the first man does not know whether he should leave his friend and go for help, or stay with his friend with the chance of never getting help. The circumstances could be such that there would be no clear solution to such a problem; yet something would have to be done; the man must either stay or go.) In this type of perplexity, I would suggest that there is no obligation, absolute or relative, once the agent has recognized the impossibility of rational decision. There is no obligation, for no judgment of conscience is possible.

Following the above lines of reasoning, every sincerely made judgment of conscience is absolutely binding on the moral agent. Relativity of obligation only appears where there is some possibility that there may be different ways in which the same rule would apply to different cases in different sets of circumstances. But we are not talking about the obligation of a general rule here, we are talking about the obligation of a singular judgment. There can be nothing relative in the judgment that I ought to do this action under these concrete circumstances.

I would exclude from consideration, in connection with obligation, the cases of so-called "permissive" conscience. These instances of permissive judgment amount to a decision that of two objects of choice one is not rationally preferable to the other. Hence, no rational choice is possible and there can be no question of obligation. In other words, the liberty of indifference discussed by Leibniz and some of the later Scholastics is not an example of moral freedom. There must be some rational motivation for a choice, if a person is to be morally obligated to make a reasonable choice.

If it is true, then, that all subjectively certain judgments of conscience are obligatory in an absolute sense, why has there been frequent discussion as to the absolute or relative character of moral obligation? I think this problem can only arise when one attaches obligation to moral law, or to some other generalized standards of morality. The kind of obligation which we may attribute to moral law will vary, depending on our way of understanding law and its component terms. If we take each moral law to be a somewhat universal precept, then obviously there can be some question as to the degree or quality of the necessity to obey this precept under changing circumstances. Traditional scholasticism insists on the absolute obligation attaching to the primary precepts of natural moral law. A good many modern moralists would deny that any moral law is a matter of absolute obligation. The root of conflict lies partly in terminology, partly in a different general philosophic outlook. Here again, to avoid argument about vaguely understood generalizations, I would direct your attention to a particular case.

Think of a man who is violently attacked by a demented person. This man under attack must quickly decide what to do. He is convinced of the rightness of the moral percept that "murder is evil." This precept does not solve his problem. He may still wonder whether he should kill this demented person in order to defend himself. He may not know whether this act of killing is murder or not. If he thinks that such killing is murder, he may again wonder whether the precept, "murder is evil," is absolutely obligatory in all circumstances. He may come to the conclusion that, in these special circumstances, he is justified in "murdering" the demented attacker. He would then claim that the precept, "murder is evil," is of relative obligation.

However, it is possible to construe this precept so that it will be absolutely obligatory. This may be done by interpreting murder as killing a human being under circumstances which are not rationally fitting. With such a strict meaning for murder, we could judge that killing in self-defense is not a case of murder. As a consequence, we could conclude that there is an absolute moral obligation to avoid murder in the strict sense.

Quite commonly Catholic moralists maintain that there are some species of moral actions which are essentially bad. There would be an absolute obligation to avoid such actions. Other thinkers deny that there are any essentially immoral types of action. We find an excellent example in the interminable discussions of the propriety of telling lies. Not all people understand lying in the same way. The Thomistic definition, *locutio contra mentem,* suggests the act of using a sign to convey the opposite of what one actually thinks true. This is a very technical definition; it does not contain the notion of the deception of another person; it stresses the difformity between voluntary signification and thought, *within one person.* There is something abusive and unreasonable in the act of consciously expressing what one judges to be wrong. We can easily see how this sort of definition leads to the conclusion that lying is immoral, irrespective of its consequences to other persons. It is actually classified as a form of self-abuse. Thus understood, lying becomes a species of action which man is absolutely obliged to avoid.

Other equally sincere moral thinkers may understand lying as a social action, involving two or more persons. Thus, to lie will be to use a sign in such a way as to deceive, or at least intend to deceive, another person. With this meaning not all lies are essentially immoral. This usage covers equivocations and deliberate reservations of the type excluded by the Thomistic definition. With the "social" meaning of lie, the rule: "one should not lie," is not absolutely obligatory in all cases. With the Thomistic definition, the same rule becomes absolutely binding.

Much time and effort are wasted by men who continue to dispute because of diverse meanings of the basic terms of discussion. Many great philosophers have pointed out this simple truth. Particularly in the area of moral philosophy the problems are too urgent for solutions to be impeded by terminological differences. It is high time all moralists recognized the need to come to some common agreement on the use of elementary terms in their subject.

As a start toward such agreement, I am suggesting that we could well admit that the obligation attaching to many moral laws is relative to changing circumstances. Second, I suggest that certain very primary and elementary rules of morality are matters of absolute obligation, when their terms are strictly understood. Finally, I submit that moral conscience, in the sense of the personal judgment that this action under these singular circumstances is right or wrong for me, is never relative but always absolute in its obligation.

8. *Decision-Making and Moral Action*

It is well known that most of the philosophies that have stood the test of time maintain that human activity is aimed at some goal.[1] Recall the famous opening lines of Aristotle's *Nicomachean Ethics*: "Every art and every inquiry, and similiarly every action and pursuit, is thought to aim at some good; and for this reason the good has rightly been declared to be that at which all things aim."[2] Indeed, we know that Aristotle is here but reporting and approving the general consensus of Greek literature (manifested in the great dramatists as much as in the philosophers): the life of reason must follow a certain rational pattern (the *logos* or *nomos*) and this entails a goal or purpose (which is called the *telos*).

A similar point of view is found in the thought of Thomas Aquinas and later Catholic philosophers.[3] Many of us are familiar with this teleological approach to human action. Though Francis Bacon and his contemporaries did their best to throw out of philosophy and science all considerations of end or purpose, under the mistaken impression that final causality is less scientific than efficient causality, the explanation of action, structure, functioning, and even energy, in terms of their goals was never wholly eradicated from the modern mind. Biology never wholly lost its teleological orientation (and it is worth remembering that Aristotle was trained in ancient biology). The notion that organs have specific functions to perform for the welfare of the whole organism, that living beings grow through a succession of preliminary stages toward a peak condition of optimum maturity (ontogenesis), and

[1] University lecture sponsored by St. Louis University Graduate School, spring term, 1958, under the general theme, "Decision — Man's Unique Privilege and Responsibility."

[2] Book I, ch. 1, 1094al–3; Oxford trans., ed. W. D. Ross.

[3] St. Thomas Aquinas, *Summa contra Gentiles*, III, c. 2–3.

indeed the many transformistic theories of evolution — all presuppose a concept of some vital goal toward which these changes move more or less successfully.

Mechanistic and behavioristic techniques of analyzing human conduct profess to get along entirely without introducing ends or goals of human life. Yet purely mechanical explanations of living activity seem now to be outmoded. The literature of present-day social psychology is surprisingly insistent on this point. Thus we find one group of psychologists saying bluntly: "Almost any set of psychological problems, especially those in the fields of motivation and personality, inevitably involve goals and goal-directed behavior."[4] These research psychologists have made very interesting studies of what they call *levels of aspiration* and, significantly enough, one lengthy experiment deals with responses to success and failure in throwing rings at a target! (Whatever the philosophical heaven that Aristotle now inhabits, he cannot but be pleased at this research.)

This is not an isolated development in social psychology. In a representative textbook[5] we read: "Earlier we said that an attitude has the character of a commitment to a policy. In this respect it represents a dynamic assessment of a given situation with reference to an end." Here is teleology restored to psychological respectability! The very language of this sentence, "assessment of a given situation with reference to an end," is reminiscent and suggestive of the sort of analysis that has been used for centuries in Aristotelico-Thomistic studies of successful human action. We shall see more of this later. For the moment it is enough to suggest that the most fruitful approach to the study of human decision-making will be in terms of an examination of the goals to which men aspire. In other words, our discussion will be teleological.

TWO TYPES OF PROBLEM-SOLVING

One of the chief areas in which human reason comes into use is in problem-solving. This is so obvious that the most American of all philosophies, *pragmatism,* tended to define all scientific and

[4] K. Lewin, T. Dembo, L. Festinger, and P. S. Sears, *Personality and the Behavior Disorders* (New York: Ronald Press, 1944), Vol. I, p. 333.

[5] S. E. Asch, *Social Psychology* (New York: Prentice-Hall, 1952), p. 580.

philosophic endeavor as the conscious response to given problems. There is much to be said for this view. In a sense, man is marked by his ability to face and solve in different ways the perplexities which emerge in his life. The capacity to see the same situation from diverse angles and in terms of plural consequences is characteristic of the human intellect — and apparently lacking in the cognitive awareness of brute animals. The agent guided by instinct has no behavior problems.

Man attempts to solve two kinds of problems. The first I should like to call the *play problem* — not because it is unimportant but because it has no direct and practical consequences. In this category are all pure puzzles and theoretical difficulties. Examples of the play problem would range from crossword puzzles, through the questions of pure mathematics, to the difficulties faced by modern physics and indeed by metaphysics. Let me again assure you, most emphatically, that in calling these *play problems*, I have no intention of denying their significance or importance. The point about them is this: the solver of play problems is impelled to his work by a sort of divine curiosity; he is motivated by a craving to know the answers and by that alone. If it turns out that, in the process of their solution, he may sharpen his wits, or discover something of practical utility to himself or his fellowmen, these indirect consequences are not pertinent to the craving to solve the pure problem.

The man who is fascinated by the play problem may mystify his more practical brother: he is the chess player who makes no profit from his skill; he is the pure scientist who is impatient with those who ask him about the utility of his discoveries; he is the thinker who stands apart from his enterprising fellows, as the contemplative is distinct from the practitioner of the active life. Indeed, he is like Mary in relation to Martha — certain that he has chosen the better part.

Perhaps it will seem odd to you, when I say that we can learn little about decision-making from the solving of such play problems. Your reaction may stem from your belief that philosophers must be the prime example of this addiction to impractical problems. I would agree with you — but hasten to remind you that not all philosophers are pure metaphysicians and that you may encounter, at times, that anomaly to his craft, the practical philosopher.

However that may be, the surprising thing about the play problem is that it requires little or no decision-making on the part of its solver. This feature is well exemplified in pure mathematics. Given certain postulates, a problem will arise, move forward, and reach its denouement in the mind of the thinker — almost as if the problem had a life of its own. The answer to the problem arises from rigorous thinking but involves no decision on the part of the thinker. The greater his skill, the more is he impressed with the feeling that he is a witness of a sort of impersonal operation or process which develops in him but, in a sense, apart from him. To those who speak the language of existentialism: the pure scientist and mathematician is the least *engaged* of all thinkers. His only personal commitment is to begin the process of pure thinking; once started, he is not required to throw his weight about, to decide anything. Things decide themselves for him. He is like a man who decides to get on a boat for Europe: there is nothing more for him to do about it until he has reached his destination — unless he be an extraordinary swimmer!

If you think that I am exaggerating the impracticality of mathematics, let me quote a few lines to illustrate my point:

> Not only is mathematics independent of us and our thoughts, but in another sense we and the whole universe of existing things are independent of mathematics. The apprehension of this purely ideal character is indispensable, if we are to understand rightly the place of mathematics as one among the arts. It was formerly supposed that pure reason could decide, in some respects, as to the nature of the actual world: geometry, at least, was thought to deal with the space in which we live. But we now know that pure mathematics can never pronounce upon questions of actual existence: the world of reason, in a sense, controls the world of fact, but it is not at any point creative of fact, and in the application of its results to the world in time and space, its certainty and precision are lost among approximations and working hypotheses.

These are not the words of some addled idealist but of one of the coauthors of *Principia Mathematica*.[6]

[6] Bertrand Russell, "The Study of Mathematics," in *Mysticism and Logic* (New York: W. W. Norton Co., 1929), p. 69.

In contradistinction to the play problem there is the *practical problem*. This new sort of perplexity has consequences to its solution which enter into the very fabric of the life of the solver, or of his fellowmen. Sometimes the same set of circumstances will provide a play problem to one man and a practical problem to another. If President Truman made the decision to use the atom bomb on Hiroshima, it was a practical problem to him. To us who may think of it now, no matter how we try to project ourselves into Truman's shoes, it can be but a play problem to decide how we would have made that decision.

The practical problem is one which requires a personal commitment on the part of the solver of it. This is something which existentialism has stressed.

And what is this point precisely? It is the rather obvious conclusion that a decision is a highly personal act, including much more than intellectual judgment. Think of the man who finds himself suddenly out of a job, his family starving, the mortgage about to be foreclosed on his home, who decides to go out that night and rob a service station. And then think of the next door reader of the morning paper, who is in no financial trouble, who reads about this robbery and judges that the robber was wrong. The robber made a decision under the influence of a tremendous anxiety, an emotional freight which the newspaper reader could not have. The robber was *engagé*, personally involved in these circumstances. To him the problem of his life was practical and vital. To another man, the robber's problem is secondhand, hypothetical, theoretical, simply not practical, a play problem.

We can *learn* much about decision-making from a consideration of practical problems. We cannot be *taught* much in that area. The reason is that personal experience cannot be communicated by a teacher. If you have not suffered a toothache, I cannot tell you what it feels like. I can make comparisons which will enable you to form, by analogy, an abstract notion of the meaning of the word "toothache." But when you finally experience your first twinge in that upper molar, you will say: "I never realized that it was like this."

It is similarly impossible to teach anyone how to make good practical decisions. And if anyone comes along professing so to teach you, avoid him like a plague; he is a charlatan. Decision-making is a skill, as swimming is, but more difficult. No one can teach you to swim; they may make it easier for you to learn but this is something which you must acquire through you own efforts. The French have a proverb which sums it up: *en forgeant on devient forgeron.* Roughly translated this means, if you want to be a blacksmith you must work at it.

DIFFERENT KINDS OF PRACTICAL DECISIONS

It is helpful to distinguish clearly between decisions as to means and decisions as to goals. The consideration of means is much easier than that of goals. A means is something that is done or used for the sake of a given end. The end or goal, on the other hand, is prized for its own sake and never as a means. For example, one may regard the obtaining of a college degree as an end. To this many things may serve as means: attendance at classes, studying, buying books, the money to pay for tuition, and so on.

The value of a means can be determined by establishing its relation to the goal in view. Using mathematical language, we could say that the means is a function of the end. However, the goal *qua* end must be valued for its intrinsic worth. In the language of Thomistic philosophy this can be put neatly: a means is a *bonum utile,* a good which is useful because it gets you something else; while an end is a *bonum honestum,* a good which stands alone and is desired simply for its own sake.

Reconsideration of the foregoing example of the college degree reveals that a subdivision of goals is now required. When obtained, the college degree turns out to be a means to a further end — it is not simply satisfactory in itself. Such an end we call proximate. It is to be distinguished from the sort of goal which would never become a means to some more remote end. This latter sort of goal, always prized for its own sake, we call an ultimate end. To express this distinction in another way: if one is asked *why* he desires a certain end, then if this end is but proximate, he may give his reason in terms of a higher value; but if this end is ultimate, then it must be valued for itself alone and no other answer can be given to the question *why*.

DECISIONS AS TO MEANS

The traditional Thomistic analysis of the problem of making a decision as to means to be used to attain a certain goal is very well worked out. It is presented in the text of St. Thomas in the various places where he discusses the acts appropriate to a prudent man.[7] If prudence means skill in thinking out problems of action, then we can discern three successive acts of prudence. The first such act is called *counseling* by present-day psychologists (e.g., Carl Rogers) and that is what Aquinas named it, *consilium*. It is a cognitive action, or process, of gathering together, as it were, the various possible means which might be used to achieve an already determined goal. Counseling further involves a reasoning process in which these available means are compared and weighed: this is the process of *deliberation*. Skill in such deliberation regarding the relative value of means depends on many psychological factors — on a good memory, on an ability to "size up" a problem quickly and practically, on the capacity to profit from experience, and on the ability to carry through one's thinking to a reasonable conclusion.[8] No one is born with these capacities fully developed nor can they be taught; they may be acquired by hard personal effort.

This first stage of weighing the means might be illustrated by the problem of choosing a college to attend. Say that a person has already decided to go to college. (This is his decision as to a goal which we have not yet discussed in detail.) He must still make a decision as to what college to attend, where, when, and so

[7] St. Thomas, *In III Sententiarum*, d. 23, 1, 4, sol. 2, ad 3m; *Summa contra Gentiles*, I, c. 93; *In III de Anima*, lect. 4, n. 630; *De virtutibus cardinalibus*, art. 2, c.; *S.T.*, I–II, q. 57, a. 4–5, c.; II–II, q. 47, a. 8, c. Cf. Charles J. O'Neil, "Prudence, the Incommunicable Wisdom," in *Essays in Thomism*, ed. R. E. Brennan (New York: Sheed & Ward, 1942), pp. 187–204, 382–387.

[8] On the integral parts of prudence: V. Bourke, *Ethics* (New York: Macmillan, 1951), p. 297; for their utilization in psychological counseling consult: Charles A. Curran, *Counseling in Catholic Life and Education* (New York: Macmillan, 1952), pp. 411–425.

on. Limiting the example for the sake of brevity to the choice of one of three colleges *A*, *B*, and *C*, we can see that deliberation consists in a sort of preliminary evaluation of the respective merits and availability of these three means to the end. In such a deliberation, one college may be excluded as a means (say it is too expensive) and, of the two remaining, *C* is discovered to be much preferable to *B*. This is the point at which the person makes the second act of prudence, namely *practical judgment*. It concludes the deliberative process in a terminal, cognitive act of preference. In our college example, the agent would judge as follows: from all points of view college *C* is the best place for me to go.

Now this example is oversimplified: one may terminate in a judgment which is not so practically clear. He may end with the sincere conviction that there is no great difference between colleges *A*, *B*, and *C*, and thus they appear as equally valuable means to his end. This is a possible conclusion. It does not help much. No real preference is established by it and it offers no rational guidance for choice.

If more information can be obtained about the means, then a reasonable person will get it and in a further process of deliberation establish a cognitive preference for one means. However, if this cannot be done, then no reasonable evidence is available for the eventual making of a choice or decision as to means. I think that such a stalemate occurs but rarely in the actual problems of life; for, besides the extrapersonal character of the available means, there are usually psychological factors which motivate the person from within to embrace one means rather than the others.

Once arrived at a judgment of preference, one last act of prudence remains. The practical thinker now may *command* himself to use or not to use this preferred means. This act (which Thomists call *imperium* or *praeceptum*) is the closest approximation to a *decision* that we may find in cognitive procedure. It is a knowing action but it verges upon a volitional action. In our example, it might be expressed: "I should go to college *C*;" possibly as an imperative: "Go to college *C*."

All the preceding occurs in the order of thinking, not of doing. The transition to action must be made by the agent *willing* to carry out his cognitive decision. This brings us to the moment of choice, where decision-making becomes most personal. One may perform all the prior acts of prudence for the sake of giving advice to another man but one cannot make an act of choice for another person. Choice (*electio*) is the wholly personal commitment to a definite line of action (or omission) as a means to a given end. Note that Thomists use the term *choice* in this restricted sense: one chooses means; one never chooses ends. That there is some act of personal commitment to an end, as such, is obvious. However, we shall discuss that act of opting an end later: it cannot be choice, in this linguistic usage, because we lose the important distinction between means and end when we treat the commitment to an end. Both are decisions, of course, but we are now discussing the choice-decision which consists in electing to use a certain means for an end which has already been decided on.

Now the foregoing analysis is but a sketch of the Thomistic teaching on decision-making in the order of prudence. Despite its venerable age, and old-fashioned terminology, I recommend it to you. You must study it further in order to put the teaching to personal use. You will not waste your time in making such a study. Indeed it will save valuable time to do so.

Those of you who are trained in the classical languages will find the various Latin terms for decision, which Thomas Aquinas uses, reminiscent of the language of Cicero, Seneca, Macrobius, and the Roman lawyers. *Consilium* suggested to the Middle Ages the etymology of *con-sidium,* the sitting down together of a group of people to look at the ways of achieving a goal from all thinkable sides. *Judicium* expresses the moment of stating the right solution: *jus-dicere. Praeceptum* has the literal meaning of taking one means and setting it before or above all others. Another term for decision, *sententia,* suggests getting at the sense, the best meaning, or the significance of a practical problem. Indeed, we still use the term today in legal language to express verbally the judge's decision in *sentencing,* passing final judgment on, a condemned criminal. The precision and delicate shadings of meaning attached to such terms are indicative of the value of language study as an approach to our subject.

Modern psychology has much to offer, too, in its studies of decisions as to means. One introduction to this material may be found in the work on *Personality and the Behavior Disorders* which I have already cited. The important distinction between the verbal goal and the true goal of a human agent is much stressed in these studies.[9] Very frequently a person professes to be aiming at one result when actually he is striving for some quite different end. Obviously one's consideration and choice of means are actually made in terms of the true goal rather than the verbally expressed one. A politician, for instance, may say that he is working for the public welfare but his decisions and actions may show that he is actually aiming at personal power or graft. Statistical and graphic interpretations of responses to success and failure in the use of various means to a goal are found in this psychological literature.[10] However, psychological thinking on the decision problems is "at present a bit chaotic" and we are warned that much more research is needed before application to value systems will be possible.

GAMES' THEORY AND DECISION

Some of you may have come upon games' theory: it is a fascinating development in applied mathematics and many people think that it can be brought to bear on the decision process. Games such as chess or bridge are governed by very definite rules which may be regarded as the postulates of the system within which a certain number of possible moves or plays may be calculated and evaluated and decided on, at any given stage of the playing. The initial moves or plays quickly exclude certain alternative lines of action and it is possible rather rigorously to establish optimum choices, once the game has progressed somewhat. In 1928 J. von Neumann published a pioneer article on this subject: "On the Theory of Playing Games."[11] Twenty years later, with O. Morgenstern, von Neumann wrote one of the standard works in English: *Theory of Games and Economic Behavior*,[12] which

[9] Lewin *et al., op. cit.,* p. 336.
[10] Cf. *ibid.,* pp. 357–376.
[11] "Zur Theorie der Gesellschaftsspiele," *Mathematische Annalen,* 100 (1928), pp. 295–320.   [12] Princeton University Press, 1947, 625 pages.

rather confidently applies the theory to the basic concepts and problems of economics.

Von Neumann starts with the blunt statement that the end of economics is profit. "We shall therefore assume," he says, "that the aim of all participants in the economic system, consumers as well as entrepreneurs is money, or equivalently a single monetary commodity."

To this I would offer a mild criticism. It appears to define economics in terms of one type only: capitalist economics. In this context it is an astonishing assumption. There are other economic systems with other ends. That of the later Middle Ages was rather highly developed and its professed end was the maximum availability of goods of consumption and production to all men in Christendom.[13] In such an economics, the profit motive meant nothing. This does not mean that the Middle Ages had no avaricious men but that the governing economic theory aimed at something other than profit.

Today it is difficult to ignore the widespread functioning of quite another nonprofit system of economics. This is the economics of the U.S.S.R. and its associated states. The end of this system is *verbally* the distribution of goods to all men according to their needs; *really* the goal of Soviet economics appears to be the promotion of world revolution, the destruction of the capitalist system, and the consequent political power of its promoters. In any case, socialist and communist economics is not aimed at mere money-making and this is a hard fact which von Neumann should have kept in mind. One cannot expect to offer a scientific appraisal of economic decisions if one limits the consideration to but one species of economic system.

However, it is very interesting to observe how von Neumann applies games' theory to the problems of capitalistic economics. Throughout he uses the means-end analysis. Almost as if he were a Thomist, he describes certain goods that are desired by most men. He asserts that "the individual who attempts to obtain these respective maxima is also said to act 'rationally.'" He offers a clear

---

[13] This point is well brought out in Henri Daniel-Rops, *Cathedral and Crusade* (London-New York: Dent-Dutton, 1957), pp. 244–258.

exposition of what is involved in using right reason in the practical order. He speaks of the need to survey the various "paths" to an optimum position. This parallels the Thomistic discussion of the process of counseling to a practical decision. He points to the indefiniteness of a qualitative appraisal of the relative values of various means and rather pontifically suggests that the whole thing can be cleared up by the use of quantitative methods. These are the mathematical procedures worked out in games' theory.

It is when von Neumann comes to actual economic problems and their resolution that we meet with our first discouragement. He selects extremely oversimplified economic situations for his calculations. One such case is that of Robinson Crusoe on his desert island! How he can be viewed as a capitalist, or a profit-seeker, I don't know. It would seem that money or any symbol of exchange value would be a least desired commodity for poor Robinson. Say he acquired his first million: what would he do with it?

Yet I am far from judging that mathematical techniques are without utility in reasoning to a practical decision. Von Neumann is very clear in stating that the procedure is not at all a calculus of probabilities working toward an indefinitely remote limit. Rather, the number of possibilities of action in a given decision-problem is finite, and often quite small. Speaking generally, "Decision theory applies to statistical problems the principle that a statistical procedure should be evaluated by its consequences in various circumstances. . . ."[14] Those of you who know mathematics can take it on from there as far as I am concerned. For those who are nonmathematicians but find me confusing, I should like to quote the definition of a decision used by one games' theorist: "Let $Z = (Z, \Omega, p)$ be a sample space, and let A be an arbitrary space of actions or decisions. Then a function d which is defined on Z and which maps Z into A is called a decision function."[15] If you follow that, then games' theory may help you to make many decisions.

[14] D. H. Blackwell, *Theory of Games and Statistical Decisions* (New York: Macmillan, 1954), p. vii. For a comparable effort to apply "systems analysis" to value judgments and ethics, cf. Charles R. Dechert, "A Pluralistic World Order," *Proceedings of the American Catholic Philosophical Association*, XXXVII (1963), pp. 167–186.

[15] Blackwell, *op. cit.*, p. 81.

DECISIONS AS TO ENDS

Given time, sufficient information, some experience, and a little logic or some other skill in reasoning, any routine thinker can come up with a good decision as to the best means to use to achieve a given end. But how does he decide on the end?

First of all we should recall the point about proximate ends. Where any question about them arises they can be justified or rejected by referring them to more remote ends. It is a favorite trick of positivists to treat ends as if they were entirely of this character. A famous work by L. von Mises uses this dodge.[16] He speaks throughout of the problem of deciding on means for certain ends or goals.[17] He insists that he is always talking about the ends which men do desire: things like money, power, a college degree. He refuses to consider what he calls an Absolute End, in Hegel's sense. However, he assumes throughout that men desire these proximate ends because their attainment is considered to bring personal *satisfaction*. Von Mises never discusses his option for *satisfaction* as an end which is really, or allegedly, common to all men. This is a neat way of avoiding difficulty but it is not philosophically adequate.

The adoption of a final goal, of a supreme value, is not capable of explanation as a choice of means. There must be some other way of getting at it. Suppose we consider the contrast between means and ends in some special fields of human activity. In business first: how does one decide that one's dominant purpose in life is money? It is possible that many people who embrace profit-making as a goal do so out of some nonreflective motivation which never rises to the clarity of a decision. This could be the case of the boy who grows up in a commercial family, knows all along that he is expected to take over the father's store, and does so without thinking much about it. He may never have made a conscious commitment to this way of life. Particularly, if everything goes well in the business he may live and die without a doubt as to his vocation and without guidance from any truly personal

[16] *Human Action: A Treatise on Economics* (New Haven: Yale University Press, 1949).
[17] *Ibid.*, pp. 11, 28.

decision in life. Let's not speak contemptuously of this person: how many of us are doing our present job because we formally decided that it is best for us? How many of us are here because we have drifted with the flow of life's circumstances, never really facing any important issues, and rather developing a sort of expertness in avoiding those uncomfortable crises which demand a decision?

Yet there are in business life some highest-level decisions on policy. Say the one-man owner of a business has to decide whether to go out of business or take in partners who will supply needed capital. If he can relate this decision to a further goal, he can approach it as a means-decision. But there may be situations where such a decision appears, at least, to relate to no further end. If it be such, then the decision is of an entirely new type and it is very difficult to understand how it is made.

Or consider a legal example. A judge giving a decision in a court of law is guided by the existing law and the precedents to his case. Actually his judgment is in the order of a means-decision. But think of a legislator preparing a law against smuggling, to which he must decide to attach a suitable penalty. Suppose legislator *A* decides that the penalty should be loss of the contraband goods plus a jail sentence of six months to a year. Suppose legislator *B* decides the penalty should be a fine of ten times the amount of the contraband, plus a life term in jail. How do they make such decisions?

It is truly difficult to give a good answer. Yet these examples can usually be handled in terms of the foreseeable consequences of such policies or laws and this is to turn them into means-decisions.

We reach our limit case in difficult decisions in the moral order. Men find themselves working for various ends in life, often discarding objectives which they adopted before maturity. It used to be that when you asked little boys what they wished to be when they grew up they would say policemen, or priests, or cowboys. I don't know what little boys say now in answer to nosy adults but I do think that they often change their objectives as they grow older. Grown people are not much smarter though. They decide on some of the silliest things as their life's goal.

And now let me say briefly what is the Thomistic solution to this question: How do we decide on our overall goal in life? Bluntly it is this: *you can't and don't have to make such a decision!* When we are born we are already members of the human species. This means that we have a special kind of nature which is different, for instance, from that of a dog or of an angel. We are not free to choose or decide what kind of nature we will have: we are men. This sort of nature is *necessarily* pointed toward a definite life goal. Nothing that we can do can change this finality of human nature. Even suicide cannot remove us from the human race; we can end our life on earth but we cannot kill our soul: this is what immortality means. You are human, you have the nature of men, and you are stuck with it. You can never become anything but a human being. So, what is your optimum objective in living? Simply, it is to develop and perfect the capacities of your nature so that after you die, you will be able to do well the things of which man is especially capable. These things consist in the good use of reason, in *understanding* and *willing* as perfectly as is possible.

Theologians can tell you a little more about this — I will not venture into their domain. My final point is very clear. You are free to decide that Thomas Aquinas and the whole Judeo-Christian teaching on this finality of man is wrong. If you reject it, you do so at your own peril. You are like the man on the ocean liner bound for Europe — you may decide that you don't want to go to Europe, that you prefer Australia, but you will end up in Europe and you will not like it. Man is free to accept the goal of his human nature and thus make the best of it. He is also free to resent it and thus to terminate his life on earth in final disappointment. All other decisions are commitments to means, or to proximate ends which turn out to be mere means in relation to this ultimate goal of life.

III. *NATURAL LAW AND ETHICS*

9. *Two Approaches to Natural Law**

All authors agree not concerning the definition of the natural law, who notwithstanding do very often make use of this term in their writings. . . .

This sentence from Thomas Hobbes[1] was true when he wrote it and it is still true. Natural law, as the term is used by moral, legal, and social theorists, has a wide variety of meanings. It is not the purpose of this essay to detail the extent and history of these ambiguities, though such a study would have practical value. Rather, I should like to describe two contrasting attitudes toward natural law to suggest that one is better than the other. In what follows, references to certain writers in the history of philosophy are used for illustrative purposes only, not to condemn or approve their theories, or to demonstrate my point by any appeal to their authority. As a matter of historical fact, some of them (Hobbes is a good example) use both approaches. For the sake of clarity, let us call these approaches *A* and *B*.

In approach *A,* natural law is considered to be a set of rules or precepts conveyed to man by immediate inspiration. This communication is frequently thought to have a divine origin. Natural law thinkers who take this approach usually offer a definite list of precepts. Hobbes does so.[2] Because it is brief, his third law of nature may be cited as an example: it is simply, "that men perform their covenants made." This is offered as the "fountain of justice"

* *Natural Law Forum,* I (1956), pp. 92–96; reprinted in *Commonweal* (September 7, 1956), pp. 562–563.

[1] Hobbes, *Philosophical Rudiments Concerning Government,* in Selections 283 (Woodbridge ed., 1930).

[2] See the parallel chapters from *Leviathan* and *Philosophical Rudiments* in Hobbes, *ibid.,* at 268–329.

and is used as the basis for an attack on Coke's "specious reasoning" in the *Commentaries on Littleton*.[3]

Where does Hobbes, or any similar thinker, get such a precept
of natural law? That the precept is not so simple and universally
accepted as Hobbes thought is evident to anyone who reads the
ethical literature of Europe. From Kant and Bentham onward,
the most hotly disputed moral question has been that of the obligation to keep promises. People who list these precepts usually
make some effort to "deduce" them from one primary moral judgment. This judgment is considered to be naturally known. Early
modern thinkers hasten to add that these rules are also promul-
gated in Holy Scripture, or by some other means of divine inspiration.[4] Some thinkers, then, with theistic convictions are quite frank
in admitting the immediate sources of their lists of rules of natural
law. Catholic writers often do this in much the same way that
Hobbes does. Where religious inspiration is weak or absent, as in
the case of some contemporary British moralists, resort is made to
an intuitive origin of basic moral judgments. In such cases it becomes more and more difficult to justify any code of laws for man's
behavior.

Another variant of approach *A* consists in the appeal to the condition of men in a "state of nature." Excellent examples of this
procedure are found in some ancient and medieval writers, but
we do not lack illustrations in English literature. John Locke, for
instance, in common with many men of his period, supposed the
American Indians to be living in a state of nature.[5] It was generally imagined that these happy savages actually lived without
the burden of positive laws, in peaceful obedience to the laws of
nature. Rousseau's version of the theory is well known. Some
thought that no contemporaries were actually living in this condi-

[3] *Ibid.*, at 298.

[4] Thus Hobbes ends chapter three of the *Philosophical Rudiments:* "the laws
of nature . . . are not in propriety of speech laws, as they proceed from nature.
Yet, as they are delivered by God in holy Scriptures, as we shall see in the
chapter following, they are most properly called by the name of laws. For the
sacred Scripture is the speech of God commanding over all things by greatest
right" (*ibid.*, at 329).

[5] Locke, *Treatise of Civil Government,* in Selections 62–80 (Lamprecht ed.,
1928).

tion but that, at some idyllic period in the history of man, there had been people in a state of nature. All that is necessary, then, to discover the natural law is to divest ourselves of this hampering garment of man-made laws and to listen to the voice of nature. The implication is that natural law is instinctively and immediately evident.

For less romantic thinkers, approach *A* takes the form of innatism or aprioristic rationalism. In this version, the mind of man is thought to be endowed by nature with a sense of duty, or even with certain initial rules of conduct. All of this is prior to sense experience. These innate promptings to goodness need only be developed in order to secure natural justice. While Kantian legal thinking makes little use of the term *natural law,* it appears closely related to the attitude of this approach.

Doubtless there are many other variations of this way of getting to the natural law. The significant thing is that no advocate of approach *A* pays much attention to the scientific study of nature, whether in man or in the world about him. The facts of human experience, the growth of human customs, the logic of competing moral and legal theories are but useless burdens to the man who already knows, or thinks he knows, the rules of life by virtue of a special communication. Some of the theoretic thinkers in the American colonies were thus impatient of man-made laws and legal theories, precisely because they claimed to find their precepts of civil justice in the Bible.

A quite different attitude toward natural law is characteristic of approach *B*. Here, there is no claim of direct inspiration from God, though one may be convinced that God is the ultimate source of order and justice. Nor is there any need for reference to an actual or imaginary "state of nature." Neither innate nor intuited moral precepts are required for this approach. The central notion is that certain types of activity are appropriate, or inappropriate, to certain types of agents under given circumstances. This approach is evident in the practical thinking of some of the classic Greek philosophers, though we are not required to think that they exhausted its possibilities. Socrates, Plato, and Aristotle figure in its history, as do the Stoics. They felt that man, as a reasoning animal, could act in ways not open to the irrational brute. They judged that some activities quite natural to brutes were not to be performed by men. They indicated the importance of the surrounding circumstances of human action and analyzed the conditions of voluntariness.

It is certainly not necessary to this approach to say, with Plato, that human nature is a really existing and unchanging essence. Such extreme realism was rejected by Aristotle. Indeed, if such a human nature were actually present in each man, it would be difficult to explain why men do not always act in conformity with it. And if they did, there would seem to be little need to legislate or to theorize on the nature of laws. The laws of such a human "nature" would be obeyed as automatically as the laws of physics. Greek necessitarianism is foreign to approach *B*.

On the other hand, I do not think it possible to develop a theory of natural law on a purely nominalistic basis. It is true that individual things are the only existents; universal essences do not exist. Men differ as individuals but they resemble each other more than they do dogs or trees or stones. There are observable types of beings. It is possible to distinguish different types of actions. This is what makes it possible to formulate laws, for a law always has some generality to it. It is a statement that a certain type of action is suitable, or unsuitable, to a certain type of agent, under certain typical conditions.

Again, in approach *B, nature* refers not merely to the nature of man but also to the natures of other things with which, and in regard to which, men may act freely. One of the features common to individual men (and not to dogs, trees, or stones) is an ability to understand a general rule and to conform to it in certain situations only. Such conformity is not automatic, wholly predetermined by antecedent conditions, as it appears to be in subhuman agents. Certain of men's actions, such as the natural processes of digestion, are naturally and physically predetermined, as they are in other animals. It is nonsense to enact human legislation to govern such events. Other actions of men, such as walking, may be voluntary. They are not wholly predetermined. These voluntary actions are governable by general precepts or law. Yet the striking thing about such laws of voluntary activity is not that they *must* be obeyed but that they *may* be disobeyed.

Approach *B* endeavors to discover such laws by studying the specific type of agent that man is, and by attending to the circumstances under which men perform voluntary actions. The more general the expression of such law, the less attention does it pay to circumstances. In its maximum generalization all circumstantial conditions would be omitted. The old formula, *good should be done, evil avoided,* is a rule devoid of special conditions. Such a rule is not immediately practical: no one can go out and just do good. More practical precepts are reached by observing and stating the actual conditions of voluntary action. Such a process is not an analytical deduction from the formula stated above. Only experience can lead to the discovery of what is good action in the concrete. However, crude experience is not enough to suggest immediately the patterns of right conduct in voluntary activity. Some hard thinking must be done. There is no substitute for practical reasoning, either in moralizing or in legislating.

Hence, this approach to law is both empirical and rational. Without experience, we know nothing of the nature of human agents, human actions, and their circumstances. Experience covers not only ordinary sense perceptions but also the findings of the various sciences. Of course the social sciences are important sources of information for the legal thinker and the moralist.[6] But, since man may perform voluntary actions modifiable by any parts of the universe, all the special sciences (biology, physics, chemistry, mathematics, and so on) are sources of significant and practical information. Whatever can be discovered about the nature of things is pertinent to the regulation of human conduct.

This is not to say that everything said by scientists is to be accepted at face value. Some scientific reports convey actual information about observed things or events. These are something like the "first-order facts" mentioned by Professor Northrop.[7]

[6] See the interesting and, I think, tenable exposition of the relation of sociological jurisprudence to natural law jurisprudence in Northrop, "Ethical Relativism in the Light of Recent Legal Science," 52 *Journal of Philosophy* (1955), pp. 651–622.

[7] *Ibid.,* at 657.

Such information is very useful to one who is concerned with the laws of human conduct. Other things said by scientists are generalizations and interpretations of certain data. These are also of practical utility. Still other things said by scientists are highly personal conclusions, even guesses, hypothetical constructs, and deliberate overemphases of partial data. These statements of the third type (which appear to me to abound in some of the social sciences) have not the same practical status as the hard facts of experience.

Thus, if a scientist reports that in studying a hundred cases of disrupted personality he has found evidence of sexual aberration in each and all, this is morally and legally significant. If he further reports that all psychological abnormality is due to sexual peculiarity, this opinion is not of the same practical value. It is not easy to distinguish what is sound and what is unsound in a scientific report. This simply underlines the point made earlier: there is no easy substitute, in jurisprudence or in morals, for hard thinking. Science does not absolve practical thinkers from their obligation to make a rational appraisal of the relation of projected patterns of activity to the nature of the human agent and to the surrounding conditions of that activity. Any method or theory which suggests that it will give ready-made answers, without much need for practical thinking, is suspect.

It is evident that my preference is for approach *B*. I do not reject *A* because it appeals to divine law. My criticism of it centers on its claim to short-cut experience and reasoning by appealing to some sort of direct and immediate grasp of natural law. This appears to be but a travesty on natural-law thinking. It is with some hesitation that I conclude by suggesting that approach *B* is Thomistic. My hesitation is solely due to my fear that I may be misunderstood by non-Thomists. I do not mean to say that one must call himself a Thomist in order to develop a legal theory along the lines of approach *B*. At least I should like to go on record as thinking that Thomism is not to be identified with approach *A*. True, St. Thomas speaks of natural law as a "participation" in the divine law. Yet I have the strong conviction that this participation does not mean a privileged communication, coming directly by divine inspiration, but rather the process of working out rules of human behavior from the data of human experience, using the ordinary rules of logic and scientific method. Such procedure is a natural approach to law, moral or civil, because its data are the presentations of natural experience, its method is as natural as any other type of practical reasoning, and its results are as good as the admittedly imperfect nature of the human mind permits.

10. *Natural Law and the Contemporary Mind**

In connection with the death of a professional boxer as a result of injuries suffered in the ring, a storm of moral indignation against prizefighting has recently arisen. Religious News Service, in April, 1962, reported that the Vatican Radio had condemned professional boxing as an immoral sport, with the following added statement:

> The Church has made no official pronouncement, but there is no need for any specific announcement, the principles of the natural law are clear and it takes only intelligence and an unbiased mind to examine them.

While in one sense accurate, this statement is calculated to arouse confusion in the minds of some Catholics and violent opposition and resentment on the part of many sincere and intelligent non-Catholics. If "only intelligence and an unbiased mind" are required to know such detailed prescriptions of natural law, it is difficult to explain why so many people appear ignorant of its precepts. In fact, there is a basic confusion between the role of natural law as it functions in personal thinking about one's own moral actions and as it is studied by the moral scientist. As natural law works in the first case, it is functioning in the *operative* mode. Right use of natural law in the performance of one's own human actions is a matter of prudence. Every responsible human being has some knowledge of the import and possible results of his own controllable activities, and he has some appetitive inclinations that may be said to be basically natural and right for a human agent. In this first sense, it is accurate to say that one needs only basic intelligence to know implicitly the principles of natural

* From: *Teaching Thomism Today*, edited by G. F. McLean (Washington, D. C.: Catholic University of America Press, 1963), pp. 307–329.

law. However, explicitly to investigate the meaning of natural law, to explain and defend one's general formulations of its rules — in other words, to teach either moral theology or ethics from a natural-law viewpoint — is to work in the *cognitive* mode. Here prudence is not the governing habit: moral science is.[1] The teacher of moral science does not teach by performing his own moral actions rightly; he teaches by analyzing the processes of practical reasoning and judgment, by investigating the conditions under which typical moral problems arise, by showing how somewhat universal, but practical, judgments on human behavior may be justified cognitively. It is all very well to claim that right appetition or inclination is of the essence of natural law. It is — in the practico-practical order. But the teacher cannot directly communicate to others his own right inclinations, even presuming that he has them. Moral science and the technical study of natural law are exercises in the speculativo-practical order. It is from this latter point of view that we will approach natural law.

The expression *natural law* requires explanation of both component terms. St. Thomas Aquinas' understanding of these words is based on his total *Weltanschauung,* on his view of man, the universe, and God. Thomistic practical science is a continuation and extension of speculative wisdom (both philosophical and theological) into the realm of action. To think well about good activity, we must first think well about the beings that act, and about the environments in which they operate.

There is one way of looking at law which is not Thomistic and which should be excluded from our consideration. Many people have regarded law as the *fiat* of some powerful will. In this voluntaristic view the lawmaker must be in a position of authority over his subjects, he must will to bind his subjects to certain actions and omissions, and he must intend to reward and punish his subjects for their obedience to, and infractions of, the edicts of his will. Now this is not the way in which St. Thomas thought of law. His famous definition (*rationis ordo ad bonum commune, ab eo*

---

[1] Elsewhere (*Ethics* [New York: Macmillan, 1951], pp. 223–229) I have made this distinction in terms of the operative moral syllogism and the cognitive moral syllogism.

qui curam communitatis habet, promulgata[2]) is so familiar to students of Thomism that we tend to overlook its full meaning. As an ordinance pertaining to reason, law must be an expression of *recta ratio*. In turn, *ratio* is a polyvalent term. It signifies the *Ratio Dei,* divine providence as regulative of the whole of creation.[3] It further signifies the real interrelations of all existing things and the reasonable relating of all things to God as their end.[4] And, finally, *ratio* signifies the human power of reasoning (the intellect performing its act of ratiocination) as informed by a practical knowledge of the natures and relations of the beings involved in any practical problem. This third meaning is central to the understanding of *recta ratio.*[5]

Commenting on Dionysius' statement: "This *ratio* is the simple and existing truth of the existent," Aquinas indicates four chief meanings of *ratio:*[6]

> He [Dionysius] says first that in sacred Scripture God is called *Ratio,* and this may be gathered chiefly from scriptural texts where God is spoken of as the Word, as in John 1: "And God was the Word." For, as Augustine says, *logos* in Greek means both reason (*ratio*) and word (*verbum*). Now, there are four ways of understanding the term *ratio.* First, it is used to designate a cognitive power: and in this way God is called reason causally, in the sense that He is the bestower of all knowledge, of reason and mind and wisdom, and all such. In a second way,

[2] *S.T.,* I–II, 90, 4, c. For a remarkable set of studies, cf. P.-M. Overbeke, "Saint Thomas et le droit, commentaire de II–II, 57," *Revue Thomiste,* 55 (1955), 519–564; "La loi naturelle et le droit naturel selon saint Thomas," *R.T.,* 57 (1957), 53–78, 450–498; "Droit et morale, Essai de sythèse thomiste," *R.T.,* 58 (1958), 285–324, 674–696.

[3] For the expression, *ratio divinae providentiae,* and an explanation of how "*divina providentia secundum rationem quamdam res dispensat,*" see *Summa contra Gentiles,* III, c. 97. My translation (*On the Truth of the Catholic Faith,* [New York: Doubleday Image Books, 1956], Bk. III, Part 2, pp. 66–72) renders this meaning of *ratio* by the phrase "rational plan."

[4] This meaning of *ratio* is brought out by St. Thomas in: *S.T.,* I, q. 21, a. 1; *S.C.G.,* III, cc. 97–99.

[5] *S.T.,* I–II, q. 66, a. 1, c: "Manifestum est autem ex dictis quod causa et radix humani boni est ratio. Et ideo prudentia, quae perficit rationem, praefertur in bonitate aliis virtutibus moralibus, perficientibus vim appetitivam inquantum participat rationem."
   That *recta ratio* applies both to *scientia* (as in the case of moral science) and to prudence, cf. *S.T.,* II-II, q. 55, a. 3, c: "Dicendum quod prudentia est recta ratio agibilium, sicut scientia est recta ratio scibilium."

[6] *Expositio in librum De divinis nominibus,* c. 7, lect. 5.

it is another word for cause, as when one asks, "For what reason did you do this?" (that is, for what cause?) : and in this sense God is called *Ratio*, not only because He is the cause of all things but also because He foregathers causally within Himself all secondary causes, not by way of composition but of uniformity and simplicity. Third, *ratio* means a process of calculating *(computatio)*, as in Matthew 18:23-24, "he began to settle the account *(rationem coepit ponere)* with his servants." God is also called *Ratio* in this way, because He is the supreme reckoning of things, pervading all and reaching, as the Book of Wisdom, 8:1, says, "from end to end mightily, and ordering all things sweetly." Fourth, *ratio* means something simple that is abstracted from many instances, as when we say that the *ratio* of man is that which belongs to the nature of man, when by means of consideration it is abstracted from individual men.

Observe how *ordinatio,* as used in the Thomistic definition of law, is quite logically juxtaposed with the word *ratio*. Indeed, the notion of order is already implicit in the meaning of *ratio*. As St. Thomas explains, in setting up the famous definition of law, *rationis enim est ordinare ad finem* — it is the function of reason to order toward the end.[7] When we speak of an ordering of things, we mean an intelligent arrangement of them, and we also mean a controlling and even a commanding of them. It is very important, here, to recall that Aquinas considered the act of commanding *(imperium)* a direct function of practical reason, not of will. This is a cardinal point on which later Scholasticism and modern legal philosophy abandoned Thomism.[8] For the Thomist, some speculative understanding of the real and universal inter-ordering of all things in the created world, and of their further real ordering to God as final cause, is prerequisite to a practical understanding of the laws of human behavior. Such laws are not arbitrary *fiats* but are expressions of the practical order that is intelligible in reality. This is why the First Part of the *Summa Theologiae* must be understood before one reads the moral discussions of the Second Part.

[7] *S.T.,* I–II, q. 90, a. 1, c.
[8] This historical change in the meaning of *imperium* is treated in: T. E. Davitt, *The Nature of Law* (St. Louis: Herder, 1951). In his article, "Medieval Theories of Natural Law: William of Ockham and the Significance of the Voluntarist Tradition," *Natural Law Forum* VI (1961), pp. 65–83, Francis Oakley concludes, "the voluntarist interpretation of the natural law tends to carry over into a positivist interpretation of law in general" (p. 83).

The term *natural* in the phrase *natural law* has also several meanings. Consider the variety of senses in which the noun "nature" is used. A nature is the essence of a specific kind of being, considered as the principle of special activities: it is in this way that we speak of the nature of man. There are many such natures in the universe, those of dogs, trees, water, iron, men, and so on — each nature being universally knowable and distinguishable by the actions that it exhibits in a given environment. The physical and biological "laws of nature" are generalizations of what we come to know of such behavior patterns. They are discovered by scientists but they are not man-made. That acids behave in a different way from bases is not the result of the legislative wills of chemists: the nature of an acid is really different from that of a base. Similarly, the nature of a man is really different from that of a horse or a dog. True, there are functions that are common and generally natural to all animals, including man. However, it is equally observable that there are specific differences within these broad genera. Again, these differences are not legislated by the wills of biologists: they are really there in the natures of living things. Most important to natural-law considerations is the observation that men exhibit activities that are really different from those of other types of animals. If we did not know this in any other way, we could learn it from modern anthropology. Men are the only animals that develop a specific culture.[9] The basic tendencies, or needs, of human life are distinctive of a special class

[9] Thus Robert Redfield, in his "Introduction" to B. Malinowski, *Magic, Science and Religion* (New York: Doubleday Anchor Books, 1948), p. 10, remarks: "The criticism so often leveled at Malinowski that he generalized from a single case loses much of its force if the assumption may be admitted that there are a common human nature and a universal culture pattern. No writer ever better justified the assumption."

Even as naturalistic a scientist as Sir Charles Sherrington concludes *Man on His Nature* (New York: Doubleday Anchor Books, 1955), p. 289, by saying: "Man's life is held to be a life apart and above the rest. . . . The planet is *man's* planet."

Several recent studies by Charles Fay explore the relations between ethics and anthropology; see his article, "Toward a Thomistic-Anthropological View of the Evolution of Obligation," *Natural Law Forum*, VII (1962), 41: "This conclusion, that all humans presently in existence differ from at least some men of the Ice Ages in ways that are relevant to the human exercise of moral acts, could not have been drawn independently of the discoveries of contemporary anthropologists and other scientists."

of living things. This is why, as we shall later note, man-centered sciences can be of great service to the investigation of natural moral law.

Of course, natural law may be quite properly designated from above (from the point of view of *ratio superior*) as a participation in eternal law.[10] This approach is open to the moral theologian — who knows something about eternal law. It is even possible for the practical philosopher who has reasoned to the existence of God as first and final cause of the universe to understand the general subordering of the regulations of human moral reasoning to the eternal judgments of such a God. However, philosophers have no direct knowledge of the details of eternal law. We are forced to work out by laborious processes of reasoning, based on our naturally acquired knowledge of man and his working environment, the rules of good human behavior. St. Thomas Aquinas has tried to do this, using the factual knowledge that was available in the thirteenth century. He formulated and discussed about forty natural-law precepts.[11] They include some very general moral judgments (such as: man ought to act in accord with reason; man ought to do no injury to other men; justice ought to be preserved) and other more restricted but still universal judgments (such as: agreements ought to be kept; man ought to educate his children; man ought not live in concubinage; man ought to be truthful). It is instructive to note how naturalistic is St. Thomas' consideration of these judgments. Even when teaching theology, he tried to assemble reasonings based on the experience of everyday life. Thus, on the rule that one husband ought not have plural wives, he argues that a plurality of wives is not unnatural from the point of view of man's generic animal nature. His reason is that it is possible for a man to have children by several women. Next he argues that the specific rational nature of man suggests that more than one wife is inappropriate because such plurality occasions

10 *S.T.*, I–II, q. 90, a. 2, c: "Et talis participatio legis aeternae in rationali creatura lex naturalis dicitur."

11 For a table of these rules, with indications of the main places in which they occur in the text of St. Thomas, see the *Appendix* to this paper. For this list of *Natural Law Imperatives*, I am indebted to the work of Sister Mary Georgetta St. Hilaire, *Precepts of Natural Law in the Text of St. Thomas*, St. Louis University dissertation, 1962.

quarrels in the home. Finally, he speaks as a theologian and says
that a Christian has a special reason for practicing monogamy,
founded on the analogical argument that the Church is the one
spouse of Christ.[12]

We should not take the precepts of natural law that Thomas
Aquinas has stated and discussed as a complete code of natural
laws. He carefully avoids such codification — and for a very good
reason. No list of precepts formulated by a human investigator
could represent a full statement of natural moral law. The point
of St. Thomas' teaching is that the actual regulations of morality
must be kept fluid and open in character. In each generation of
mankind, and in various places in the world, the circumstances
of moral activity vary. When moral reasoning achieves a valid
universal judgment, this constitutes a rule of natural law. The
more specific the rule, the more circumstances does it embrace.
No code of absolute and unvarying precepts can or should be
attempted. It is possible, for instance, that when professional
boxing was first started the sport was morally approvable. It is
also possible that, today, this so-called sport *as now practiced* is
not morally approvable. The point is that boxing may not now
have the same *ratio,* the same intelligible character, that it once
had.

Notice that this flexible view of natural law is quite different
from the notion that precepts of morality are based on what is
appropriate to man in an alleged "state of nature." This odd
theory found few adherents in the Middle Ages but it had many
supporters in the early modern period.[13] It is especially characteristic of the classic political philosophers of England and France.
Actually, there has never been such an ideal "state of nature" and
this imaginary construct has little resemblance to a Thomistic
understanding of natural law. It is this pseudo concept of a state
of nature that has done much to discredit the name of natural
law in contemporary philosophy.

This brings us to the question of the status and relevance of

[12] *In IV Sent.,* 33, q. 1, art. 1; this work is the formal record of the first
theology course taught by St. Thomas.
[13] Cf. above, pp. 96–97, for some indications of this notion in Hobbes, Locke,
and Rousseau.

natural-law morality in our contemporary world. On this matter there are four points to be observed. First of all, natural-law thinking is functioning today in the practical politico-legal order in an extraordinarily active way. Several present-day nations are using approximations of natural law in at least some parts of their civil and criminal codes of law. In Latin America, West Germany, Italy, France, and Japan, even in the United States of America, there is an important revival of interest in the natural-law theory.[14] Germany and Japan are the countries in which natural-law legislation and jurisprudence seem to have the greatest impact. New constitutions, new state laws, new approaches to court procedure had to be devised in these two countries because they were forced to abandon their totalitarian institutions after the past war. It is encouraging to note how many influential legal minds in Germany and Japan have turned to natural law as a source of legislative and judicial reform.

Second, there has been a noteworthy increase in the study of natural law by professors of jurisprudence in the United States. In the area of the philosophy of law, positivism, pragmatism, sociological evolutionism, naturalism, and even linguistic analysis, divide the field. However a significant number of jurists and law school professors shows a lively interest in the possibilities of natural-law theory. This is true not merely of Catholic centers (where such a development might be expected) but especially in some of the outstanding secular institutions. In the law schools at Yale, Harvard, Columbia, Wisconsin, Chicago, Indiana, Ohio State, Texas, and other such universities, the theory of natural law is at least getting a hearing today.[15] This is not to say that a Thomistic version of natural law is widely known. What the movement boils down to is that a good many American lawyers are now being taught that natural justice has some meaning and validity, that

[14] Since the *Natural Law Forum* began annual publication in 1956, eight surveys of the role of natural-law thinking in various nations have appeared, plus the general article by Johannes Messner, "The Postwar Natural Law Revival and Its Outcome," *NLF*, IV (1959), pp. 101–105.

[15] See the list of editors, in any issue of the *Natural Law Forum*, for the representatives of these institutions. The work of Lon Fuller and F. C. S. Northrop is discussed in: Scott Buchanan, *Rediscovering Natural Law* (Santa Barbara: Center for the Study of Democratic Institutions, 1962).

there is in some sense a set of natural values which transcend
positive laws. This is a very important change in American legal
education.

Third, the past twenty years have seen a gradual movement
among some social scientists, notably anthropologists, toward
something that resembles natural-law thinking. The social sciences
first developed as descriptive disciplines which avoided generalizations and abhorred normative statements.[16] More recently, a number of first-rate anthropologists have modified this stand. I am
thinking of people such as Kluckhohn, Redfield, and Montague.
They still avoid saying that their scientific findings provide any
norms for the good life, but they do attempt some generalizations
that have practical importance. Some anthropologists now speak
in terms of "cultural universals" which enable them to approach,
at least, a general conception of human nature. As Margaret Mead
has recently explained:

> The basic principles of nutritional science may be regarded as
> universals, derived from man's biology and from the biochemical
> composition of specific foods grown on specific types of soil.
> They are as applicable in one culture as in another. . . . Stripped
> of the cultural traditions of the country within which the sci-
> ence of nutrition had developed, it can be applied anywhere.
>   Although a system of jurisprudence provides us with a very
> different set of problems, it would be worthwhile, I believe, to
> experiment with the model of stripped universals when we are
> faced with attempts to diffuse our legal system beyond the boun-
> daries of the civilization within which it grew. We have seen
> that recognition of natural rights, to life, property and repro-
> duction, is found in all societies, although with profound varia-
> tions in interpretation. . . . Is it possible to regard law as having
> such a set of universals, which can in any way be compared with
> scientific principles such as govern nutrition, or can we only
> arrive at a scentific study of the law by way of the study of
> comparative legal systems, each seen as part of a particular
> culture and one line in a long historical chain of legal inven-
> tions?[17]

Clearly, Dr. Mead is trying to break through the wall of nomi-

---

[16] An account of the European situation, early in this century, is given in:
S. Deploige, *The Conflict Between Ethics and Sociology* (St. Louis: Herder, 1938).
[17] "Some Anthropological Considerations Concerning Natural Law," *Natural
Law Forum,* VI (1961), pp. 51–64; the quotation is from p. 64.

nalism which has prevented most social scientists from offering any general guidance on the sociolegal level to mankind. That her tentative suggestions are made in a discussion of natural law and anthropology is not without hope for the future.

On the other hand, and this is my fourth point, one has to admit that in contemporary ethics the theory of natural law plays but a small part. Catholic ethicians continue to appeal to it but the general course of ethics runs elsewhere. The dominant trends in academic ethics in the United States move in the direction of emotivism and naturalism. Neither of these schools pays any attention to natural law. In surveys of contemporary ethics, natural-law theory is regarded as a type of theological approbative ethics and dismissed as a sectarian doctrine.[18] This strongly negative reaction is well illustrated in an article by Kai Nielsen.[19] He argues that the concept of an unvarying human nature is not scientific, that there is no proof that commonly shared ethical views must be God-given, that natural-law ethics confuses fact and value. More basic is Nielsen's challenge to the teleological character of Thomistic natural law. His attack on the whole notion of final causality points up the importance of increased interest in this topic on the part of metaphysicians. Nielsen is willing to grant some value to Thomistic ethics but he sees no point in its appeal to divine regulation. As he puts it:

> I am not in the least suggesting that all is dross in Aquinas. It is abundantly clear that he is one of the great moral philosophers. Calling attention to the importance of understanding ourselves and our place in nature in determining what we ought to do is a permanent and useful insight of the Thomistic-Aristotelian tradition, though I think in connecting it with the rational commands of the Deity this insight has been badly blurred.[20]

Note the last sentence of this comment: he sees no value in appealing to divine commands. Doubtless he understands such commands

[18] T. E. Hill, *Contemporary Ethical Theories* (New York: Macmillan, 1950), treats natural-law ethics as a metaphysical theory, along with idealistic and self-realization positions.

[19] "An Examination of the Thomistic Theory of Natural Moral Law," *Natural Law Forum*, IV (1959), pp. 44–71.

[20] *Art. cit.*, p. 69.

as the interference of God's will in the affairs of a universe in
which He is but a benevolent despot. This confuses Thomism with
voluntarism.[21] In any case, it is well to note a rather dominant
antitheological bias in much American ethics. Historically and
doctrinally, the resources of Catholic theological scholarship demand a better presentation in English than they are getting at
present. Some excellent writing on special moral problems has
appeared under the names of theologians like G. Weigel and J. C.
Murray but there has not been enough theological publication
on the more general questions of methodology and procedure that
are distinctive of the best Catholic scholarship. Often writers like
F. Copleston and Jacques Maritain are taken as spokesmen for
Catholic theology, when actually they are moral philosophers.
We need some English works of the caliber of the studies published in French by Dom Lottin and P.-M. Overbeke.

Catholic scholarship, both theological and philosophical, could
also adopt a less negative attitude toward modern science. One
sometimes gets the impression that the bulk of Catholic thinking
on matters of science has not advanced much beyond the scientific
knowledge of Aristotle. But the factual knowledge of man and his
world has increased tremendously as a result of the activities of
modern physical and social scientists. I do not suggest that we may
find new and different primary rules of morality in modern science.
Such universal and broad rules do not automatically solve concrete
problems. One can be fully convinced that it is unjust to kill another man, except in self-defense or for some equally serious reason, and still not know whether the use of nuclear weapons in
modern warfare is ever justifiable. One needs to know something
more than a thesis about the natural right to private possessions
before he can make a judgment on the morality of membership
in a labor union. Too often, exponents of natural-law morality
think and speak as if they had some wonderful code of laws in
which all moral difficulties have been settled in advance. Of course
there is no such miraculous code.

A recent work in French illustrates my point: it is a study of

[21] For a criticism of legal voluntarism, cf. below, pp. 123–124, 127.

the relation between natural justice and social science.[22] In it Jacques Leclercq argues strongly that very little has yet been done to work out the natural-law judgments that modern life demands. He thinks that little is being done by natural-law thinkers to study the social nature of man. Social science is doing this, according to Leclercq, and is putting more and more stress on the influence of environment. "We must *search* for what natural law consists in," Leclercq says, "and to determine this, we must study."[23] He makes no secret of his conviction that what Catholic moralists require is a much more complete knowledge of the facts of modern life. That some of his views are startling may be gathered from the following typical passage:

> Now, social environment can be changed: moralists should be concerned with this from their own point of view. They have as their function to see to it that men practice morality, and so they should demand that we put all men in conditions permitting it to be practiced.
>
> One aspect of the question of living in slums, for instance, is that when a whole family sleeps in one room the girls and boys at times share the same bed, and in rural conditions cattle spend the night with men in the only room in the house, so cases of incest and bestiality are multiplied along with a decrease of moral responsibility which is all the more evident because under these conditions the development of personality is equally attenuated. For these moral deviations to disappear, all that is required is to improve the living conditions. Preaching, on the contrary, has no effect.
>
> This means that these faults, which are moral in the sense that they are contrary to the rule of morality, are in reality sociological disorders. It is vain to preach morality to people who do not find themselves in an environment that allows them to observe it. In the case of families that enjoy a certain level of upbringing, which is dependent on a certain level of economic well-being, care is taken to separate boys and girls, to make them sleep in different rooms: but this requires a certain kind of living quarters. Similarly, a given level of poverty occasions a multiplication of thefts; for these thefts to stop, what is required is a change in the social order.[24]

[22] Jacques Leclercq, *Du droit naturel à la sociologie*, 2 vols. (Paris: Editions Spes, 1960). Canon Leclercq is a professor of moral philosophy at Louvain University. For a briefer sketch of his position, cf. "Natural Law the Unknown," *Natural Law Forum*, VII (1962), pp. 1–15.   [23] *Art. cit.*, p. 12.

[24] *Du droit naturel à la sociologie*, II, p. 102; translation by the present writer.

Observe carefully what Father Leclercq is trying to tell us. The average professor of ethics or moral theology teaches as if all men were not only rational but also well fed and properly housed. Perhaps most of his students are. But it is equally obvious that the majority of men in the world today live under conditions that are subhuman. How can we teach an abstract, natural-law morality to those millions of our fellow Americans, many of them Negroes, who actually live in circumstances as shocking as those described by Jacques Leclercq? He doesn't mean, certainly and I don't, that all moral responsibility is a matter of economic or social determinism. However, it does take more than an unbiased mind to make good judgments on the kind of problems selected by Leclercq. We do need to know the actual conditions under which men face their moral problems.

The use of right reasoning, in the moral science of St. Thomas, makes provision for circumstantial considerations. Briefly, the determination of generic types of human actions, and the judgment that some such abstractly considered kinds of activity are fitting for human beings and other types are not, are but the beginnings of moral science. One may properly speak of these broad judgments as natural-law precepts. To become more specific and more practical in moral reasoning we must pay more attention to the circumstances of human activity.[25] This is fully recognized by St. Thomas. As our ethical judgments are more definitely specified and move closer to the practico-practical order, more circumstances are included in these judgments. These circumstances must be known with factual accuracy, in order that our ethical conclusions may have practical validity and application. There is no point to a condemnation of professional boxing, unless we know and make manifest the conditions under which this "sport" operates. I wonder whether the spokesman for the Vatican Radio knows, for example, that the great majority of professional boxers in the

[25] Discussing whether circumstances specify a sinful act, or change its character, St. Thomas insists that they do (De Malo, q. II, art. 6, c). He adds that it is not right to try to distinguish sins simply as offenses against various legal precepts; then he shows how variations in circumstances must be included in the reasoning of a moral scientist. This whole treatise on circumstances (De Malo, q. II, art. 6–9) is a much neglected part of St. Thomas' thinking on natural-law morality.

United States are young Negroes who look to this profession as one of the few ways in which they may hope to advance their economic status. For them, boxing is not a sport but a grim opportunity to make a better living. I wonder, too, how the mortality statistics in American boxing compare with those in European automobile racing? My aim is not to defend one or the other sport but to suggest that, while moral judgments are not simply factual conclusions, they do require us to know the pertinent details of the problems under consideration. It is obvious, I think, that the kind of information that social and other scientists have can be of real utility to the natural-law thinker.

Nothing of what has just been said should be taken in depreciation of the value of a solid background in speculative philosophy. To understand the Thomistic approach to natural law, one must know the metaphysics and philosophies of man and nature that form the groundwork for practical reasoning. I would again emphasize that one of the most practical metaphysical insights is the concept of final causality. Consideration of the end-directed character of human life and action is essential to natural-law morality. We need the assistance of thorough speculative discussions of basic axioms such as the proposition that every agent acts for an end.[26] Not only is the notion of final causality a vital part of the presentation of Thomistic natural law to non-Thomists, it is central to our own commitment to the moral ideals of natural law. This is but one illustration of the importance of speculative understanding to the practitioner of practical reasoning.

Finally, a word may be said on the subject of the type of certitude that is proper to moral science and natural-law thinking. Here we should not look for the certainty of metaphysics. Practical moral science moves on the level of moral certitude. St. Thomas was aware of the limitations of such reasoning, as he shows in a formal discussion of the methods used in the various disciplines:

> In the event that its thinking deals with mobile things that do not remain uniform, a science is less stable because its demonstrations often proceed by probability, due to the fact that what

[26] Cf. G. P. Klubertanz, "St. Thomas' Treatment of the Axiom, 'Omne Agens Agit Propter Finem,'" in *An Etienne Gilson Tribute*, ed. C. J. O'Neil (Milwaukee: Marquette University Press, 1959), pp. 101–117.

is contingent sometimes occurs in a different way. So, too, the more a science approaches singulars (as is the case with operative sciences like medicine, applied chemistry, and moral science), there is less possibility of certainty because of the multitude of items that must be considered in such sciences; for, if any one of them is omitted, error may follow, and also there is the variability of these items.[27]

Natural law is sufficiently knowable for all practical purposes. To know it well enough to teach its theory to others requires long study. Such a task is not impossible but it imposes a certain humility on those who profess to speak in the name of natural law.

APPENDIX

Natural Law Imperatives From the Text of St. Thomas[28]

1. *Man Ought to Maintain Society*
   C.G., III, 85; 129
   In Ethic., I, 1, 4
   De Regno, I, 1
   S.T., I–II, 94, 2; II–II, 109, 3, ad 1

2. *Man Ought to Love His Neighbor*
   C.G., III, 117
   S.T., I-II, 100, 3, ad 1; 5, arg. 1 et ad 1; ad 5; 11; II-II, 114, 1, ad 2
   De Duo Praec. Carit.

3. *Man Ought Not Do to Another What He Would Not Have Done to Himself*
   In IV Sent., 33, 1, 1, ad 8

4. *Man Ought to Preserve Justice*
   S.T., I–II, 100, 8, ad 1

5. *Man Ought Not Injure Anyone*
   In III Sent., 37, 1, 4
   Quodl., III, 12, 1
   C.G., III, 129
   In Ethic., V, 12, 1018; 1023; VI, 11, 1277
   S.T., I–II, 95, 2; 100, 3; 5, ad 4; 7, ad 1

6. *Man Ought to Possess Goods in Common as Regards Use*

7. *Man Ought to Possess Goods Privately as Regards Management*
   S.T., I–II, 94, 5, ad 3; II–II, 66, 2; arg. 1 et ad 1; 66, 7

[27] In Boetii De Trinitate, q. VI, 1, c; translation from The Pocket Aquinas (New York: Washington Square Press, 1960), p. 40.
[28] Compiled by Sister Mary Georgetta St. Hilaire, see note 11, supra.

8. *Man Ought Not Steal*
    Quodl., II, 4, 8
    In Ethic., V, 12, 1023; 1029
    S.T., I–II, 94, 4; 6; 100, 1; II–II, 57, 2, ad 2

9. *Goods Ought to Be Restored to Their Owner*
    S.T., I–II, 94, 4; II–II, 57, 2, ad 1

10. *Man Ought Not Kill Another Man*
    S.T., I–II, 100, 1
    In Duo. Praec. Carit.

11. *Man Ought to Live Agreeably With His Fellowmen*
    S.T., I–II, 94, 2; II–II, 114, 2, ad 1

12. *Man Ought to Honor His Benefactors*
    In Ethic., V, 12, 1024
    S.T., I–II, 100, 7, ad 1

13. *Man Ought to Honor His Parents*
    Quodl., II, 4, 8
    S.T., I–II, 100, 1; 5, ad 4; 7, ad 1
    In Duo. Praec. Carit.

14. *Man Ought to Support the Ministers of the Common Good*
    S.T., II–II, 87, 1; 4, ad 3

15. *The Evildoer Ought to Be Punished*
    In IV Sent., 26, 2, 2, ad 1; 36, 1, 1, ad 3
    Quodl., II, 4, 8
    In Ethic., V, 12, 1023
    S.T., I–II, 95, 2; II–II, 85, 1, ad 1

16. *Persons Not at Fault Ought Not Be Punished*
    In IV Sent., 36, 1, 1, ad 3

17. *Persons Suffering Through No Fault of Their Own Should Be Relieved*

18. *Captives Should Be Redeemed*
    In Ethic., V, 12, 1024

19. *Agreements Ought to Be Kept*

20. *Ambassadors Ought to Be Safe With the Enemy*
    In Ethic., V, 12, 1019

21. *Man Ought to Tell the Truth*
    S.T., II–II, 109, 3, ad 1; 114, 2, ad 1

22. *Man Ought to Procreate Children*
    In IV Sent., 33, 1, 1; 2, 2, 1, ad 1
    C.G., III, 126; 136; IV, 78
    In Ethic., V, 12, 1019
    S.T., I–II, 94, 2; II–II, 152, 2, arg. 1

23. *Parents Ought to Rear Their Children*
    In IV Sent., 33, 2, 2, 1, ad 1
    In Ethic., V, 12, 1019
    S.T., I–II, 94, 2

24. *A Child Ought Not Be Treated Against the Will of His Parents*
    Quodl., II, 4, 7
    S.T., II–II, 10, 12; III, 68, 10

25. *Man Ought Not Procreate Children Outside Wedlock*
    In IV Sent., 33, 1, 3, 1; ad 4; 2, ad 1; 3
    Quodl., II, 4, 8
    C.G., III, 122
    S.T., II–II, 57, 2, ad 2; 154, 2

26. *Man Ought to Be Concerned to Know His Offspring*
    C.G., III, 123; 124
    S.T., II–II, 154, 2

27. *Man and Wife Ought to Remain United Until Death*
    In IV Sent., 33, 1, 3, 1; 2, 1; 2, 2, 1
    C.G., III, 122; 123
    S.T., II–II, 154, 2

28. *One Man Ought Not Have Many Wives*

29. *One Woman Ought Not Have Many Husbands*
    In IV Sent., 33, 1, 1; ad 1; ad 4; ad 8; 1, 2
    C.G., III, 124

30. *Man Ought to Love God*
    De Veritate, 17, 2
    C.G., III, 129
    S.T., I–II, 100, 3, ad 1; 11

31. *Man Ought to Worship God*
    C.G., III, 119
    S.T., I–II, 99, 3, ad 2; II–II, 81, 2, ad 3; 85, 1, sed contra et corpus; 85, 1, ad 1

32. *Man Ought to Show Gratitude to God*
    S.T., II–II, 86, 4; ad 1

33. *Man Ought to Obey God*
    In II Sent., 24, 2, 3
    De Veritate, 16, 1, ad 9

34. *Man Ought to Confess His Sins to God*
    In IV Sent., 17, 3, 1, 2, ad 1

35. *Man Ought to Act in Accord With Reason*
    De Veritate, 16, 1, ad 9
    S.T., I–II, 94, 3; 4; ad 3

36. *Man Ought to Love Himself*
    S.T., I–II, 100, 5, ad 1

37. *Life Ought to Be Preserved*
    De Veritate, 22, 5
    De Malo, 6, 1; 16, 4, ad 5
    S.T., I–II, 10, 1; 94, 2; II–II, 64, 5

38. *Man Ought to Eat*
    In IV Sent., 33, 1, 1
    S.T., II-II, 152, 2, arg. 1 et ad 1

39. *Man Ought to Observe Moderation in Eating*
    In IV Sent., 15, 3, 1, 4; 33, 1, 3, 1, ad 4
    C.G., III, 129
    S.T., II–II, 147, 3

40. *Man Ought to Seek the Truth*
    In IV Sent., 33, 1, 1
    De Veritate, 22, 5
    De Malo, 6, 1
    S.T., I–II, 10, 1; 100, 5, ad 5; II–II, 166, 2

11. *Foundations of Justice**

In a series of lectures at Notre Dame University in the early 1960's, Margaret Mead described the coming of British justice to the people of New Guinea.[1] When she first visited these people in the 1920's, they had no way of settling their disputes without physical combat. Under a mandate following World War I, a few Australians introduced these people to court practice. Returning to New Guinea after about twenty years, Miss Mead found a functioning system of political justice administered by the natives "with only moral sanctions."[2] She concludes that the people of New Guinea had never cared for fighting and that they were quite ready to adopt some rules of law and order. Further, she suggests that it may be possible to discover, anthropologically, a minimum set of moral and legal convictions that are held by all peoples. As she puts it: "We have seen that recognition of natural rights of life, property, and reproduction, is found in all societies, although with profound variations in interpretation."[3]

It is this pregnant and philosophically suggestive conclusion that I should like to examine here. What is natural justice? What are the bases for our notions of what is just?

DEFINITION OF JUSTICE

To make a start, let us consider a nominal definition of justice. The first statement in Webster describes justice as: "the principle of rectitude and just dealing of men with each other."[4] Now we

---

* From: *Proceedings of the American Catholic Philosophical Association,* XXXVI (1962), pp. 19–28.

[1] "Some Anthropological Considerations concerning Natural Law," *Natural Law Forum,* 6 (1961), pp. 51–64, is a digest of these lectures.

[2] *Ibid.,* p. 58.

[3] *Ibid.,* p. 64.

[4] *Webster's Collegiate Dictionary* (Springfield, Mass.: Merriam Co., 1948), p. 548.

could all think of some possible revisions in this dictionary definition; not much is explained by saying that justice is "just dealing,"
and "rectitude" may be simply another word for "justice." We may
even have some hesitation in limiting justice to dealings among
human beings. But we can at least begin with this statement and
exclude two meanings that are not central to our investigation.

There is, first of all, the religious meaning of justice as *supernatural justification*. Those who read St. Anselm know what is
meant. The Christian teaching that fallen man has departed from
the state of "original justice" and that he must be elevated again.
through the working of divine grace, to a state of restored justice
so that he may be able to perform supernaturally meritorious acts
— this teaching employs the term "justice" in a special way. We
will not attempt to treat this theological usage.

Second, let us exclude the notion of *general justice*. Since this
term is open to various interpretations, not all of which are imper-
tinent to the core meaning of justice, let me state how I understand
it. Wuellner, for instance, gives as a second meaning of justice,
"human goodness."[5] It is correct that justice is so used to cover the
principle, or general condition, of all good human acts. In this
sense, the morally good is coextensive with the just. This is a position taken in some types of Scholastic philosophy: justice becomes
the completely universal principle of a good life and all moral
virtues are types of justice. However, I do not think that this is a
Thomistic view of justice. We will restrict justice to the area of
interpersonal relations (as Webster and St. Thomas do) and exclude from justice simple acts of temperance, fortitude, and prudence.

In the dictionary definition cited above, justice is called a *principle* of rectitude. This word "principle" can mean two things: a
personal quality or an interpersonal equality in the real order.
On this, as on many key points in the tradition of Western
thought, Plato has something to say about both views. The fourth
book of the *Republic* suggests that justice may be found on a large
scale in a well-ordered state. State justice is an existing balance
and harmony of all classes in an organized society. Thus Plato

[5] *Dictionary of Scholastic Philosophy* (Milwaukee: Bruce, 1956), p. 66.

says: "when each order — tradesman, Auxiliary, Guardian — keeps to its own proper business in the commonwealth and does its own work, that is justice and what makes a just society."[6] This meaning seems close to the notion of social justice which has figured so prominently in recent papal encyclicals. It also lies behind, I believe, Thomas Aquinas' discussion of justice as a virtue. He always seems to presuppose a social and political context in which a real balance of personal claims may be achieved objectively. Justice for St. Thomas is not merely *willing* the good to others, it requires that one *do* what is possible for their good.[7]

On the other hand, Plato also describes justice within the individual man as a "well-tempered harmony" of all three parts of his soul (concupiscent, spirited, and rational) working together.[8] In this, he approaches the notion of justice as a personal virtue or quality. This personal concept of justice is developed in Aristotle and the Stoics and becomes a commonplace in philosophical and legal literature through Cicero's famous formula: "justice is a habit of the conscious soul which assigns his own value to each person and also preserves the common welfare."[9]

Will comes to the fore in standard definitions of justice with Justinian's codification of civil law. From the sixth century on, all writers know that "justice is the constant and perpetual will which renders his right to each person."[10] This is a definition which even St. Thomas has trouble explaining.[11] With St. Anselm in the eleventh century, rectitude of willing is stressed in his much quoted statement that justice is "rightness of will preserved for its own sake."[12] In the next century, Peter Lombard entirely obscures the matter by quoting a chance remark of St. Augustine's as if it were

6 *Republic* IV. 434; Cornford (New York, 1956), p. 129.

7 *S.T.*, II–II, q. 79, a. 1, c.

8 *Republic*, IV, 441; Cornford, p. 140.

9 *Rhetoricorum libri duo qui sunt de inventione rhetorica*, II, 53: "iustitia est habitus animi, communi utilitate conservata, suam cuique tribuens dignitatem."

10 *Iustiniani Digesta*, Lib. I, tit. 1, leg. 10 (*Corpus Iuris Civilis*, ed. Mommsen-Krueger, Berlin: Weidmann, 1928, Vol. I, 29b): "iustitia est constans et perpetua voluntas suum unicuique ius tribuens."

11 *S.T.*, II-II, q. 58, a. 1, c: "praedicta iustitiae definitio conveniens est, si recte intelligitur."

12 *De veritate*, c. 12; see McKeon, *Selections from Medieval Philosophers* (New York: Scribners, 1929), Vol. I, p. 179.

a formal definition. "Justice," Peter solemnly assures us, "consists in helping the unfortunate."[13] With this reduction of justice to mercy Peter Lombard "caused confusion among intellectuals," as Dom Lottin puts it.[14] Small wonder that St. Thomas never produces a definition of justice that is simple and clear-cut, as are his formulations of the other cardinal virtues. The dead weight of a confused tradition is too much for him. What is very clear is that he does not think that justice is needed in order to will one's own good: that is done by each person quite naturally. Hence we might suggest the following as a working Thomistic definition: *Justice is the habit of will whereby one desires and accomplishes in external acts what is good for other persons, and reasonably equal for all persons.*

THEORIES OF JUSTICE

Many attempts have been made to explain the ultimate basis of justice. Let us consider six such theories, starting first with the worst. This is *legal positivism.* It is a theory to which lawyers, civil and canon, are much addicted. According to this view, the law exists and justice is simply the application and interpretation of the law. It is idle to look for any reasons why the law is so: it simply is, and that is all there is to it. As Paul Weiss has said:

> The positivists, ancient and modern, have . . . looked at nature in the light of positive law. The laws of nature were held by them to be, like positive law, conventional, constantly changing, empirically discovered, and humanly produced . . . what is said to be stable and just is a useful fiction . . . and the positivists allow that once a convention has been established it may operate without human intervention or control.[15]

A second theory that provides no valid ground for justice is *legal voluntarism.* This is the widespread view that the law, and consequently justice, is whatever the lawmaker wills. The lawmaker may be either God or some political authority. In this theory all that one has to do to discover what is just is to find what the legislator intended — and if his intention is not manifest one can

[13] *Libri Sententiarum,* III, 33, c. 1, 3 (Quaracchi, 1916, II, pp. 697–698).

[14] O. Lottin, "Notes sur la vertu de justice," in *Psychologie et Morale* (Louvain: Mont-César, 1949), tome III, seconde partie, I, p. 286.

[15] *Our Public Life* (Bloomington: Indiana University Press, 1959), pp. 148–149.

presumably do what one likes. This is also a theory dear to the
hearts of legal experts; hence it is frequently combined with some
version of legal positivism. In a pure position of legal voluntarism,
there can be no ground or reason for the volitional *fiat*.[16]

Evolutionary relativism constitutes a third position. Justice is
what is required and enforced at any given time and place in the
growth of human customs. What is observably just in one stage of
cultural development is obligatory and enforceable — but such
justice is quite relative to the culture and social mores of mankind
at any given era in history.

The *class interest* theories of justice, in ancient aristocracies and
in proletariat jurisprudence of our twentieth century, represent
important species of relativistic justice. They countenance no unchanging justice common to all men but they admit some shifting
ground for jurisprudence in the actual accretions of human customs or in the idealized values of certain groups of people.

All four of the foregoing views of justice share one common feature which may be stated negatively. They deny that there is any
really universal foundation for justice in the nature of man and in
the character of his environment. In other words, these theories
are variations of nominalism in the field of human relations. Contrasting with such theories are two views of justice which do affirm
some kind of really universal basis for judging right action among
men.

Thus there is a fifth theory which might be called *metaphysical
naturalism*. This is the approach that is found in the fifth book
of Aristotle's *Nicomachean Ethics* and in St. Thomas' exposition
of this work. It might be better to call it legal realism, except for
the fact that this name has been appropriated by some legal positivists who like to think of themselves as hardheaded, tough
minded "realists."[17] Metaphysical naturalism recognizes a certain
uniformity, and indeed universality, in human beings and in the

16 For the gloomy history of the transition of Scholastic thinking to legal
voluntarism, during the late thirteenth and the fourteenth centuries, cf. T. E.
Davitt, *The Nature of Law* (St. Louis: Herder, 1951).

17 Cf. the pertinent comment of F. J. de Sloovère, "Natural Law and Current
Sociological Jurisprudence," *Proceedings of the American Catholic Philosophical
Association*, XVII (1941), pp. 137–142.

universe in which men live. In this view, justice is a fairness in interhuman dealings, based on certain intelligible and real relations among persons, involving other really existing beings with somewhat constant, though not perfectly known, universal characteristics. What-is-right (the *justum* in the concrete) in such a real context is a rationally appraised balance of the interests (or goods) of all persons involved, at times taken individually, at times collectively.

Metaphysical naturalism provides valid but perhaps not ultimate or complete reasons for living in accord with justice. There is a sixth and ultimate position, the *divine wisdom* theory, which roots justice in God's perfect understanding of the universe that He has made.[18] What-is-right is not so much what God *wills* (though it is in fact that) as what God *knows* to be equitable in all interpersonal relations. Divine wisdom judges the activities of all persons, not only universally but in all their concrete individuality and particularity. This practical wisdom of God is the ultimate foundation of justice, yet it is only imperfectly knowable by men on earth. Philosophers and legal theorists know little of it; even theologians must admit that their grasp of the secrets of divine wisdom is hardly adequate.[19]

St. Thomas Aquinas, as a theologian, made use of both metaphysical naturalism and a divine wisdom theory in his discussions of justice. He is clearly aware of this duality: "There is, however, a twofold rule of human life. The first is the natural law impressed by God on the minds of man, through which man naturally under-

[18] Cf. Augustine's admonition: "Respice ergo, transcende, vade illuc ubi semel locutus est Deus, et ibi invenies fontem justitiae." (*Enarrationes in Psalm.*, LXI, 21.)

[19] St. Thomas Aquinas, *Expositio in Job*, c. 11, lect. 1 (Parma, XIV, 49): "Leges enim humanae, quia non potuerunt earum latores ad omnia singularia respicere, ad universalia quaedam respiciunt, quae ut in pluribus accidunt. Qualiter autem universalia statuta humana sint factis singularibus applicanda, relinquitur prudentiae operantis: unde in multis homo potest deficere a rectitudine; quibus tamen non contrariatur legi humanitus positae. Sed lex divina, secundum quod est in sapientia Dei, ad omnia particularia et minima se extendit: et sic non potest contingere quod homo in aliquo a rectitudine discordat, et non contrarietur legi divinae. Quia igitur homo ad ipsam legem divinam, prout est in secreto sapientia Dei, inspiciendam pertingere non potest, et per consequens nec ejus multiplicitatem agnoscere; contingit quod aliquando non putet se contra legem Dei agere, cum tamen agat, vel parum delinquere, cum tamen multum delinquat."

stands what is good from the likeness of divine goodness . . . the other is the external law, divinely handed down."[20] He develops this point later[21] when he compares the human view of justice with that of God:

> In comparison with divine justice, all human justice may be regarded as practically nothing. Not only is it impossible for a man to appear just when compared with God but, even more, in such a comparison man seems unjust. Similarly, things that possess some beauty may seem ugly in comparison with the most beautiful objects. . . . Now this leads to the conclusion that, no matter how just and blameless a man may be, his justice and innocence cannot be primary, for they are regarded as nothing in comparison with God and the question of divine judgment.

The same theme of the unique and ineffable character of divine justice runs through St. Thomas' *Commentary on the Psalms*.[22] His frequent statement that all our justices are but nothing in the sight of God is, of course, an echo of Isaiah 64:6.

This view of the supremacy of justice in God's wisdom is not the same as the theory that the divine will is the root of all justice. There is a unique text in the *Questions on Truth*, where Aquinas takes a definite stand against legal voluntarism.[23]

> Since justice is some sort of rectitude, as Anselm says, or an establishment of equality, according to Aristotle, the essential character of justice (*ratio iustitiae*) must depend on where the basic standard is primarily discovered, for it is in accord with this standard that the equality and rightness of justice are established in things. Now will does not have the essential character of a primary rule; instead, it is a ruled rule, for it is directed by reason and understanding, not only in us but also in God. However, in our case intellect and will are really different and thus our will and the rightness of our will are not the same; but in God understanding and will are really identical and thus the rightness of His will is the same as His will. So, what the essential character of justice primarily depends on is the wisdom of the divine understanding which establishes things in their proper relations to each other and to their cause. It is in this character (*ratio*) of proper relationship that created justice consists.

[20] *Exp. in Job*, c. 23, lect. 1.
[21] *Ibid.*, c. 25, lect. 1.
[22] *In Psalmos Davidis Expositio*, 25, 1; cf. also 42, 1.
[23] *De veritate*, XXIII, 6, c.; cf. the translation by R. W. Schmidt, S.J., *Truth* (Chicago: Regnery, 1954, Vol. III, 119), from which my English version differs but slightly.

To say that justice depends on a simple act of will is to assert that divine will does not proceed in accord with the order of wisdom — and this is blasphemous!

Compare this forthright declaration with the fourteenth-century opinion of Pierre d'Ailly. Here we have an explicit voluntarist who says: "just as the divine will is the first efficient cause in the genus of agents, so is it the primary law or obligatory rule in the genus of agents imposing legal obligation."[24] Or notice the subtle shift in the relation of will to intellect that is introduced by William of Ockham, who first insists that "every right will is in agreement with right reason but it is not always in accord with a previous act of right reason showing the reason why the will should so act." Then he adds a classic statement of divine voluntarism: "But from the very fact that the divine will wills this, right reason dictates what must be willed."[25] As a result of this voluntaristic position, Ockham proceeds to make moral good and evil stem from an obligation that is wholly extrinsic to the nature of man and created reality, and indeed to the nature of God Himself. In his lectures on the second book of the *Sentences,* Ockham finally claims that God can even will that a human act of hating God would be "without any moral malice."[26]

We are heirs to this voluntaristic tradition of law and justice. Many of the great names in the history of modern jurisprudence and politicolegal philosophy are at least partial voluntarists: Martin Luther, Francis Suarez, John Locke (in his early *Essays on the Law of Nature*). Thomas Hobbes, Hugo Grotius, Samuel von Pufendorf, and even William Blackstone.[27] Such voluntarism, however, is always reducible to positivism and nominalism; for, in the final analysis, the view that a pure fiat of will is the standard of justice means that there is no rational and real foundation for law.

This is also why we have the greatest difficulty in grasping St. Thomas' divisions of justice. Few Thomists now understand that

[24] *Quaestiones super I Sententiarum,* I, 14, 3 (ed. Lyons, 1500, fol. 173r); see the comment on this passage in: F. Oakley, "Medieval Theories of Natural Law: William of Ockham and the Significance of the Voluntarist Tradition," *Natural Law Forum,* VI (1961), 75, and his note 49.

[25] *In I Sent.,* d. 41, q. 1, K.

[26] *In II Sent.,* q. 19, P; cf. Oakley, p. 69, note 23.

[27] Oakley, *art. cit.,* pp. 72–73.

equity is not only a species of justice but the highest kind of justice. Perfect equity is identical with divine justice. All other types
of justice are but imperfect participations in equity.[28] Legal justice
is not primary; it is a secondary analogue of equity.[29] From the
viewpoint of voluntarist legal theory, legalistic justice became
primary and equity was reduced to a principle for the mitigation
and relaxation of strict justice. Eventually equity came to be regarded as a form of mercy!

Again, the Thomistic division of justice into distributive and
commutative has degenerated to the point where many writers
speak of commutative as strict justice and of distributive as if it
were not justice at all, but rather some sort of liberality. In the
view of Aquinas, distributions and commutations are simply two
different kinds of real transactions among persons, both of which
require to be justly regulated. In distributions, what belongs to the
community (whether agreeable or disagreeable) is proportionately
assigned to individual members of the community for their private
good. In the case of commutations, private goods are equally exchanged between persons for the sake of the private good of both
persons. Both commutative and distributive are justices in the strict
sense; but both are secondary analogues of equity. Since legal
justice looks to the common good, distributive and commutative
justice may both be used to implement a legal decision. However,
the supreme habit of just action in all areas is equity, for it considers both the public and the private good in all details.

CONCLUSION

May I make it perfectly clear now that I think the study of
divine wisdom as the source of justice is the work of the theologian? The only useful philosophical approach to justice is through
a rational appraisal of existing natural beings and their behavior.
Philosophers should try to understand all that they can about

[28] St. Thomas formally describes equity (*epieikeia*) as a "pars subjectiva justitiae" in *S.T.*, II–II, q. 120, a. 2, c. He adds concerning equity: "de ea justitia
dicitur per prius quam de legali; nam legalis justitia dirigitur secundum
epieikeiam."

[29] For the story of the deterioration of the concept of equity in canon law
literature, cf. the article by a judge of the Roman Rota, Msgr. Charles Lefebvre,
"Natural and Canonical Equity," *Natural Law Forum*, VIII (1963), pp. 122–136.

human beings and how they operate. It is not enough to define man as a rational animal and deduce from this definition the normative laws of just action. Rather, we should call upon our total experience of human living, upon all the resources of our humanistic tradition, upon all the useful evidences of psychology and the social sciences, in order to frame a philosophy of justice. More than this, we should try to know the real world in which men act now; not the world of Aristotle, nor even of a medieval philosopher of nature. Practical philosophy needs the factual reports of the most up-to-date physical sciences. We should cherish the new knowledge that scientific observations afford. To gather in such knowledge, to interpret it reasonably, to apply it practically — this is the only realistic way to work toward a philosophical understanding of justice.[30]

[30] For a presentation of such a program in moral science, cf. Jacques Leclercq, *Du droit naturel à la sociologie*, 2 vols. (Paris: Spes, 1960).

12. *Natural Law and Human Rights**

For more than two thousand years in the history of Western civilization thinking men saw the truth of the proposition that man is by nature a social or political animal. They realized that, while a human being may *exist* in isolation from his fellowmen, he cannot *live well,* or fully, without human society. Certain human needs require the very natural association of family life, and other aspects of man's nature can only be developed and satisfied in that larger social union which is called the political community.

It was also clear to these classic thinkers that each human being living in the society of his fellowmen must make certain adjustments between the natural love of his own private good and the equally valid aspirations of other individual men for their goods.

Moreover, it was quite apparent that each member of human society had to give some consideration to the welfare of the whole human society to which he belonged. All reasonable men saw that these adjustments between one's private good and the goods of other men required an intelligent appraisal of the claims of all the people who make up a community and, above all, that they required goodwill to other men.

This habit of recognizing and constantly willing the good of other men, as well as one's own good, is justice. The rules or precepts of just human behavior make up the moral law as it applies to the social life of mankind.

It is evident, then, that there is a type of law which expresses a fundamental rightness in the intercourse of men. This is the natural moral law.

* Radio address originally entitled "The Natural Law — and the Rights of Man," delivered on the Catholic Hour, National Broadcasting System, October 12, 1952. Printed in the pamphlet: *The Natural Law — A Return to God* (Washington, D. C.: National Council of Catholic Men, 1953), pp. 12–18.

In one sense this law is nothing but a flowering and a fulfillment of the social nature of human persons. That natural law
has a more ultimate basis in the justice of God, the Creator of
human nature, was a more profound insight which Judaism and
Christianity brought to the classic philosophy of natural law that
the ancient Greeks and Romans had developed.

This reasonable and natural and right way of looking at the
pattern of men's aspirations and actions in human society went
unchallenged until about three hundred years ago. Then an English political philosopher, Thomas Hobbes (who had a very unsatisfactory family life and suffered much disappointment in his
broader social contacts), wrote two books in which he vigorously
denied the whole notion that man is disposed by nature to live
happily in society.

Hobbes not only disliked women, he distrusted men too. His
argument was very simple and very specious: if all men naturally
desire the same things, he said, then all men are natural enemies;
their primary disposition is to quarrel and fight like wolves over
their spoils.

Hobbes convinced many of his readers that the natural condition
of mankind is not the peace and friendliness of classic political
thought but rather, as he put it, the war of all men against all men.

Coupled with this amazing distortion of the natural tendencies
of man was Hobbes's additional theory that social and political
institutions, including laws, are the result of a purely arbitrary
and artificial agreement among men to limit and restrict their
conflicting desires, in order to establish a precarious condition of
social peace. In this theory the laws of justice are the expression
of an unnatural and scheming decision of each man to give up
certain of his natural claims to the goods of human life, provided
that every other member of human society will agree to make a
similar sacrifice.

From this point onward, much English legal and political
thinking is governed by the absurd notion that the basis of human
law is neither natural nor moral but rather a calculated and arbitrary departure from the natural tendencies of the human person.

On the continent of Europe, Hobbes's theory of the "unnatural" law had little immediate effect. It was not until the next century had elapsed that another malcontent, Jean Jacques Rousseau, brought forward the astounding view that laws make lawbreakers!

To this Frenchman it seemed obvious that if there were none of these artificial laws' then there would clearly be no criminals. The thing to do, as he saw it, was to abolish the whole fabric of legal and moral rules and let men live as the brute animals do, and as he thought primitive peoples did, in accord with the untrammeled instincts of the human species.

Contrary to Hobbes, Rousseau felt that human nature is basically good and peaceful; but by diverse processes of misreasoning both men reached a somewhat similar conclusion: there is no *natural* moral and social law; all laws of human behavior are the result of purely arbitrary agreements or compacts.

But human life does require law and order, and a later generation of political and legal theorists, believing that the natural law doctrine was dead, turned to another source of law.

In the late eighteenth and nineteenth centuries the notion became prominent that the nation or state is an absolute being, having its own substance, nature, and proper actions. Soon the state was regarded as a supreme lawmaker, the source not only of political enactments but even in some sense of moral rules. What was good and bad, right and wrong, in the intercourse of men was to be determined by national, not natural, laws.

Now since human laws govern the exercise of the rights of man, the historical stage was set for the diabolical theory that all human rights are granted to men by the supreme authority of the state.

An immediate consequence of this totalitarian view is the conclusion that what the state has given the state may take away. If a citizen enjoys the right to live, to marry and raise a family, to choose and practice his vocation in life, to think and express his views, to work out his own destiny — these rights (under the theory of totalitarianism or statism) have been conferred on each human being by the supreme authority of the state and they may be withdrawn from any man by process of state action.

With the widespread abandonment of the natural-law teaching

in recent centuries, this is the pitiful condition in which millions of men find themselves today. Creatures of the state, of the party, of the leaders of a certain ideology, they find that all their rights, their moral powers and claims, are but state privileges — phantom claims, to be tolerated or abrogated at the whim of those who wield the supreme authority of the state.

This is not only true of those countries which are admittedly totalitarian. Many of our fellow Americans have lost their awareness of the distinction between *political* rights and *natural* rights. Fortunately they have retained an instinctive repugnance for totalitarianism and statism. They lack, however, a conscious awareness of the reason why man is not merely a creature of the state, of why human rights are truly inviolable and unalienable.

But our forefathers knew that moral rights have a sounder foundation than political expediency. They knew that morality is rooted in the nature of the human person and that natural rights stem from the law of God. To see this, we need only turn to a brief examination of the *Declaration of Independence*.

The opening paragraphs of this *Declaration* are verbally familiar to all of us. We can easily recall the solemn affirmation that it sometimes becomes necessary for a people, a group of human beings, "to dissolve the political bands which have connected them with another, and to assume among the powers of the earth, the separate and equal station to which the Laws of Nature and of Nature's God entitle them. . . ." We remember, too, how this classic document proceeds to list explicitly certain true propositions of the "Laws of Nature":

> We hold these truths to be self-evident, that all men are created equal, that they are endowed by their Creator with certain unalienable Rights, that among these are Life, Liberty and the pursuit of Happiness. That to secure these rights, Governments are instituted among Men, deriving their just powers from the consent of the governed.

I say that these lines are verbally familiar: we recognize them as old friends, to be greeted with love and respect but certainly not to be too closely inspected, for we have formed the habit of taking them for granted.

But I wonder how many of us know what these words mean, understand them, and realize how far our present ways of thinking may have departed from the convictions expressed with a passionate but reasoned restraint in these immortal paragraphs?

They constitute the appeal of a wronged minority group — not to international law, or to the British parliament, or to a League of Nations, or to a United Nations, but to the moral conscience of mankind.

Certainly many of those, if not all, who signed this *Declaration* believed that such an appeal to the ethical and religious judgment of society at large was an effective means of justification for the momentous step which the American people were then about to take. The basis of this well-founded belief lies in the conviction that there is a supreme law, transcending the legal codes of states and national governments.

Some of the men who framed and signed this document were deists: they believed that God does exist and is the Creator of all, but they did not think that this God had given any supernatural revelation to men.

These few eighteenth-century deists felt that natural reason was the sole source of religious conviction. Theirs was not the faith of fundamental Christians, certainly not of Catholics, but on the other hand deism was not wholly wrong, for it saw partially and with much obscurity the workings of the Creator in the things of creation. To the deists, "Nature's God" was a remote and inaccessible Being but He was a real divinity, the ultimate source of law and order.

Other signers of the *Declaration* — and we may judge that they were in the majority, for deism never appealed to large numbers of men — were theists. To them, as to Catholics today, the supreme law was the law of God.

This divine law, they thought, as Catholics do now, was conveyed to them in two ways: more perfectly through supernatural revelation, less adequately but still quite validly through the use of natural reasoning about the facts of ordinary human experience.

Historians are correct, then, in telling us that the wording of this *Declaration* is something of a compromise, since the intentional ambiguity of the phrase "Nature's God" permitted both deist and theist to subscribe to the statement, each to understand it in his own way.

Yet there was no need for compromise or ambiguity in the first name used for the precepts of the moral law; these were for the Founding Fathers, and still are, the *Laws of Nature*.

To avoid any misunderstanding and to make the point quite explicit, the *Declaration* proceeds to list certain self-evident truths which express part of the content of the natural moral law.

The first proposition is that all men are created equal. What is implied in this truth is not physical equality (for even Hobbes had pointed out that men are not actually equal in strength or stature or physical capacity) — nor was the point that all men have the same mental abilities — nor was it even the notion that all men enjoy equality in courts of law. The fundamental meaning of human equality lies in the fact that each human being is a person, a complete member of his species and possessed of the actual use of intelligence.

This was a declaration of the independence of men — not of animals or plants, nor of states or institutions — but of the only moral agents here on earth, human persons.

It is characteristic of human persons, of all men as the *Declaration* reminds us, that they possess certain God-given rights which cannot be taken away from them. Not all of these natural rights are mentioned here, but we are told that a person has the right to live, the liberty of choice and action, and the right to work out his own destiny in the search of happiness.

This enumeration of three general human rights is quite sufficient to make clear the distinctive quality of human personality. Obviously a person must have life, and above this, the opportunities to perform the kind of human actions which make up a good life. There is otherwise no special value in being human.

The reason then why a man has certain natural rights is not to be found in the enactment of some civil law, nor in the granting of privilege by state authority. Man possesses these moral rights because he cannot exist and function as a member of his species without them.

Truly, human actions are quite different from the workings of a machine or the instinctive functionings of a brute animal. A man works in a human way when he thinks intelligently about his proposed course of action and then chooses to act in line with his rational judgment of the matter. He has a right to do this because he is born that kind of agent. A dog does not have a right to perform human actions — to take thought of the future and freely to choose his course of conduct by virtue of that thought.

A state may and should work so as to protect and encourage the use of basic human rights on the part of its citizens, but it would be a complete absurdity for a state to attempt to confer the use of human rights upon a dog. Only men have natural moral rights because men alone have the natural endowments, the personal powers, which give reality to the actions stemming from these rights.

In a very profound sense moral law and moral right are the same thing. It is reasonable and just for each man to seek his own good but not at the cost of depriving another human being, or the community as a whole, of his or its good. Justice or rightness of will demands that we adhere to a certain reasonable order or balance between our personal advantage and that of the next man.

Natural moral law is the expression of those rules of right human conduct which may be used to decide the inevitable conflicts between the demands of individual persons, and between the claims made in terms of a private good and the common good of a group of men.

If we are asked why man should have these moral rights, and why he should obey the natural moral law, we may first give the answer of realistic philosophy. Man must have the use of these rights, within the limits of a reasonable respect for the similar rights of others, or else he cannot achieve that ultimate happiness which all men cherish.

But what is happiness for man? Surely if life has taught us any lesson it is that perfect happiness is not to be found on earth or in this life. No good or perfection of soul or body is capable of satisfying the natural human craving for something better and something more lasting. We can be satisfied only with the goodness of a perfect being. This is a philosopher's way of saying that God alone can fully satisfy man's desires. The Christian philosopher knows that this happiness comes only with the beatific vision in heaven.

He also knows that this is the ultimate justification of the natural law. If morality is to be something more than an ever changing set of rules of expediency — if the natural law is to be an absolute and not a relative standard of conduct — it must rest on an Absolute Being. This is God, of course.

This is the message of Catholicism today and it is the thought which I would leave with you. It has always been the message of Christianity and it was given poetic expression at the beginning of St. Augustine's *Confessions:*

> Thou hast made us for Thee, and our heart is unquiet until it finds its rest in Thee.

13. Nielsen's Examination of Natural Law*

The *Natural Law Forum* was founded as a medium for discussion of the validity of legal thinking stemming from the persistent tradition that there are certain rules of justice superior to human customs, the enactments of human legislatures, and the chance opinions and possible prejudices of given groups of men. That the name "natural law" has come to be associated with this view is not an unmixed blessing. It is a name that repels many thinkers and it admits of a wide variety of meanings. In any case, the *Forum* is open to the expression of expert comment, both for and against the theory of natural law.

Pursuant to this policy, several valuable pieces of criticism have been printed. The contributions by Nakhnikian[1] and Nagel,[2] in earlier issues, seem to me to have been outstanding in the philosophical category. In the 1959 issue there appeared a forceful critique written by Kai Nielsen.[3] It is to Nielsen's article that my remarks are directed, not in a spirit of rebuttal but of cooperative discussion.

It should be noted in the beginning that Nielsen directs his criticism to the Thomistic theory of natural law and not against other possible versions of the theory. Many of the editors of the *Forum* are not Thomists and would insist that there are other bases for natural-law thinking than the philosophy of Aquinas. Doubtless Nielsen understands this fully. Indeed, he indicates at several places in his article that he sees some value in the efforts of

* *Natural Law Forum*, V (1960), pp. 112–119.

[1] "Contemporary Ethical Theories and Jurisprudence," *Natural Law Forum*, II (1957), pp. 4–40.

[2] "On the Fusion of Fact and Value: A Reply to Professor Fuller," *Natural Law Forum*, III (1958), pp. 77–82.

[3] "An Examination of the Thomistic Theory of Natural Moral Law," *Natural Law Forum*, IV (1959), pp. 44–71.

certain American naturalists to elaborate a theory which might have some affinities with natural law. This should be noted by Thomist readers: Nielsen's critique is not an advocacy of ethical skepticism.

To make a start, I should like to say a word about Thomism as a philosophy. There is, first of all, the thought of Thomas Aquinas — a thirteenth-century man. It is very difficult for the historian to determine the precise limits and meaning of this original Thomism. Aquinas was a teacher of Catholic theology at two universities: Paris, a religiously "commited" institution; and Naples, a royal, or state, university. In the course of his studies and teaching, he read and adapted to his use many purely philosophical works. He also used the writings of non-Catholic theologians, both Mohammedan and Jewish. The precise status of what one might call a purely natural philosophy, in the thought of Aquinas, is the source of controversy among Thomists today. Some think it possible to bracket the theology of St. Thomas and to treat the remainder of his thought as one would Platonism, Cartesianism, or Kantianism. Others (including both Gilson and Maritain) insist that Aquinas' philosophy cannot be considered in isolation from his religious convictions. They see him as a "Christian philosopher"— much indebted to his religion for his understanding of reality and of man's problems.

The foregoing is written frankly. Not only are non-Thomists puzzled when they try to extricate the philosophy of Aquinas from its theological setting; some Thomists are in a similar quandary. A strong group of modern Thomists will have nothing to do with a "so-called philosophy" of St. Thomas, separated from its theological context.

There are also twentieth-century Thomists who have taken the opposite view. Some think that Thomism is a philosophy much like any other kind of philosophy. Some recent Thomists have developed personal philosophical positions that are related in various ways to the thirteenth-century thought of Aquinas. This is not the place for further details on the ramifications of Neo-Thomism; suffice it to say that modern Thomism is far from monolithic.

All of this makes it difficult to discuss Nielsen's critique in a brief paper. I do not know whether he is primarily concerned with natural law as presented in the text of Aquinas, or in the several works of Jacques Maritain, or in the historical exposition by Copleston. If I write from my own view of what Thomism means today (as, in the last resort, I must), then I add a fourth variant.

To illustrate, let us consider the status of physics (philosophy of nature) in Thomism. There is no question that Thomas Aquinas made some use of a type of physics that stemmed very largely from Aristotle's *Physics*. However, there is much room for argument as to the importance of this material in the overall thought of Aquinas. Some people think that his metaphysics is but a projection and extension of this physics. Others (and I am one of them) think that he came to his metaphysical position rather independently of contemporary physical science. This latter group of Thomists tends to agree with Nielsen that medieval physics is outmoded and no sound basis for a theory of law. Maritain has always placed more emphasis on the philosophy of nature than has Gilson, for instance. Father Copleston gives the impression that he would not wish to revive the physics of Aristotle in the twentieth century. My own view is blunt: if Thomistic natural law thinking today requires acceptance of Aristotle's *Physics*, then I do not favor such thinking.

Here we come to the heart of the matter. Probably Nielsen does not see much difference between a medieval physics and a metaphysics. They talk about natures in both. Yet the Thomist metaphysician makes the greatest effort to understand the judgment that being is not confined to bodily existents. The kind of natural-law reasoning identified with much present-day Thomism centers on another metaphysical judgment: there are certain specific "natures" (e.g., dog, tree, man) which can be understood universally. These natures are not regarded as existing individual things, nor are they fictions of the human mind. What, then, are they? To answer this question is difficult because of the weight of much modern thinking which tends to discredit the notion of a universal. Take the judgment: "water freezes at 32 degrees Fahrenheit under certain conditions of pressure and purity." What is the meaning of "water" in this proposition? Of course it is an object of thought, but the point is that the judgment is not arbitrary. The judgment implies that a number of things, recognizable as "waters" in different times and places, behave in this way. If someone finds a new kind of "water" that does not freeze in this way, then he has found a new nature. Much physical science still deals precisely with such natures. This is so of the descriptive rather than the mathematical sciences. The ordinary chemist is not interested simply in the sulphuric acid in his own bottle. He desires to know certain properties typical of this acid, whenever and wherever it is found. Water is a universal object of study and understanding (and practical use); it is real or thingish because there are many individual instances of existing "waters." A circle is also a universal object of understanding but it is not real, because there are no instances of circles existing as individual things. This is the reason why physical science is not mathematics.

No Thomist professes to have an exhaustive knowledge of the real "natures" of things. Nor do I know any serious representative of Thomism who claims to be able to deduce the rules of natural law from his knowledge of the "nature" of man. Other natures than that of man are involved in human activity. To put it very briefly: it is a different matter, consciously and deliberately, to drink water, liquor, and sulphuric acid. Our variables are three different liquids that produce different results within the man who performs much the same action in drinking them.

It is practical and morally advisable to know which of these liquids to drink. Such information does not enable us to judge immediately that natural law "tells us" that a man ought to drink water and not acid. Unfortunately many Catholic writers have fallen into the habit of speaking as if it did. Notice that I have passed over the problem of what to say about drinking liquor: it is obviously much more complicated. Circumstances, other things than the natures of man and liquor, must be known before one could make a practical judgment on it. There are many fringe cases like this where the average person is frankly puzzled at times in trying to determine what is right. It is not advisable to give the impression that mere adherence to natural-law thinking provides immediate and infallible judgments on all moral issues. On the other hand, there are some actions that are, under usual circumstances, suitable for a man to do, and others that are not. These homely examples illustrate the first point that I wish to make: "natures" — in the realistic sense suggested above — are important to our understanding of the theory of natural law. More than human nature is involved. And we do not learn about these "natures" from Aristotle's *Physics* but from our own experience of reality.

At this point it may be helpful to distinguish two kinds of knowledge of natural law: (*a*) the way in which most men (not moral scientists) may grasp natural moral law; and (*b*) the way in which a moral expert reflects on, and endeavors to offer a scientific or philosophical explanation of, natural law. This distinction is important to our reading of Maritain. He writes, of course, as a moral expert, but about what he sometimes calls "natural" (untrained, unreflective, nonphilosophical) moral knowledge. When Maritain speaks of nonconceptual, connatural knowledge, or knowledge by inclination, he is talking about level (*a*) above. He is asserting that the ordinary person grasps certain natural-law notions or attitudes in a vague, nonreflective manner. This ordinary grasping is a combination of low-grade cognitive and affective activity. Sometimes it is close to animal feeling. Such a "natural" knower is related to the moral scientist in somewhat the same way that a natural singer is to a trained teacher of singing.

Maritain is trying to describe the bases within the moral agent for his own moral decisions. Maritain cannot make these ordinary moral experiences any clearer than they actually are in the average person. Consider the so-called synderesis principle: *Good should be done; evil should be avoided*. To say with Maritain that this generalized rule is known to all men is not to claim that all, or even most, men can and will state the rule when called upon to justify their moral decisions. Rather, Maritain's view is (and it is the position of most Thomists) that practically all men show some concern (both affective and cognitive) for right and wrong. I say most men. Some unwary Thomists may say that all men do. However, as Hobbes and Locke and Nielsen and others have said, there are some classes of men who do not show that they can discriminate between right and wrong. These atypical people are: very young children, fools, and certain highly sophisticated ethicians. I think we can exclude the first two classes: time will cure the children; and insane people are not regarded as responsible, legally or morally, precisely because they lack an awareness of such values. The professors of ethics are not the ordinary people that Maritain is talking about. I realize that I am passing over the really difficult point here. Some appeal to what is "normal" is made, consciously or unconsciously, in talking about such exceptions. This introduces the notion of what a nature is for, of finality in natures.

Thomists think that every action and every real thing that exists has some end. This is teleology. It is Aristotle's old theory of final causality. For Aquinas, finality has a different explanation, however, from that given by Aristotle. St. Thomas took it that God is the Creator and providential Governor of man and his universe. Aristotle did not. In the Thomistic view, God's intelligence directs all natural things and actions, in an orderly way, to their ends, just as an archer aims his arrow at the target. All finite natures have, in this position, a vector quality which God gives to them. This is true of man's nature too. However, Aquinas thought that men control some of their activities and may direct them toward the end of man, if they wish. Man is free. Otherwise man would be a physical but not a moral agent.

Now a critic may say: this is belief; we don't know that there is such a God; Aquinas' arguments for the existence of a providential Deity are not convincing. Such criticism would demand a discussion beyond the scope of an essay such as this. The Thomistic reasoning requires a good and thorough knowledge of classical metaphysics. Aquinas' arguments can hardly owe everything to his Christian training. Some parts of these arguments are taken from the pagan Aristotle; some elements are suggested by Mohammedans (Avicenna and Averroës); important forms of the famous "five ways" are found in the learned Rabbi Maimonides. May I say three things about this criticism. First, for anyone who is interested in a modern Thomistic presentation of the arguments for the existence of God, I should recommend a standard book: G. Smith, *Natural Theology* (Macmillan, 1951). Second, the acceptance of the exist-

ence of God is vital to a Thomist. Third, if Thomism is correct
about God's regulative care of man and the universe there should
be some observable evidence of this finality in the nature of things.
A person who is not sure about God could still look at himself
and his world of experience to see whether things exist and work
as a Thomist claims they do. In other words, even if we bracket
the problem of the existence of a providential Deity, there is still
something that a Thomist can talk about with his colleagues.

Is there evidence of end-directedness in the activities of men and
of other things in nature? That there is some such evidence is not
usually disputed. The biological and social disciplines make considerable use of purposive analyses. The concept of the "function"
of a physiological member is teleological. Oddly, most evolutionary
theories introduce some surreptitious notions of purpose. Self-perfectionism is an internal form of teleology: it is the kind of finality
that we find in the biology of Aristotle. At one point, Nielsen remarks that anthropology does not back up the Thomistic notion
of a purposive human nature. I can hardly think that he is serious
about this. Without quoting chapter and verse, I should like to
remind him that there is a strong movement in recent American
anthropology in this direction. Some of the leading names in the
field (Kluckhohn, Malinowski, Kroeber, Redfield, Evans-Pritchard,
Montague) see man as a very distinctive nature. Indeed one of the
basic assumptions of anthropology is that man is the only culture-
producing animal.

However, there are two great objections to natural finality. One
arises from the mathematical sciences, the other from a consideration of chance events. A Thomist has to admit that mathematical
physics makes little, if any, use of finality as a means of explanation.
This does not surprise him. Classical mathematics had no place
for purposes or ends. As early modern science moved from qualitative to more and more quantitative methods of interpretation, it
gained in accuracy and simplicity of verification — but it lost something in the process. The price that it paid was the loss of contact
with many of the properties of reality that make life worth living.
A tree is not the same thing to a mathematical physicist that it is
to Joyce Kilmer. But people have to live with Kilmer's tree and

not with a mathematical construct. Legal and moral decisions operate on the level of ordinary human experience. This is why morality
and legal thinking receive very little help from mathematical science. They have different interests, different values. As far as the
criticism of finality, based on mathematicized science, is concerned,
my suggestion is that such science deliberately excludes those qualitative aspects of reality in which teleology finds its justification.

The criticism from the evidence of chance deserves serious consideration. Let me say, first, that no man (not even a Thomist!)
knows all the causes of a given event. What a man does know is
that certain patterns of action, in most cases, produce certain results. Sometimes he finds that a certain line of actions intersects
with another causal series (that he has not known about) and gives
rise to an unexpected result that can be called a chance event.
Still informative is the classic example of the farmer digging a
well to get water; he finds a treasure buried by robbers with the
intention of hiding the treasure. The discovery is intended by
neither the farmer nor the robbers. It is a chance happening but
this does not mean that causality is inoperative. In a sense, the
example involves too many causes.

To say that most events in nature are fortuitous is, however, quite
another matter. As soon as chance begins to be the regular thing,
it loses its fortuitous character. The basic assumption of the investigator of nature is that there is some regular pattern to be
discovered. When a man tries to govern his own actions as well as
he can (or, in the case of a lawmaker, when he tries to govern the
actions of a group of men), his aim is to minimize the unexpected,
the chance results. His very program is predicated on the expecta-
tion that he can plan for the future and that chance will not, in
the long run, predominate. There is not much point to legal or
moral thinking if one takes the opposite view.

There is, finally, a point of criticism that is found throughout
Nielsen's appraisal of Thomistic natural law theory: you can't get
an *ought* from an *is*. The fact that things exist or happen in a
certain way does not mean that they should do so. This is a well-
known dilemma in contemporary ethics and value theory.

I think that this difficulty is set up by taking the terms *is* and *ought* (or fact and value) in a narrow, unrealistic sense.

Consider the *ought* part of it first. This term expresses some sort of obligation or necessity. The necessity implied cannot be absolute in the sense that agents who come under it must do what is required and cannot do otherwise. One does not tell a man that he ought to obey the "law" of gravity — he cannot avoid it. But the foregoing use of "absolute" in connection with necessity is only one way of employing the term. In the time of Kant (when most philosophers were theists and very conscious of the weight of moral duty) one could talk about an "absolute" moral necessity in a different way. God was there as an absolute lawgiver, dwelling in power and majesty above all men. In such a view God may function as an absolute monarch: what He requires *ought* to be done, or else. To many thinkers in the eighteenth and the nineteenth centuries, the "or else" implied very real sanctions. If you didn't obey God's commands you ended in hell. This sort of *ought* is compatible with human freedom (and so is not a type of physical necessity), but it is an obligation imposed on all men whether they choose to recognize it or not. (Parenthetically, it is well to note that the Thomist thinks that God does so command men, and that it is not possible for men to evade moral duty by not thinking of it; but the force of this necessity is lost if God is left out of the picture.)

What Kant did with this has caused trouble in philosophy ever since. He tried to see whether you could retain this strong meaning of the moral ought, even if you ignored sanctions (punishments and rewards), and even if you ignored God as the absolute lawmaker. He asked the odd question: Can man find within himself a sufficient source for such a duty, such an absolute *ought?* (This is one of those Irish questions to which Kant was addicted — something like his question: How can we know a thing-in-itself if we define the *Ding-an-sich* as that which is outside knowledge?) Ever since Kant's time, moral philosophers have been plagued by this question: How find an absolute *ought* if we do away with absolutes?

It seems rather obvious to me that without God in one's moral view the moral ought can only represent a conditional necessity. Kant saw this and introduced God as guarantor of the *summum bonum.* Otherwise, ought names an "if *A*, then *B*" sequence. Some British writers on ethics ridicule the idea that a moral ought is anything like the statement that a carpenter ought to use a certain tool to achieve a desired result. However, a conditional necessity is difficult to construe in the practical order, unless we introduce the notion of the utility of certain means to achieve a given end. That is probably why most British ethicians have still a lingering respect for social utilitarianism. The good of society is a respectable goal and may be used to decide many moral questions. It does not help, however, with some of the most difficult questions of private morality.

If we bracket the existence of God as moral legislator, then we must reduce our meaning of the moral *ought* to the notion of utility for a certain end. One way of putting this is to admit that no man is forced to work for happiness, or well-being, or self-perfection. Any person may reject the whole concept of working for an end that is suitable to his nature. In doing so, he has repudiated the only basis on which a moral ought can be given a workable meaning apart from divine law. To me, a naturalistic moral *ought* means that a person must do certain actions and avoid others, or take the consequences of an unfulfilled and imperfect human life. This is a reason for trying to do one's best but it is not an absolute one.

Turning to the other side of the problem: what is the connection between the *is* and such a conditional oughtness? Here again the meaning of our terms and our experience has been unnecessarily narrowed down. In good part due to the influence of Hume (it seems to me), reality has been reduced to a sort of atomic theory of unrelated events. In such a theory, what is given is a collection of sense "facts" that have no real interconnections. If that is the character of the *is,* then I should say that no oughtness arises from it.

But this atomism of sense data is not by any means self-evident or logically established. In the past few generations of English philosophers, it has brought nothing but bankruptcy in practical philosophy. I am getting a little tired of being accused of "dogmatism" because I question the validity of a Humean analysis of

man's experience. What is real may very well be closer to the world
of the average man-in-the-street than to the sense data of Bertrand
Russell. I am not suggesting that philosophers revert to the sim-
plistic position of the common-sense school. But I would strongly
maintain that the average man's world is not an unreality; it
merely fails to tell the whole story. He knows that there are trees.
dogs, water, other men, and so on, in his environment. He knows
that these things are related to each other, and to himself, in ways
that he does not impose by his own thinking. The reality of such
relations is very important for practical thinking. If I am the son
of a certain man, that is as much a fact as the perception of red.
But a relation such as this provides an experiential basis for oughtness. I obviously owe something to my father that I do not owe
to other men.

Consider a more simple example. Two boys each own four
marbles. One boy takes two of his friend's marbles, and his friend
protests. This seems to be a moral claim of a very obvious kind.
We have an interpersonal situation comprising several realities that
are interrelated. If no other circumstances are added to modify
the example, it is clear that the boy *ought* to return the two marbles to his friend. This is the "right thing" to do — what Aristotle
called the *justum*. It is not that boys or marbles, considered in
isolation, demand such a return. Rather, the governing reality in
this case is the fact of possession, based on some reason that can be
given to substantiate it. In the example, the effort of the boy to
establish a new fact of possession is based on no reason for the
transfer.

To know such relations is beyond the realm of sense experience.
You do not *see* that a boy owns a certain number of marbles; you
must try to understand the complexus of prior related facts on
which his claim is based. The beginning of such knowledge lies
in sense experience, but the grasp of the meaning of ownership is
an affair of understanding, of reasoning. G. E. Moore made the
naturalistic fallacy famous. In doing so, he perpetuated a far more
dangerous moral fallacy: the notion that if good is not a natural
property it must be a nonnatural one. These are not the only
alternatives. Good, right, wrong, and other such moral terms name

complex relations, not properties. It takes understanding to grasp them. Thomism has a long and perhaps overcomplicated explanation of the working of the human intellect. It differs radically from most modern theories of knowledge. What is essential in it is the claim that man knows on two levels: he senses individuals and he understands universals.

In regard to the philosophy of law, the understanding of universal relations, meanings, implications, tendencies, goods, and obligations is of primary importance. So it appears to a Thomist. A law is not a sense "fact"; whatever else it is, a law is some sort of universal. It applies to many possible subjects in a variety of circumstances. Clearly a theory of knowledge that reduces all human experience to atomized, isolated, unrelated sense impressions cannot give an account of law. Nor can it account for obligation, moral or legal.

I am far from suggesting that Thomism offers a fully developed explanation of all that natural law implies. More attention to the multiple experiences of modern life is needed. More cooperation with social scientists is advisable. Modern Thomists are not yet doing a proper job of making their position clear to their colleagues. Nielsen does a real service in demanding a better presentation of the natural-law theory. Of course, communication is a two-way affair; it cannot all be accomplished by Thomists. To me it is encouraging to see a non-Thomist offering a searching criticism of Thomism.

IV. CONTEMPORARY PROBLEMS

14. *Censoring Mass Media**

For most people — certainly for me — there is something negative and repellent in the very notion of censoring. Possibly this is why the literature on the subject is meager in quantity and often inferior in quality. Yet censoring is an important activity within most organized societies and it is probably a good thing for us to take a close look at it.

Since precision in terminology is helpful to the solution of most difficult questions, a start may be made by suggesting working definitions for the key terms in this topic. These statements of meaning are tentative, not intended to predetermine our conclusions, and subject to revision if they are found defective. Three terms seem to require clarification: "censoring" — "media of mass communication" — and "moral."

As to the first, let us start with a standard definition and see what we can do with it. Censorship is described in the *Encyclopedia of the Social Sciences* as "the policy of restricting the public expression of ideas, opinions, conceptions and impulses which have or are believed to have the capacity to undermine the governing authority or the social and moral order which that authority considers itself bound to protect."[1] This statement is, I think, subject to some revision. It would be well, first of all, to shift the emphasis from *censorship*, which is a general policy, to censoring as a concrete action. I will propose, then, a definition of censoring, rather

---

* From: *Problems of Communication in a Pluralistic Society* (Milwaukee: Marquette University Press, 1956), pp. 113–137; reprinted in *Marquette Law Review*, 40, 1 (1956), pp. 57–73.

[1] Harold D. Lasswell, "Censorship," *Encyclopedia of the Social Sciences* (New York, 1930), III, p. 290.

than of censorship. Second, we can state the conscious subject matter of human expression more concisely than "ideas, opinions, conceptions and impulses." Here it is obvious that differences in one's philosophical or psychological approach make for variations in terminological preference. For myself, I should prefer to speak simply of the expression of "thoughts, feelings, or volitions." In any case, I do not mean to place great stress on this change. More important, I think, is a third change to be made. In the last part of the quoted definition, these conscious events are qualified as those "which have or are believed to have the capacity to undermine the governing authority or the social and moral order." It seems to me that we might better apply the qualification to the *expression,* rather than to *what* is expressed. My intent is not to close discussion on the subject matter of public communication; instead, I wish to include not only possibly objectionable items that may be expressed but also possibly objectionable modes of expression. It is often not what is said that is potentially harmful but the way in which the communication is made. Moreover it seems possible to condense these qualifying phrases while still retaining the meaning of what is regarded as socially objectionable.

It is proposed, then, to speak of censoring as the act of restricting the public expression of thoughts, feelings, or volitions, which expression is considered by the censoring agency to be contrary to public or private good.

Concerning the second phrase, "the media of mass communication," our need is not so much for a formal definition as for some itemized analysis of the available means of expression, and for some suggestions as to the relative importance of these means within the ambit of our topic. I should say immediately that I do not intend to attempt an exhaustive description and evaluation of all significant media of communication. It is possible to group these means under four categories. One group employs written and printed words: in this first class will fall newspapers, books, magazines, and pamphlets. A second class utilizes oral speech: this would include conversation, public orations, radio, recordings, and schoolteaching. Visual but nonverbal presentation characterizes a third group of media: here we might place pictures, cartoons, sculpture, and comic books. Finally, some media use various combinations of verbal, oral, and visual signs: examples of these complex forms are stage plays, movies, and television.

There are important diversities among these classes of expressive signs. In law, the original distinction between libel and slander, for instance, depended on the notion that defamatory statements in the form of written words are more permanent than those in oral form. Etymologically, *libel* means a small book or pamphlet, whereas *slander* means any type of defaming. However, this distinction in terms of media has come to take a secondary place in legal practice, having given way to a more practical and utilitarian difference based on the relative permanence of the calculable effects of defamation. Thus libel is what is deemed permanently defamatory, whereas slander is considered transiently such.[2] Obviously the potential for harm to society or person varies from one type of medium to another. There is an observable moral, as well as legal, difference between the possible injury of a chance remark made in private conversation and the same statement as printed for large and continued circulation. And when we think of the defamatory potential of a presentation through movies or television, we easily realize the complexity and difficulty of making moral and legal decisions on the harmful uses of these new media.

To the moralist, diversities of media constitute circumstantial conditions of the act of expression or communication. Circumstances are of the utmost importance in determining the moral quality of an action. Yet I think it advisable to forgo lengthy discussion of the many variations which might be introduced by a detailed consideration of these many means of communication. The reason for my renunciation is not disinterest but the realization that it would take many days of discussion to cover our topic adequately in this way.

I propose to consider all means of communication as basically similar uses of signs to convey thoughts and attitudes. Indeed, in what follows I shall keep primarily in mind that medium which is most typical: the printed word. Censoring of the press will be

2 See Z. Chafee, *Government and Mass Communications. A Report from the Commission on Freedom of the Press*, 2 vols. (Chicago: University of Chicago Press, 1947), I, pp. 77–130.

the focal point of my discussion. Other media are not excluded but are peripheral.

The third and last term requiring precision is "moral." Within the context of the overall title of this conference, it is indeed hard to say what this word means. A pluralistic society, such as that in which we live, admits of plural and divergent ethical views. Yet I, as a student of ethical theory, cannot grant equal validity to all these varied approaches to morality. My problem at this moment, then, is whether to speak from the point of view of what I consider right and wrong in human conduct — or from the point of view of the plural and divergent moralities to which significant persons and groups within our society are actually committed. If I do the former, I shall doubtless appear narrow and unduly prejudiced in my approach to these problems of censoring: in fact, I could be guilty of an overt act of censoring, without apparent justification, the expression of competing moral positions. If I do the latter, endeavoring to speak for a variety of ethical positions, I shall find myself using several different meanings for morality and supporting views which are inconsistent with each other, even mutually contradictory.

To this theoretical dilemma there is, I take it, a practical solution. After all, our courts and legislative bodies are continually faced with the necessity of taking a stand on moral issues. I recognize the importance of constitutional guidance and precedent in legal thinking, but I am also convinced that moral reasoning and judgment play an important role in making the law of the land and in interpreting it. However this may be, I submit that there is a common denominator of moral conviction underlying our superficially pluralistic society. It is from the viewpoint of this fundamental morality of our democratic way of life that I propose to work. This is not a question of concealing my personal commitment to the ethics of modern Thomism, but it is rather a practical effort to discover a point of departure acceptable to most thinking persons in our pluralistic society.

Perhaps it is a mistake to use mathematical terms in this matter. I do not aim to combine all known systems of morality into a grand synthesis. Were this to be done, these divergent theoretical positions would cancel each other on many points of principle and application. The result would be a gray neutralism in morality, from which no definite decisions could be taken. Instead, I would seek to find those commitments in the moral area which seem to represent the very roots and ideals on which our democratic society has waxed strong, and to which our most thoughtful citizens might give assent.

Fully to treat this ethics of American democracy would be a lengthy matter. In order to avoid prolixity I have looked about for a statement of such a basic moral position by a writer with a religious, educational, and philosophic background different from my own. I have found such a statement in a book written by W. E. Hocking, formerly of Harvard University.[3] It is not that Hocking says all that could be said, or that I agree with him entirely — but his book is one to which I can point and say: "Here is what the ethics of democracy is, in great part." Naturally, I cannot summarize this work of two hundred and fifty pages but I can indicate my general agreement with his framework of principles.

Further to show what this morality means, I shall attempt to state its chief contentions in a few brief points. Of course the formulation and extent of each of these statements are matters for debate. My purpose in the following nine items is simply to sketch some of the accepted standards of morality in our society. These statements are necessarily brief and unsupported by scholarly or philosophical justifications. It is my hope that you will, at the very least, take these statements as what some American moralists regard as the touchstone of our social mores.

I.   Each human person is the equal of every other person in his basic rights.

II.   These rights are claims to some degree of self-fulfillment.

III.   These rights are not mere privileges conferred by the state; to some thinkers who remember the Constitution, they are conferred by the Creator; to others, they appear to stem from man's higher nature or from his conscience.

IV.   It is morally good and right for each person to seek and

[3] *Freedom of the Press: A Framework of Principle* (Chicago: University of Chicago Press, 1947). Cf. also: Marten Ten Hoor, *Freedom Limited, an Essay on Democracy* (Tuscaloosa: University of Alabama Press, 1954).

work for his own perfection and happiness, provided he recognizes, and does no direct injury to, the similar rights of other persons and of his community.

V. Governmental authority is exercised primarily for the common good of all persons subject to such authority, and secondarily for the private good of individual persons within the same group.

VI. It is possible to determine from experience, and from reflection thereon, certain standards of moral judgment whereby a distinction may be made between what is good and what is bad for the community and for the individual person.

VII. There are some actions, and some omissions of activity, which, under given circumstances and stemming from conscious intention or culpable negligence, are bad and deserve restraint or punishment.

VIII. A morally valid law is the general and overt expression of a regulation calculated to promote the common good of those persons subject to the legislating authority.

IX. Applications of such laws in a morally approvable way require further reflection on the character and dispositions of the individual person subject to the laws and on the pertinent circumstances in which he may act.

If we take the foregoing definitions and statements of principle as preliminary to our consideration of the moral problems of censoring, we may next proceed to an examination of the situation in which such problems arise.

MAN'S RIGHT TO KNOW

That every man possesses a basic moral right to acquire some knowledge can hardly be questioned. This general right to know may, on occasion, require restriction; but, on the whole, it appears to be as primary and self-evident as any right ever claimed by mankind. Indeed, since the act of knowing is directly related to the exercise of reason, traditionally regarded as the specific characteristic of man, it could well be argued that man has a greater moral claim to knowledge than to any other value.

Furthermore, it seems especially important for a democratic society to recognize the validity of this right. First of all, the conten-

tion that all human beings are of equal worth as persons leads to
the conviction that all men share in the claim to some knowledge.
Second, for the proper functioning of democratic institutions, all
citizens of a democracy must be enabled to know the things needed
for active participation in the civic and social life of their community. A society of intellectual zombies cannot function as a
democracy.

So much has been written of recent years on the character of
this right to knowledge and the freedoms associated with it, that it
is probably unnecessary to reemphasize it here.[4]

Intimately associated with the right to know is the communication of knowledge to other persons. Indeed, where person *A* has
some potentially useful knowledge and person *B* needs that knowledge, a situation is set up such that if *B* appears to have a right
to this knowledge then *A* acquires a definite obligation to consider
whether or not to communicate his knowledge to *B*. Suppose, for
instance, that *A* and *B* are driving their automobiles along a country road. *A* comes first to a washed-out bridge and manages to
stop on the brink of disaster. He makes a U turn and meets *B*
driving at high speed toward the site of a possible accident. In
this situation, it is clear that *A* is morally obliged to use all ordinary
means to convey his knowledge of the danger to *B*. Not all exercises of the right to know entail an accompanying obligation to
communicate knowledge to others; it is enough for us to note the
possibility of such entailment in certain cases. From this we may
recognize the possible moral connection between one man's right
to know and his being obliged to communicate his knowledge to
another.

Here is where our first moral problem arises. Is the right to know
absolute and unconditioned? And, as a consequence, is the right
to communicate information and attitudes quite unlimited? To
find a moral answer to this general problem, it is necessary to
consider the nature of freedom. It is noteworthy that in most of

[4] Mark Van Doren, *Man's Right to Knowledge and the Free Use Thereof*,
introduction by Richard R. Powell (New York: Columbia University Press,
1954). For a comparable statement by European Catholics, cf. Louis de Raeymaeker *et al.*, *Liberté et vérité* (Louvain: Nauwelaerts, 1954), printed in English
as: *Truth and Freedom* (Pittsburgh: Duquesne University Press, 1955).

the literature concerned with the free use of the right to know, and in most works on press and academic freedom, one basic assumption is made by American discussants. This assumption is that *freedom* is an *absolute* value.[5] Nearly all suppose that freedom is quite generally understood and that it is independent of all other values.

However, I think that freedom is *not* universally understood. My reason for this judgment is that one finds underlying these essays on free thought, free research, and free speech, the tacit and almost invariable assumption that to be free means simply to be unrestrained by external impediments. Now this meaning of freedom is neither primary nor most important. To me freedom has another and more important aspect: this is the positive meaning of freedom, consisting in the concrete possession and use of the ability to do something. What I mean is this: you are all *negatively* free (in the sense of being unrestrained by other persons or institutions) to play Bach on the piano, to study quantum physics, and to do any number of other excellent things. No one is stopping you. Yet, in point of concrete fact, most of us are not free to do these things. We know full well that negative freedom in regard to such actions is an empty freedom, even though many people continue to speak as if it were all-important. On the contrary, if we lack the ability or skill to do something, it is idle to assert our freedom in the matter. For negative freedom to have actual applicability, *positive* freedom must be present.

The objection may be offered that the foregoing instances are loaded, that they are cases of highly specialized skills, that in regard to most actions we may presume positive freedom, whereas we often have to fight for negative freedom. This objection is partly valid. I do not deny the importance of the negative meaning. What I do claim is that the positive aspect must not be ignored. Consider a situation in which artistic or scientific skills are not involved. Suppose that we find a small country in which the citizens have been ruled by dictators for generations and decide to liberate these unfortunate people. We drive their present dictator into exile and say to the people: "Democracy is obviously the best form of gov-

[5] An important exception is Dean Ten Hoor, cf. *supra*, note 3.

ernment. No one is holding you back. Go ahead and rule yourselves democratically." It is quite possible that such a people cannot do this. In such a situation negative freedom is inoperative because there is little or no positive freedom. If people do not know *how* to rule themselves, it is useless to tell them to do it.

This stress on the positive side of liberty is today almost forgotten, though it was an obvious thing to men in the past. The contrast is clearly evident in two books published by the University of Chicago Press for the Commission on Freedom of the Press.[6] Speaking of the approach to press freedom, Professor Chafee (Harvard Law School) says (*Introd.*, p. viii) : "Another departure from the traditional conception was the recognition that freedom *from* something is not enough. It should also be freedom *for* something." (Emphasis by way of italics is in the original; actually, this is not a "departure from the traditional" but a return to a commonplace notion in ancient and medieval philosophy.) Likewise, Hocking argues for the positive as well as the negative notions of freedom (pp. 54–56) : "To be free is to have the use of one's powers of action, (i) without restraint or control from outside and (ii) with whatever means or equipment the action requires." In his two following paragraphs, Hocking then distinguishes freedom *from* something and freedom *for* something, as does Chafee, and as I would. However, some other members of this Commission on Freedom of the Press, whose objections are recorded in footnotes, show that they are quite incapable of understanding the point. They (particularly Professor John M. Clark of the economics department at Columbia University) insisted that the absence of restraint is the essential meaning of liberty. Hocking is eventually forced to say that "the negative meaning of freedom remains the chief element of the conception." This I would not admit; freedom to me is essentially the power to do something, and only secondarily the absence of restraint on the exercise of such power.

Man grows up with the equipment for knowing, and he is supplied by the world about him with objects of knowledge. He also acquires when young the ability to communicate his knowl-

6 Two volumes by Z. Chafee, Jr., and the book by Hocking have been cited previously.

edge to other men. This is all it means to say that man has natural rights to know and to communicate his knowledge to others. These rights are not granted him by the state or by any other institution. They are moral rights, not merely legal rights. Man would possess them outside, and apart from, organized society. Legal recognition of such rights adds nothing to their basic character. To say the contrary is to support one of the chief contentions of totalitarianism: that the individual person is utterly dependent on the state for all his powers.[7]

LIMITATIONS OF THE RIGHT TO COMMUNICATE KNOWLEDGE

If freedom to know is conditioned by its relation to the kind of knowledge *to which* the right is asserted, and by the capacity of the person asserting his right (and that is what the foregoing implies), this does not mean that man has only the right to know what is right or true. It is sometimes necessary to know what is false and wrong. It is sometimes necessary to admit that a man has a right even to err, provided he does not deliberately seek out error. Otherwise, the free quest of knowledge becomes impossible. What limits man's use of his powers of knowledge is twofold: his own limited capacity and his obligation to respect the rights of other persons. If this is so, we may turn to the related question: is man's right to communicate knowledge to others unconditioned? I think it is obvious that this is not an absolute right.

The state — and quite possibly other organized societies — is morally entitled to see to it that this right of communication, like any other moral right, is properly exercised. Some reasonable limitations must be imposed on the use of all moral rights; otherwise it becomes impossible for all persons to enjoy the use of their rights in society. Primarily, the individual person should recognize the need for restraint and should impose some degree of self-control on his utterances. If all persons were prudent and just, no other form of limitation would be necessary. But many persons are not morally adult, and so it is sometimes necessary for external force to intervene and set limits to the use of the personal right to convey

[7] "To identify rights with legally recognized rights is to render one's self helpless before the authoritarian state. . . . On this issue we are with the Declaration [of Independence]." Hocking, *op. cit.*, p. 59.

information to others. This is the general moral justification for censoring.

The kind of utterances or expressions which require limitation must be carefully considered. In general, objectionable communications are such that they unnecessarily injure the common good of a group of persons, or the private good of one or more persons.

Let us first think of the unjustifiable communication of knowledge or attitudes injurious to the common good. It is widely granted that, under certain special circumstances, the use of the media of public communication requires state restriction, or censoring. In time of war, for instance, to permit open publication of the news of troop movements, plans for attack, disposition of materiel and such things, is self-injurious to a state. Few men will deny the need for some censoring under such circumstances. Disagreement on this sort of censoring arises mostly in connection with its extent and the manner of its application.[8] Moral justification for wartime censoring is found in the axiom that the state must have authority to use all legitimate means necessary to maintain its existence. There is no point in having states unless we grant them this authority. Thus it is reasonable enough to admit some state control of communications channels in the circumstances of war.

Difficulties appear when we consider whether such restrictions are justifiable under circumstances of peace. Many indications would point to the undesirability of censoring the media of international communication in time of peace. Unfortunately, there are periods of unstable peace, times in which war may be just around the corner. In such times, which we have come to call the intervals of "cold war," it is quite possible that some forms of state censoring of otherwise quite useful knowledge are morally permitted. After all, it may be quite as self-injurious to give information of martial value to a potential enemy before he makes war, as to give it to him after he has attacked. I think we may take it, however, that in time of genuine peace the free and open communication between all peoples is a most desirable thing from a moral

[8] On this type of censoring in the U.S.A. during World War II, see R. E. Summers, *Wartime Censorship of Press and Radio* (New York: Wilson, 1942), with extensive bibliography, pp. 287–297.

point of view. Indeed, one might suggest that undue limitations of such international communication are the main instruments of misunderstanding and ill feeling among nations.

The name "national security" is used for the foregoing value which state censoring is intended to protect. If that is its proper use, then we frequently misuse the term today. For there is another situation to which censoring can be applied — whether with moral justification or not — and that is to the communication of information concerning governmental activities to the citizens under that government. Too often, national security may be used to justify restraint of the free communication of such information. Censoring of news regarding official plans and activities is easily extended beyond what is necessary to protect a country against its enemies. The motives for such unwarranted extension may vary; often they are reducible to a desire on the part of government workers to avoid public criticism. This is only to suggest that state censoring, like any other use of public authority, can easily be abused.

Let us consider a hypothetical case. Suppose some officials in a country learn, or suspect, that their country is in danger of invasion and injury on the part of intelligent beings able to fly to this earth from another planet.[9] Let us suppose, further, that these government officials decide to suppress all news concerning this possible danger — with the purpose of avoiding public hysteria. Granting the sincerity of these officials in this hypothetical case, it is debatable whether their position is morally justified. It is moreover questionable whether the notion of national security covers the situation. One of the reasons for questioning such censoring lies in its impracticality. A means is not a good means if it fails to work in most cases. If there were some actual danger to the public, it could be very ill-advised to keep all knowledge of it from the people for the sake of avoiding panic. In the due course of affairs the public would have to learn something of the situation eventually. Secrecy on such matters would postpone but not remove the actuality of general hysteria. The effect of improper censoring is to break down confidence in the government which uses it.

[9] For an accusation of such censoring: D. E. Keyhoe, *The Flying Saucer Conspiracy* (New York: Holt, 1955).

Another undue extension of the concept of security is found in the tendency of one branch or division of government to keep material secret from other branches of government. Here again I would suggest for your consideration a hypothetical case.[10] Say a country has a secret defensive weapon, such as radar; say this weapon exists and can be used by certain technical experts; say this news has been kept so secret that even the commanding general in the area supplied with the weapon does not know of its potentialities.[11] This seems ridiculous and clearly an overextension of the policy of military security. To discuss such a situation properly one would need full knowledge of it. This is precisely what secrecy prevents. What I am suggesting is that some reasonable limits must be placed on censoring by various branches of government. If this is not done, the very principle of the division of powers breaks down. In particular, the censoring of information about government activities must be carefully limited in a democracy. Granted that the people need not know all sorts of technical details, it still remains true that the people should know, be able to evaluate, and be able to influence the determination of general policy. This cannot be accomplished if government agencies adopt the policy that what the people do not know will not harm them.

That some limited censoring of the media of public communication by governmental agencies for the common good may be morally justified is apparent. Note that we are not directly concerned with the truth or falsity of what is censored in this sort of material. The true may be even more dangerous to public security than the false. Moreover, the text of what should be censored in this way is not simply whether the information is harmful to the public welfare. There will be news which will immediately hurt the public morale (for example, loss of an important battle in time of war) but it may be advisable in the long view not to censor such news, for the sake of maintaining democratic processes and popular faith in the trustworthiness of officialdom. In each major case where censoring is contemplated by government,

10 Cf. Thomas R. Phillips, "Secrecy Keeps Military Data from Planners," *St. Louis Post-Dispatch* (February 16, 1956).

11 Phillips reported (*art. cit.*) that such was the case with radar equipment at Pearl Harbor in 1941.

careful thought should be given to all the foreseeable effects of censoring. No moralist would demand the gift of prophecy in government agents but it is expected that especial prudence be used in connection with the restraint of basic rights by censors. One of the chief aspects of such prudence is foresight. The long view of the most probable results of censoring is the good view. Indeed, instead of following the maxim: "when in doubt, censor," it is better to adopt the rule: "the least censoring is the best censoring."

Turning now to a second type of problem, let us consider the censoring of material potentially harmful to the common good of social groups smaller than the "great" state. (By this term I mean to designate the whole body of people subject to the government of a given country; thus the U. S. is a "great" state, Illinois is not.) Here we have something difficult to express as a question, and even harder to answer. There are minority groups within a country which constitute actually or potentially organized societies. I am thinking of social groups such as the citizens of a city, the members of a labor union, or an industrial association, such things as associations of professional people, and Churches such as the Lutheran or Catholic. These and other such groups each have their respective common goods which are entitled to reasonable protection at the hands of civil government.[12] Our question is: are such minority groups morally justified in endeavoring to limit the dissemination of information which in their best judgment is harmful to their respective common goods?

To make the question more concrete, let us face one typical instance. Are Catholics, living as citizens of a democratic country, justified in seeking government restraint of the dissemination of information on birth-control practices? Before examining this, let us remember that we are talking about a pluralistic society, a society in which there are diverse views on the moral value of birth-control data. Here we come to the heart of one of the issues of censoring. It is clear that censoring implies general acceptance of some standards of judgment of what is objectionable or harm-

[12] On the function of the "great state" as protector of the rights of smaller groups, see Johannes Messner, "Freedom as a Principle of Social Order," *The Modern Schoolman*, XXVIII (1951), pp. 97–110.

ful. Where there is no common standard of judgment it is impossible to avoid conflicting assertions of presumed rights. On the present question Catholics may assert their right to remain free from solicitation to what they consider moral evil — but others may with equal subjective conviction assert their right to free publication of material which they judge to be socially and morally beneficial. Now it is not possible for the moralist to avoid facing such conflicts of asserted rights.

Remembering that these conflicts arise because of varying notions of what is morally acceptable, I think we may say these things about them. First, each minority group has a right, even within a larger pluralistic society, to censor *for its own members* the use of media seriously considered harmful for that group. Second, one minority group in a pluralistic society does not have a moral right to demand government censoring of the expression of the foregoing sort of information *for members of other groups* who do not share the same standards. Third, any minority group has the moral right to attempt to raise and improve the moral standards of its "great" society by arguments and persuasions conducted within the law and on a factual and reasonable basis. Fourth, it does not have the right to impose its own moral views, by any form of violence, on other smaller groups within a pluralistic society.[13] This opens for discussion, for instance, the propriety of certain pressure groups aiming to improve the moral tone of media, such as magazines or movies, by group boycott.

It must be admitted that the moralist has no ready-made solutions for certain conflicts of interest among minority groups. Where the matter of censoring is involved, there are situations in which one cannot know in advance what is the best thing to do. Practical thinking often requires a willingness to compromise — not on ideal principles but on the actual exercise of presumed rights. This would be particularly so in a society constituted from groups with diverse moral attitudes. If we wish to maintain the general value of freedom, we must refrain from attempts to coerce others in their exercise of what they honestly regard as their rights.

[13] These four propositions were later quoted extensively as expressing a liberal Catholic view on censoring.

The point here, as in most other problems, is that a minimum of censoring is far more likely to prove beneficial than an attempted maximum. We would do well to recall that censoring is often, if not always, a plural-effect action. It may achieve bad results along with the good consequences. These bad results, such as general restriction of freedom of expression, excessive use of authority, and violent achievement of conformity, may on occasion outweigh the good ones.

Zealous Catholics should remember that their Church functioned up to the twelfth century without any formal censoring of books, for instance.[14] They should also take note of the quite minimal requirements of the Catholic *Index of Prohibited Books*.[15] The intent of such ecclesiastical censoring is not to close a part of the world of literature from all Catholic readers (for permission to read most any work may be secured by those who have a good reason for reading it) but to protect the moral and intellectual integrity of those who could easily be harmed by promiscuous reading. Of course, ecclesiastical censoring is not under discussion here, for a Church is not a pluralistic society in our meaning of the term.

Another typical instance of censoring in the name of the common good of a smaller society is found in certain restrictions imposed by educational institutions on faculty members. A good deal has been said and written about academic freedom from the side of the teaching profession. Often, academic freedom for the teacher is presented as an absolute and quite unconditioned freedom.[16] Though I have spent my mature life as a teacher and am as jealous of my prerogatives as any, I cannot accept this notion. It appears to me that any man, whatever his work, must recognize certain prudent limitations on his utterances. A person who teaches or does research in an educational institution is not thereby raised above all law. He is not a demigod, transcending all restraint. He should be granted freedom to teach as he thinks

[14] Cf. G. B. Flahiff, "The Ecclesiastical Censorship of Books in the Twelfth Century," *Mediaeval Studies*, IV (1942), pp. 1–22.

[15] Cf. R. A. Burke, *What Is the Index?* (Milwaukee: Bruce, 1952), with the bibliography, p. 117.

[16] Cf. R. Hofstadter and W. P. Metzger, *The Development of Academic Freedom in the United States* (New York: Columbia University Press, 1955).

best and to inquire after new knowledge and new ways of interpreting his data. He should even be accorded a certain freedom
to make mistakes — otherwise his task would demand superhuman
abilities. Yet his freedom should also be limited by concern for
the rights of other persons, for the good of his country and of his
institution of learning. He should be limited by all applicable
civil laws and by the standards of his profession. As Hocking (a
man of liberal mind and long experience in teaching) has said of
the teacher: "The right to be in error in the pursuit of truth does
not include a moral right to be deliberately in error."[17]

A third area of censoring problems embraces restraint of communication in regard to items that are calculated to injure the
private good. Here we must briefly consider the protection of
private goods, such as personal reputations, by public agencies
because these private goods constitute important parts of the
common good.

We may ask, for instance, for the moral justification of commonly applied laws of slander and libel. These laws do function
as a type of censoring. To see this, we may review the generally
made distinction between preventive and punitive censoring. Since
the time of Milton in our tradition, preventive censoring has been
regarded as more opposed to freedom than the punitive form.
I should like to question both the distinction and the conclusion.

In point of fact, punitive censorship becomes preventive after
its initial usage. If A publishes a libelous book or article and is
punished at law for this act, B, contemplating a similar publication, is usually deterred from publication by his knowledge of A's
punishment. In effect, punitive control of communication turns
into preventive restraint. All major publishers, for instance, retain
legal counsel to determine in advance of publication whether
their proposed material is subject to legal objections. In most
cases they prefer not to publish matter of a possibly objectionable
character. I do not say that there is no difference between preventive and punitive censoring; I do maintain that, from the point
of view of positive freedom of utterances, the practical difference
is small. In other words, laws of libel are forms of censorship —

[17] *Op. cit.*, p. 109.

though they do not always completely restrain the dissemination of possibly objectionable matter.

The moral basis for such laws is sound enough. It centers on the actual harm done to a person, and indirectly to his community, by certain utterances. Injury to a man's reputation resulting in the loss of a job and rather permanent unemployability is calculable in terms of dollars and cents. When accomplished with malice, or culpable negligence, this is obviously immoral. If sometimes the laws of libel, mechanically applied, lead to the punishment of persons innocently involved,[18] and if, on the other hand, moralists emphasize the importance of an agent's having some knowledge and voluntariness in regard to the possible effects of his utterance — it is still true that in most cases such laws operate in a morally justified manner.

A notorious problem in the field of censoring arises in connection with presumably obscene and pornographic material. I put the problem here because it has to do with potential harm to the private goods of individuals and, again, indirectly with the public good. It should be possible to include in this category communications calculated to incite to crime and delinquency. The name "moral censorship" is frequently used to cover restraint of this sort of thing.[19] Actually, this is no more the province of morals than are other types of objectionable expression. But sexual conduct is difficult to regulate by public law and it has become customary to consider it the special domain of conscience and private morality.

To my mind, there is little doubt that public restraint on the communication of obscene and similar material is demanded under some circumstances. The effects of such material may consist in the lowering of the moral tone of a community, with consequent overt forms of vice and public disorder. Even the most liberal-minded person sees that, when press or art media are employed as public solicitations to community disorder, such use becomes

[18] Instances are discussed by Chafee, *op. cit.*, pp. 77–130, and W. M. Daniels, *The Censorship of Books* (New York: Wilson, 1954), pp. 51–106, and throughout Summers, *op. cit.*

[19] Daniels devotes a whole chapter (pp. 51–81) to what he calls "Moral Censorship"; it is entirely concerned with problems of obscenity in printed matter.

open aggression against the public welfare.[20] This is generally recognized, for instance, in situations where children are the objects of vicious communications. It is for this reason that many people think that there is some need for the censoring of media, such as comic books, which appeal to the child — in years or in mental capacity.

In the United States practically no effort is made by the federal government to censor obscene materials. At times, the postal department engages in a sort of *ad hoc* censoring, by refusing special mailing privileges to senders of printed material deemed obscene or similarly objectionable. No definite standards for such censoring are published; it may be difficult to set up such general rules. Rigidly applied regulations can limit the circulation of works of literary genius, of high religious tone, and of classical reputation in art and literature. Moreover, it is quite clear morally that what is possibly obscene under certain circumstances is not objectionble in different conditions.

What is more often practiced is local censoring of presumably obscene or vicious matter. It is part of the irony of the situation that decisions on such material are made by police and minor municipal officials. Restrictions are effected by application of licensing and similar ordinances. Local control in this area is strongly imbedded in our democratic traditions. It is morally odd, however, for a community to rely on the personal judgment of a policeman in situations where no clear general directive seems possible. With all due regard for the sincerity and high caliber of the average officer of the law, it must be confessed that there is little in the training or background of such an official to fit him for this delicate task.

The problem of who should censor is immediately connected with the foregoing. On this point, we may note a strong tendency in legal thought to avoid federal censoring where possible. A moralist might suggest that differences in media are paramount in settling such problems. Local censoring of media which ordinarily reach only a local audience seems reasonable enough. Thus

20 See Hocking, *op. cit.*, pp. 118–126, for a full statement of this point in ethical language.

restrictions on the performance of a stage play may be the direct concern of local government. On the other hand, a medium of wide geographic appeal, such as television or radio, is hardly a subject for local censoring. Indeed, variations in local standards make it very difficult for managers of such media to broadcast materials of new and striking character. The result is a mediocrity far from golden. I would suggest that media appealing to a countrywide audience might best be controlled by a minimum degree of countrywide censoring. But this is a question on which expert legal opinion is very important.

Voluntary censoring by trade organizations, such as the movie producers' code, is only a partial answer to these problems. In fact, such censoring is not wholly voluntary. It is usually motivated in part by the fear of outside restraint, to be applied unless the entertainment or publishing industries regulate themselves. Such self-restraint only continues to function as long as public opinion is firm enough to occasion such fear.

This points up the main conclusion to be drawn from this survey of the moral aspects of censoring. The ideal community would be a society of persons sharing such high standards of morality, loyalty, and seemliness that censoring would be unnecessary. In point of fact, censoring is only called for when people fail to exercise due restraint over their personal inclinations to endanger the good order of their community in various types of communications. Censoring, then, is the mark of some degree of moral failure in a society. Those who resent and criticize it are partly right. But the thing to do is not passively to suffer the evils which censoring is designed to avoid but actively to work for standards of public conviction which would remove the very reasons for censoring.

15. *Man in the Space Age**

That mankind has entered upon a new era, the Space Age, is now obvious. For the first time, human beings have penetrated the realms beyond the earth and its atmosphere and have made astronomy, at least in part, an experimental science. The age of geographical discovery now gives way to the age of astronomical exploration. It is too early for us to speculate on the full implications of this historical change but it is not too soon for philosophers to begin to think of the new problems which may arise.

Our new era in human history is characterized by evident changes in earthly existence. The rapid development of pure and applied science in the twentieth century has modified the dimensions of human life on earth in so many ways that one may wonder whether man himself will be able to adapt to his new condition. It is the function of the philosopher to appraise the manifold of human experience, to endeavor to understand its overall meaning, and even to try to offer some practical guidance to mankind for the optimum conduct of human life in the future. If philosophers fail to do this, the mantle of the wise man will be assumed by other men, less impartial in their judgments perhaps, less informed about the lessons of our past history, less willing to reflect and to listen to the voice of reason.

It is often said that human nature remains basically the same throughout the ages of recorded history. One has only to read the plays of the ancient Greek dramatists, the dialogues of Plato, or the poetry of Vergil and Dante, to see that men of all periods are indeed very much like ourselves. The ancients loved and hated, hoped and despaired; they understood some things and failed to

* Paper delivered at the XIIIth International Congress of Philosophy (Mexico City, 1963); printed in *Memorias del XIII Congreso Internacional de Filosofía* (Universidad Nacional, 1963), IV, pp. 23–30.

understand others — just as we do today. We can take it that a baby born in ancient Athens was provided with very much the same bodily and mental equipment that a modern child has at birth.

However, man does not remain an undeveloped infant; as he grows, he reacts with his environment, and his whole personality is modified by the milieu in which he lives. The opportunities for human growth and self-expression differ from place to place, and from era to era. That is why the mature human being in the twentieth century is in many ways capable of doing things that were quite impossible for the citizen of ancient Athens. In some ways we are the same as our predecessors; in other ways we are very different.

Consider the speed and ease with which we now travel to an international meeting. This sort of thing would have been inconceivable in the time of Socrates. Trips which may now be accomplished in hours or days were then matters of months and years. In the ancient world, people from another place or continent were not merely foreigners, they were barbarians. Languages, customs, modes of life were divisive. In spite of his vast curiosity and ready understanding, Herodotus regarded the Egyptians as a different kind of people from his own. Now, in the Space Age, man has so increased his immediate environment that, in effect, we may all soon be living in the same place. Our milieu will be the world.

Today we have, or can create, the instrumentalities whereby the apparent diversities among men may be, in part, removed or overcome. We can move into the era of the cosmopolitan man. I do not suggest that all differences among men are evil or that the ideal man is the person with no distinctions of culture, of geographical adaptation, or of loyalty to the ideals of his immediate ancestors. My point is that some differences among men make trouble, while other distinctions lend interest and richness to the potentialities of mankind.

There is little doubt, for instance, that the present diversity of languages is a barrier to mutual understanding and cooperation among modern men. Man's ability to communicate effectively with his fellowman is the foundation for the intelligent resolution of world problems. At one time Latin served as the international language of science and scholarship. There may be serious objections to the revival of Latin for this purpose today. However, philosophers might do well to lend the weight of their wisdom to the promotion of some one language (even an artificial one, such as Esperanto) which would provide a medium of communication for all scholars, scientists, diplomats, and international figures. At present one learns three or more languages in preparing for the doctorate: why could not one of these languages be a tongue common to all learned men? Surely this is a proposal that is not impractical in our new era. Let the man of the Space Age be a person who can talk to all of his fellows.

The foregoing suggestion is purely instrumental: it serves but to introduce the main thought of this essay. Events in the twentieth century have simply highlighted a long-developing phenomenon, the reunification of the human race. The human being of the future may be, first and foremost, a citizen of the world and only secondarily an Englishman, a Spaniard, a Russian, or a Congolese. In the ancient and medieval world a person was named from, and owed loyalty to, the city or town or countryplace of his origin or upbringing. Socrates of Athens, Augustine of Hippo, John of Paris, Catherine of Siena — these names indicate the narrow ambit of ancient and medieval persons. The modern man has been identified by his country or nation. Rivalries between cities became wars among nations but some progress has been made toward the unity of mankind. Why can we not hope that this evolution will continue to the point where the prominent people of the Space Age will be true cosmopolitans?

This could have important implications for the moral growth of man. To the eternal question: "Who is my neighbor?" the verbal answer may remain the same. Every man is my neighbor — but in the social realities of the new age this answer should have a new meaning. Instead of moral rights and duties being operative in a small local community, the moral relations of the man of the Space Age may extend throughout the world.

The philosophical and anthropological effects of such a transition could be profound. Suppose we do make contact with intelligent beings from outer space: what would the result be to our earthly race of men? I think our relations with these "others" would at least serve to draw mankind together and to make us realize the importance of our earthly community.

A second major feature of the man of the Space Age derives from the increasing complexity of human life. New inventions, new arts, new knowledge of all kinds — all make increasing demands on the personality. Today we take it for granted that the average person will know how to operate an automobile, tune a television set, use electric cooking devices, and do a hundred other things that would have puzzled our ancestors. Human nature is somewhat plastic; the man who drove an oxcart yesterday is expected to manage a tractor today. Man in the Space Age must be mechanically more adept than his forefathers.

This is not merely a matter of manual skills and mathematical expertise. From the point of view of moral judgment, the situation and potentialities of man have changed already. Due to the rapidity with which many human activities may now be accomplished, ethical decisions must be made more quickly than in the past. Let us agree that, whatever type of ethics we consider best, one of the basic features of moral judgment is that it be based on some sort of reflection, some reasoned appraisal of what man chooses to accomplish with the activities that come, at least in part, under his personal control. As the pace of human living now increases, man's ability to assemble and interpret practical information must be accelerated in its functioning. Mechanical devices, so-called thinking machines, are of some assistance in the preliminary phases of such considerations. There are people who expect that all practical decisions may eventually be made by such machines. What will the effects on human personality be, if more and more of our practical judgments are left to the operation of nonhuman devices? Conceivably the man of the future could alienate much of his freedom by virtue of his confidence in the accuracy of the machines that he has produced.

One of the cornerstones of our past culture has been the prizing of the individual person. That each man has a dignity and worth that is to be protected at all costs, has been generally admitted. This personalistic point of view is not difficult to justify and defend, where human lives are not too numerous. In the past it has seemed a good thing to advise mankind to increase and multiply its members, for the opportunities open to men on earth appeared to be limitless. Recent developments in the health arts and sciences have much extended the span of man's life expectancy and, at the same time; have increased the capacities of human beings to reproduce in their kind. As a result, the number of human beings on earth is now growing rapidly. There has also been a great improvement in our capacity to produce food and the other basic necessities of human life. We now know that the rate of increase in the number of men on earth could continue to grow indefinitely. It is possible that there is a numerical maximum for mankind — beyond which we cannot go without seriously altering the optimum conditions of social life. Theoretically we could reach a point at which there will simply be too many people on earth. In such crowded conditions the value of the individual man may be cheapened; each life may no longer be regarded as precious. What this prospect will do to the concept of the dignity of the person may be an object of present speculation; it could become an urgent and practical problem as the Space Age grows older.

There is the remote possibility that part of the human race could emigrate to other planets. As of now, we do not know of any other place in the universe where sustained human living, from one generation to another, is practically possible. If such a new location for man were found, the new environment would doubtless be somewhat different from that of earth. New problems would arise concerning man's adaptability to a radically different milieu.

Another dimension of problematics for the man of the future has to do with the use of leisure time. In the past (and still in many parts of the world) all men had to work almost full time in order to make a living. Now many persons need labor only for a few hours a week to accomplish this same goal. People will have more leisure. What are they to do with their free time? Some of it will be spent in cultural, religious, and sports activities — but are we giving enough thought to the effect on mankind of so much time being devoted to nonutilitarian activities? I am not suggesting that we make any quick value-judgment on this question. May I simply point out that large numbers of people are spending many hours per week in bowling alleys, diligently knocking over wooden pins with balls? The same is true of many other facilities for relaxation and amusement. There is a certain health value in sports and games, of course. One wonders whether the man of the Space Age will eventually give most of his time to such leisure activities. If so, is this an ideal goal for mankind?

Anthropology has become a social science distinct from philosophy and has produced many interesting studies of peoples who have lived in the past, or who now live in remote places, under conditions and in cultures much different from those of modern civilized man. That we may learn much from such studies is true. However, one may ask whether similar investigations should not be made of men who live as we do, under what we consider to be the ordinary conditions of life and culture in the twentieth century. Surely there is room for improvement in the way that we lead our lives. Man in the Space Age could well become more conscious of the defects in his social institutions and more critical of previously accepted customs.

Up to this point, various environmental factors which modify human personality have been considered. If that were the whole story, if all men were inexorably subject to the deterministic influence of environmental conditions which could neither be avoided nor resisted, then we would not need to give any further thought to these questions. Man would evolve and we would do nothing about the process. However, this is not the full story.

Man is able to take thought about what is happening to his race and he is able to interfere with these blind forces of change. Of course, some of the effects of these forces are due to man's past interference with physical and social conditions on earth. For example, we now have the prospect of future wars which would be very different from those of the past — simply because we have discovered extremely effective ways of killing large numbers of people. In mid-twentieth century, a third world war could wipe out most of the persons now living on earth within a few weeks. I mention this obvious point, not to introduce a discussion of the problem of warfare today (urgent though that question may be) but to suggest that this is a good example of how influential a few individual persons may be. One inventor or scientist may open up entirely new advantages or disadvantages for mankind. The same invention may be turned, by personal initiative, to good or ill use. Individual persons are still to be reckoned with as factors affecting the future of the race.

With all our modern emphasis on group activities, it still remains true that certain extraordinary persons leave their permanent marks on the history of mankind. It is possible for the unusual person to react against the forces of nature, against the weight of human customs, to reorientate the ongoing processes of life and human culture. Even in the work of the philosopher there are sporadic efforts at group thinking and at dialectical procedures involving the meeting of many minds, but how important are these joint programs when compared with the efforts of the individual thinker? What great contribution to philosophy has been made by a group of men? It is true that the individual genius needs help from his associates and his success depends somewhat on his cultural and historical context. In a very primitive community, Socrates might have been but a garrulous stonecutter of local renown. However, the fact remains that millions of men live in the same environments and are provided with almost identical opportunities for thought and self-expression but only the rare person seizes these opportunities and does something that has lasting significance for mankind.

In the period of Christopher Columbus and Hernando Cortez few people could have guessed at the changes that would be introduced into human life as a direct result of their explorations in the New World. Who would then have suspected that, four centuries later, an international congress of philosophy would meet in Mexico? Our new explorers are men like Gagarin and Shepherd. We cannot fully appreciate what the consequences of their efforts will be.

In summary, I have ventured to suggest certain possibilities concerning mankind in the immediate future. Man may be able better to understand and communicate with his fellowmen — but only if he deliberately acts to remove some of the present barriers to mutual understanding. Man in the Space Age may well become a cosmopolite — just how much uniformity and how much diversity among men may be ideal is a legitimate problem for social philosophers. The possibility of human contacts with intelligent beings from other parts of the universe may still lie in the realm of science fiction — but such a confrontation may have to be met in the future. The complication and acceleration of the pace of human living are factors which challenge the plasticity of human nature — we may have to consider, rather soon, whether our rate of change exceeds the adaptability of the average man.

On the other hand, we cannot ignore the importance of the individual person and particularly of those extraordinary people who, by virtue of some inner spark of genius or dogged effort, furnish new directions to mankind. These few comments and conclusions are offered here to stimulate philosophical consideration of questions whose urgency may soon become more obvious.

16. *Material Possessions and Thomism**

Thomistic philosophy in America still lags behind European Thomism. This is less evident in speculative thinking than in the approach to practical problems. Significant contributions have been made by American scholars in the areas of Thomistic epistemology, psychology, and metaphysics. With the recent development of several centers of research in medieval studies, both in the United States and Canada, the history of St. Thomas' thought is now being studied in a scholarly manner on this side of the Atlantic. However, though America is probably regarded in many other parts of the world as the home of a practical-minded people, it can hardly be claimed that much work has been done by American Thomists on the problem of ethical, social, or political philosophy. That is not to say there is a lack of interest in these questions, or that the work already done is of negligible value.

The fact is that American Thomism is a comparatively young movement. Many of its leading writers and teachers are European scholars who perhaps hesitate to handle questions of practical import because they necessarily require a background of familiarity with American customs and circumstances of life, difficult for a newcomer to acquire. There is also, no doubt, a certain unwillingness to become involved in controversies of a practical character, because of the danger that any criticism of existing conditions or practices may be misunderstood. It is far easier to be daring and critical in the speculative order than in the practical. There is a tendency of the general reading public to regard any new or

* From: *Philosophic Thought in France and the United States*, edited by M. Farber (Buffalo: University of Buffalo Publications in Philosophy, 1950), pp. 613–627; French version in *L'Activité Philosophique* (Paris: Presses Universitaires de France, 1950), Vol. I, pp. 302–320; Polish version in *Filozofia Amerykanska*, edited by Jerzy Krzyvicki (Boston: Boston University Press, 1958), pp. 146–162.

different type of thought, if it be practical, as an attack upon the established order of things. Yet it is the function of the philosopher to criticize life and to suggest better ways of living. *Sapientis est ordinare* must apply to more than theoretical problems.

For this reason, and because of its intrinsic interest, the topic for this chapter has been chosen from the field of practical philosophy.

THE PROBLEM OF MATERIAL POSSESSIONS

Consider a group of men and women shipwrecked on a previously uninhabited island. Suppose the island affords food, materials from which clothing may be made, and locations suitable for shelter. What would be the best way for these people to arrange for the distribution and use of these things?

Suppose one of these people were to find the only source of good drinking water on the island. What are his rights in regard to this spring? What are the rights of the whole group to the use of this water?

This imaginary example intentionally simplifies the problem. Such simplification has some advantages. We may consider ourselves as emotionally disinterested spectators, judging the claims and conduct of the islanders from the point of view of what is right and best. Reasonably to make such judgments, we must already be in possession of some standards of moral value. We must have formed some views on human life and what is generally good for man. To say, for instance, that the discoverer of the spring is entitled to keep all the water in his possession and exclude the others from its use, if he is strong enough to enforce his claim, is not an initial moral judgment. This conclusion implies a previous general position, either consciously or unconsciously adopted. Such a judgment may be based on the notion that "might is right," or that "possession is nine tenths of the law," or some other prior principle. Even to say that our problem might be solved by depending on the moral instincts, or feelings, of a normal person placed in these conditions, is to presuppose a general theory of moral judgment which has been already adopted. To take such a general theory as given, as not open for examination, is not to proceed in a philosophical manner. One might start with the law-as-given, or with a certain religious faith-as-given, or with the assertion of what "science teaches" as something given, or with some other absolute initial position. The point is that every attempt to face a particular moral problem, even a pragmatic approach which professes to do without absolute standards, does imply some initial point of view which is adopted, with full awareness in some cases, with subrational faith in others. The conclusions reached from such a point of view are only as good as the starting point permits.

To postulate our starting point and promise to verify this initial position from the conclusions which we reach as we go along is not to avoid this difficulty. Many sets of moral postulates may be adopted which can be logically related to practical conclusions, after the conclusions have been made. If, at any point in the process, we endeavor to give more than logical validity to such postulates, we must revert to some absolutely given position on which our demonstration will depend. If we deny this, we have adopted the absolute view that logic, with sufficiently consistent development, becomes a philosophy of real and moral value. This is, then, to adopt a general theory of value, a meta-morality.

The moral philosopher should be conscious of what he takes as his general interpretation of what is good for man in his life. Thomistic ethics has such a position in that initial part of its development which is usually called general ethics, or ethical theory. It takes some time to present such a theory of moral values. That is not possible in a brief chapter. For that reason, some references are given in the ensuing footnotes to books which explain the general theory of Thomistic morality. What we can do here is to summarize this theory. Obviously the truly philosophic part of such a position is omitted in summary. What we are doing is something like giving the gist of Euclid's theorems without the reasoning which accompanies and justifies them geometrically.

THE THEORETICAL BASIS OF THOMISTIC ETHICS

What is taken as a starting point, in Thomistic ethics, is a certain metaphysical interpretation of the human being in his concrete setting, in a real universe. Man is viewed as a substantial agent capable of freely choosing to do, or to refrain from doing, certain real actions. These are called human acts; they do not include all the acts of man but only those which have the quality of voluntariness. To be voluntary, an act must issue from the agent himself, be at least partially under the control of his intellect, and be powered, as it were, by his own will.

Moreover, man is taken as a being having a definite kind of nature, with a definite set of functions which characterize this nature. As a species of animal, man is regarded as having a final cause, or end, which is manifested by his specific capacities. What man is best equipped to do, in comparison with other species of beings, is to think rationally. The peak of such action is not the process of discursive reasoning but the flash of understanding, the quick contemplation of truth, with which reasoning begins and finishes. It is not enough that intellectual contemplation can be achieved in any high degree of perfection during this earthly life. Though Thomists do not pretend that the beatific vision of God in heaven is a fact demonstrable from reasoning founded on natural experience, they find some evidence in the tenth book of Aristotle's *Nicomachean Ethics* (and more clearly in the *Eudemian Ethics*, 1249b20) that a philosopher may see the possibility of the vision of a Perfect Being as an ultimate end for man.

This does not mean that each individual man will actually attain this end. It is an end of the species, which may be attained by any member of the human species who lives in keeping with the highest potentialities of his specific powers. If we consider the end of the apple tree to be the production of apples, this does not mean that all such trees will do it. But an individual tree is good and perfect to the extent that it does produce apples. It fails as a member of its species to the extent that it produces imperfect or no apples.

All of this theory is frankly teleological. The only known way to judge the goodness of a function is to determine its purpose and then decide whether it is achieving this end. We may substitute other terms and ask whether the agent is useful, whether a

given action "works," whether action contributes to this or that
— but the thought implied in a value-judgment seems to be overtly
or covertly, teleological.

To say that man's moral end is to achieve happiness by as perfect an act of understanding as is possible is based, of course, on
an acceptance of human freedom and immortality together with
an acceptance of the existence of God as a Supreme Object of
knowledge. These are Kant's postulates. They are not regarded as
postulates by Thomists but as conclusions demonstrated in speculative reasoning about the nature of reality.

The determination of the moral goodness or evil of a given
human act requires more than the foregoing theory. Acts done for
the sake of the ultimate end are regarded as morally good; other
voluntary acts are morally bad. It is not easy to distinguish the
acts which belong in either category when we deal with the individual action. The ordinary moral agent, the nonethician, can only
be expected to do as well as the circumstances of his intellectual
development permit. The ethician never tries to judge the moral
value of individual human actions, and then incorporate them into
his science as ultimate conclusions. It is the work of ethics to go as
far as possible in determining the value of definite types of
human action. So the ethician must discover some means of apply-
ing the theory of the end of man to less general and more practical
questions. This is done in Thomistic ethics by distinguishing between those broad types of action which are always suitable to a
rational agent, and those which are not. Such suitability is determined by a rational consideration of the specific capacities of
man in relation to the ultimate end. Thus the act of telling a lie
(defined as: speaking in contradiction to what one thinks to be
true, with the formal intention of doing so) may be judged unfitting to a human being. Notice that this can be made into a
moral rule, because lying is defined in a strict sense, so as to exclude cases of conveying an untruth without actually intending
to do so. It is possible to work out a set of general rules of moral
behavior in this way. These are the primary principles of the natural
moral law. Less universal rules, including more of the concrete circumstances of human life, can be stated. These derivative rules of

the moral law have moral validity as long as the circumstances in them remain approximately the same. But such conditions may change, and so, the more removed are one's moral rules from the primary principles of moral law, the more necessary is it to know the actual circumstances surrounding the proposed action. The alteration of one important circumstance may change the reasonableness of doing, or omitting, a proposed action. Hence it is not possible to plot an ideal moral life ahead of time.

A concrete decision about an individual moral problem is called the act of conscience. This decision must be made by the individual agent who has done, or proposes to do, the action. It is not an act of science but of prudence. The ethician does not perform acts of conscience for any other agents than himself. No good Thomistic ethician would venture a judgment as to whether President Truman was morally right or wrong in deciding to use the atomic bomb against the Japanese people. All that can be done, in regard to such a moral problem, is to offer a judgment of what *in general,* under given circumstances, would be right or wrong. Science, even practical science, cannot go beyond universal conclusion.

It is regrettable that the foregoing has had to be stated in a categorical manner. It may give rise to the understandable reaction that Thomism is a dogmatism, rather than a philosophy. In one sense it is a dogmatism. It does endeavor to reach some conclusions which are true and right. These conclusions, when formulated to the best of one's ability, are held to be true and are taught as true. Until recently this has been the practice of the great philosophers of history. Thomism is not a dogmatism, however, in the sense that it tries to impose infrarational beliefs upon its adherents. The starting point of Thomistic philosophy is not supernatural faith but natural experience. That a man's religious beliefs influence his understanding of things is admitted. But so do his other beliefs. An atheist may, consciously or unconsciously, be just as much affected in his thinking by his atheism as a theist is by his theism. It is no doubt better to be conscious of such influences and to endeavor to understand one's beliefs. "Faith seeking understanding," is not an unreasonable motto.

ST. THOMAS' TEACHING ON THE RIGHTS TO USE AND TO MANAGE THINGS

This historical section is included for two reasons. There is first some general misunderstanding among students of Thomism as to the precise position which St. Thomas took on this problem. Perhaps because of a strong tendency of some Catholic thinkers to defend the institution of private possessions, and also because of the well-known Catholic opposition to modern Communism, it is rather generally thought that a Thomist must defend private ownership at all costs and must utterly reject any suggestion of communal theory in regard to possessions. This is not wholly true. The second reason, for a brief exposition of St. Thomas' teaching, is to indicate to non-Thomists the attitude which a modern student of Thomism may take in regard to the original thought of St. Thomas. It will become evident that it is not maintained that St. Thomas has solved all our modern problems. He lived under different circumstances from those of the present. He is not an infallible authority, to be followed at all costs. But before deciding whether he has anything to contribute to the discussion, it is necessary to examine what he did think.

Fundamental in St. Thomas' handling of the problem is the distinction of two quite different moral rights. First and most important is the *right to use* material things. Man is not an angel; he has a body which must be fed and clothed and protected. He cannot long continue his proper existence on earth unless he makes use of things for these purposes. Such use is natural to man in his genus. All animals unhesitatingly take over food and other things from their environment for their use. Such use is a necessary and natural means of life; every man is morally entitled to satisfy his material needs by using material things.[1] This is not to be confused with the right to own things. One may occupy, and thus use, a house without being its owner. In fact, both the terms "ownership" and "property" may well be avoided in the initial stages of discussion, for they suggest a private holding of things to the exclusion of other persons.

The other right, in relation to material things, is called in

---

[1] *S.T.*, II–II, q. 66, a. 1, c; *Summa contra Gentiles* III, c. 22 ad fin.

Latin: *potestas procurandi et dispensandi.*[2] Literally this means the power to acquire and dispose of things. It is roughly equivalent to the modern economist's notion of management. Apart from consumptive use, there is a group of actions which man may perform in regard to material things: he may obtain them from nature, work upon them to make them more suitable for human use, hold them over a period of time, dispose of them by exchange, sale, gift, and other ways. For convenience, let us just call this the *right to manage* things.

Now, while the right to manage things is chronologically prior to the right to use them, this does not necessarily mean that it enjoys moral precedence. This statement contains the essence of the Thomistic position. It is absolutely necessary to a good life upon earth that each human being exercise the right to use material things. You must eat in order to live. On the other hand, it is not absolutely necessary for each human being to exercise the right to manage things. Some people may live, and even live well, without holding anything as their own. We shall see that St. Thomas considers three possible forms of "management" and eventually decides that one form is best for most men. The point now to be observed is that there is only one way of exercising the right to use, and that is incumbent upon all men. It is for this reason that St. Thomas suggests that the right to use things is common to all human beings. As he expresses it: "The other thing which pertains to man in relation to exterior things is the use of them. And, in regard to this, man should not hold exterior things as private (*ut proprias*) but as common (*ut communes*), in order that one may easily share them with others in need."[3]

To put this very bluntly, it means that if a starving man has no other way of getting food, and if he asks a farmer for a melon, the farmer is morally obliged to give it to him, provided the melon is not immediately needed for consumption by the farmer and his family. Moreover, if the farmer refuses to share his excess goods, the starving man is morally right in taking the melon and eating

[2] "Dicendum quod circa rem exteriorem duo competunt homini. Quorum unum est potestas procurandi et dispensandi." *S.T.*, II-II, q. 66, a. 2, c. int.
[3] *Ibid.*

it.[4] Morally then, the right to use is more natural, more basic, than the right to manage things.

If we say that it is necessary to get, to have, some things before we can use them, it may be admitted that the notion of possession is not entirely separable from that of use. But possession is not identical with private ownership. What must be recognized is the common right of all men to use material things. This is not incompatible with private management of material things, provided the right to hold things as private possessions is not taken to exclude others, who are in need, from their use. As St. Thomas puts it: "the rich man does not act immorally, if, in taking over possession of a thing which was common from the start, he also shares it with others."[5]

Historically, three ways of handling the management of things have been tried by men: (1) private and individual possessions; (2) communal possessions; and (3) mendicancy. In the first case, one person obtains some material things, perhaps improves them by his labor, and manages their use and distribution by his own efforts. In the second case, a group of human beings (usually conceived to be larger than the family) exercises these functions as a corporate unit. The third possibility is obviously not open to all people but some men may choose to do nothing about acquiring and managing things, depending simply on the gifts of others as a means of getting the things which they must use.

While at least some men in any age may get along by following any one of these three systems of possession (the third amounts to a form of minimal possession), the question that is asked by St. Thomas is: Which of these is the most reasonable for the majority of men to practice? It should be recalled that the mendicant orders in the Catholic Church were originally groups of men living a religious life and supporting themselves by begging. Gradually these religious groups turned to a special form of communal

[4] Such taking of goods in the possession of another is not regarded as an act of theft; one may even take over things held by another to help a third person who is in extreme need. *S.T.*, II-II, q. 66, a. 7, ad 2m, et ad 3m; cf. A. D. Sertillanges, *La philosophie morale de s. Thomas d'Aquin* (Paris: Aubier, 1946), pp. 185–186.

[5] *S.T.*, II–II, q. 66, a. 2, ad 2m.

possession. St. Thomas Aquinas lived his mature life under a system of community possession; he owned no private possessions. When he discussed these possibilities he knew them as real methods of living and managing things.

His decision is that the most reasonable method is that of private possession and management of material things. A life of poverty is a fine thing when voluntarily adopted by the individual for some special motive. Forced poverty is the source of much trouble.[6] This leaves the choice between private and communal management. St. Thomas makes it clear that, to his mind, the natural moral law in its primary principles enjoins neither communal nor private possession. "According to natural law, there is no distinction of possessions, but rather according to human agreement and this pertains to the positive law."[7] Previously he had pointed out that some things are natural to man in two senses. Some actions, such as the union of male and female for the production of offspring, or the feeding of the young by their parents, are suited to human nature in a primary sense. Even brute animals grasp these things and practice them without deliberation. Other things are natural in a derivative sense; they follow from a reasonable consideration of possible ways of acting in relation to the rational nature of man. By this kind of reasonable deliberation it is possible to understand that private possession is natural, in a secondary sense, to man. St. Thomas uses the example of property to illustrate this general distinction between that which is natural to man, as it is to all animals, and that which is natural to man because human beings may use their reason to reach a reasonable agreement. He suggests that, if we consider *this field* in relation to *this individual man,* there is nothing in either to indicate that this field should belong to this man. But if we make a reasonable examination of the possibilities of this man to cultivate and use

---

[6] *Contra Impugnates Dei cultum et religionem,* c. 6, ad primum (ed. Mandonnet, *Opuscula Omnia,* Paris, 1927, IV, 85): "sicut divitiae non sunt in culpa, sed divitiarum abusus, ita mendicitas sive paupertas non est in culpa, sed paupertatis abusus, quando scilicet aliquis paupertatem invitus et impatienter sustinet; tunc enim desiderio divitiarum in multa peccata quandoque incidit."

[7] *S.T.,* II–II, q. 66, a. 2, ad primum.

this field, then we may conclude that he is entitled to be its private owner.[8]

Three reasons are suggested for the conclusion that private possession is the best system for most people to follow. First of all, a man is more careful and conscientious in procuring things which will belong to him privately than he is in managing public, or common, possession, Second, private possession is more orderly; confusion arises where everyone is looking after everything. Finally, there is less opportunity for quarrels under a system of private possessions; disputes frequently arise where property is undivided and held in common.[9] Three reasons are considered sufficient; they do not make St. Thomas an eager proponent of the system of private possessions. He simply says that it is "licit" (*licitum est*) for a man to possess things privately. It is not opposed to the natural law (*proprietas possessionum non est contra jus naturale*).[10]

We should remember that this right of private possession, or management, is strictly limited by the common right to use. The person who undertakes to hold and manage large posssessions is also undertaking the problem of seeing that they will be properly used to satisfy the reasonable needs of himself and others. A rich man is not required by Thomistic ethics to go all over the world trying to find people whom he may help. He is strictly required to give of his excess goods (and not out of charity alone, but as a matter of strict justice) to those who are in need in his immediate vicinity. With modern systems of communication and monetary exchange, this position would seem to make it difficult for a person to retain a large fortune and do what is morally right.

USURY AND THE RIGHT TO USE

An excellent illustration of the Thomistic attitude to the right to use of possessions is found in the medieval teaching on usury. A brief consideration of this doctrine may cast some light on the general theory, as well as the poorly understood notion of usury.

[8] *S.T.*, II–II, q. 57, a. 3, c; the meaning of a reasonable agreement of men (*condictum*) is discussed in the preceding article (2, c).

[9] *S.T.*, II–II, q. 66, a. 2, c. Somewhat the same reasoning is found in Aristotle's *Politics*, II, 4, 1263a21. The last reason is connected with a very old principle of common law: that common property should be divided wherever possible.

[10] *Ibid.*, ad primum.

It will be observed that the term *usury* is etymologically related to the word *use*. The only primary use for money that the medieval man knew was to spend it. Merely to put it away somewhere and keep it was not regarded as a form of use. Of course, coins have various secondary uses, such as bodily adornment, but these do not stem from the fact that coins are money but from other attributes which they possess.[11]

Now under these conditions, if one man had some extra money and another man needed some, a loan of accommodation might be made. This was usually done among friends. The man who had no present use for the money simply allowed someone else to use it, with the understanding that the sum would be returned in full later. The lender was really giving up nothing, for he was not using the money himself. When the loan was repaid, he was in just the same position as he would have been had he kept the money all the time. To try to charge a fee, or interest, on such an accommodation was considered immoral. It was regarded as an attempt to get something for nothing. It was called usury because it was an attempt to charge for a use which was not given up.[12] This is precisely an example of how moral circumstances change, and with them some secondary rules of ethics must change. It is not that the original rule becomes false; rather, the real conditions which it embodies are modified and, with this modification, the rule itself may lose its original application.

In the modern world, money seems to have acquired a new primary use. In the form of capital it appears to have become an instrument of production and distribution. Investment is a modern use which was not open to the ordinary man in the Middle Ages. Even St. Thomas could grant that a man is entitled to some compensation when he risks losing his possessions.[13] Hence, in the present world, a loan (even between friends) can involve the loss

[11] *Quaest. Disp. de Malo,* q. XIV, a. 4, c. et ad 15m.

[12] *S.T.,* II–II, q. 78, a. 1–4; *Quaest. Quodlibetales,* III, q. 7, a. 19, c. For a broader treatment of the whole medieval attitude toward money and loans, consult: Bede Jarrett, *Social Theories of the Middle Ages* (Westminster, Md.: Newman, 1942), pp. 150–180.

[13] See the discussion of the danger of a businessman losing goods in transport: *S.T.,* II–II, q. 77, a. 4, ad 2m. Consult also the four articles on usury, in the next question, 78.

of the moderate interest which comes from leaving extra money in a bank. There is no reason to suppose that St. Thomas would consider it immoral to accept a moderate amount of interest on a business loan. It is still unreasonable to take excessive interest, and that is what is called usury by modern Thomists.

THE CONCEPT OF COMMON USE AND COMMUNISM

A possible reaction to the Thomistic theory of possession for common use is that it is nothing but communism. What is the good in being industrious, thrifty, a good manager, if one is expected to give of one's excess goods to any persons who are in need? The answer would seem to be: this moral theory is quite different from communism and also from *laissez-faire* capitalism.

The Catholic attitude toward communism is much too complicated to be expressed briefly.[14] We may note two great points of difference. If we take communism, not as an ideal theory (on which basis it is very difficult to find a positive program for which it stands) but as the world view of a large segment of mankind today, many of whom insist that the economic ideal of a real communism will not be reached in any country for many years yet, then we can say that it is much more than an economic program. Apart from their views on property holding, communists have an outlook on human life which is very largely antithetic to Thomism. The majority of vocal communists seem to reject the existence of God, the spirituality and immortality of the human soul, the dignity of the individual person. If they grant any moral freedom to the individual man, it is of a very restricted character. Their interpretation of the course of human history, the conclusions of natural science, the social institutions of men excludes many of the things considered true and right in Thomism. This is not, perhaps, applicable to all communists — but the general trend of actual communism seems to be atheistic, antispiritualistic, and deterministic. Thomistic philosophers oppose communism for more than merely economic reasons.

[14] For a philosophical appraisal of communism, cf. C. J. McFadden, *The Metaphysical Foundation of Dialectical Materialism* (Washington: Catholic University Press, 1938 ; J. Lafarge, "The Philosophical Basis of Communism," *Proceedings of the American Catholic Philosophical Association*, IX (1933), pp. 47–62.

Second, in the purely economic area, Thomism is wedded neither to communism nor to capitalism. A Thomist is interested chiefly in the moral implications of any system of economics. Extreme forms of capitalism have obvious defects.[15] Despite its otherworldly attitude toward moral and social problems, Thomism is definitely concerned about providing every human being with the necessary means to work out his earthly life in a manner suited to the dignity of a human person.[16] The successful capitalist does not seem to share this concern. Nevertheless, capitalism does leave some personal freedom, even to those who are economically depressed; communism appears to be directed toward an exaltation of the material values of the group and an annihilation of the worth of the individual man. In an economy of material abundance, to which communist theorists point as a sort of Marxian heaven, most any kind of system will work. Under present conditions and those of the predictable future, modern man has the choice between forced poverty under communism or free enterprise (with the possibility of individual failure or success) under capitalism. There is no question that the second option is better. Capitalism and the whole practice of private possessing can be abused. There is good promise, however, that it could be well used by men who are properly concerned about the moral and social welfare of their neighbors.

WHAT IS VALUABLE IN THE THOMISTIC POSITION

The heart of the Thomistic theory of possessions lies not in the details of arrangements for the acquisition and distribution of things but in the original distinction of the right to use from the right to manage things. There is no "official" system of economics, dogmatically imposed on Catholics, which Thomists wish to foist upon an unsuspecting world. Nor is there any Catholic political movement working toward such an end. Thomists would like to convince the average man, by appealing to his reason, that the

[15] Cf. J. A. Ryan, "The Philosophy of Captialism," *Proceedings of the American Catholic Philosophical Association*, IX (1933), pp. 35–46; V. Michel, *St. Thomas and Today. Comments on the Economic Views of Aquinas* (St. Paul, Minn.: Wanderer Press, 1935).

[16] This theme has been very well developed by Jacques Maritain in several works, the most recent being: *The Person and the Common Good* (New York: Scribner's, 1947).

improvement of his condition in human society on earth depends on the perfecting of the moral character of the individual man. It all reduces to the proposition that no society can be good unless the members who constitute it are good.

The moral perfection of the individual person requires not only the internal development of prudence and temperance and fortitude, it also demands the outward-looking virtue of justice. To will the good for other men, as one naturally does for oneself, is a most difficult habit to acquire. Yet it would seem to be the only basis for good social life. The willingness to share earthly possessions with others who are in need is but one application of the social virtue of justice. Fundamental to all this is the conception that all men have an equal right to use material things. This is the right which is most natural.

Placing the other less natural right, to acquire and manage things privately, above the right to use is responsible for many of the evils of modern economic and social life. Private possession for common use is not offered as a foolproof system which will immediately bring about ideal social conditions. For it to work properly most men must be morally good people. Thomism is optimistic about this possibility, holding that there is much goodness left in mankind, that most men want to do what is right. If this confidence is misplaced, then no theory of possession will do any practical good.

17. *Ethics and Contraception**

Our problem could be stated in this way: Is it a reasonable thing for a man and a woman to perform the act of sexual union and, prior to or in conjunction with this action, to use some physical or chemical means to prevent a child from being conceived? I am trying to state the question without using emotionally charged terms. It is a problem on which there are strong differences of opinion, but we should be able to examine it dispassionately: What does "reasonable" mean in this context? Much of the remainder of this essay is intended to deal with that question.

The point of view that I bring to this discussion is that of a philosopher. What kind of philosopher should become more evident as we go along. I am a Catholic and know that my Church has its own answer to this problem. The enunciation of Catholic thinking on such a question is a job for a moral theologian — which I am not. (To avoid any misunderstanding, may I add that I am not a priest but a layman with three children. All of my studies were done at the University of Toronto, which is a Canadian equivalent of a state university. I have been teaching ethics for more than thirty years.) For the sake of readers who may wonder what the difference is between a Catholic who is a moral theologian and one who is an ethician, may I say that it boils down to this: ethics uses only the ordinary and natural experience of life as its starting point in considering a moral problem: moral theology may use, in addition, various data of faith, supernatural revelation, papal and conciliar pronouncements, the traditional views of Fathers and Doctors of the Church, canon law provisions,

* Originally titled: "An Ethical Consideration of Artificial Contraception," in *What Modern Catholics Think About Birth Control*, ed. by William Birmingham (New York: The New American Library, 1964), pp. 15–28.

and so on. The thing may be put more simply. The moral theologian may quote the papal encyclical *Casti Connubii* to make his point. I don't feel that I can, principally because I wish to address my discussion to people who desire to know whether artificial contraception is morally approvable, apart from what an encyclical says about it.

Some readers may react against this separation of the work of the philosopher from that of the theologian. In much Protestant thought what is called "Christian ethics" is precisely a combination of biblical morality with some sort of moral philosophy. Moreover, in the view of some Catholic thinkers (such as Jacques Maritain) it is impossible to develop an adequate and practical ethical position without some borrowing from moral theology, or from the data of religious faith. Maritain would not accept the distinction that I have made. He would say that a purely natural ethics is a mere abstraction. I disagree — but will not argue the point here. My aim is to discusss our problem from the point of view of what any person can know and understand, whether he be a Catholic or not.

Here again someone may properly ask: Don't you believe what your Church teaches, and aren't you required to agree with what it teaches on such an important moral problem? My answer is yes — but I am quite free to inquire whether there is, or is not, a philosophical answer to the same problem. Thus I believe as a Catholic that God created a world that has not always existed. However, as a philosopher I cannot prove that God has done so. I happen to think that the fact of divine creation of a temporal universe is purely an item of supernatural faith. Or let us go to a less exalted parallel. Suppose I am teaching geometry and I wish to prove that the sum of the three interior angles of any plane triangle equals two right angles. One of my students says, "I have measured all sorts of triangles and I already know that their interior angles always add up to two right angles." My answer to him is that his way of establishing this conclusion, by an induction from many measurements, is not the method of geometry. It is not that I disbelieve his conclusion; I wish to show, *by the method of geometry,* that a triangle has this invariable character.

The methods open to a philosopher are not identical with those available to a theologian, as I understand these terms. Hence I shall try to use philosophical considerations only. I do not really think that I can, particularly in a few pages, convince any and every reader of the validity of what I have to say. Actually, this problem of artificial contraception involves a whole philosophy of human life and an overall view of all reality. These I cannot detail here. On the other hand, it should be possible to make an honest effort to state my views on this problem (admitting that I have to assume certain things that cannot be fully developed) in not too long an essay.

Now let us get at the problem: Is it reasonable to practice artificial contraception? I know that it would be reassuring to many people if I could give a good clear statement in the affirmative. Emotionally I am much inclined to sympathize with young couples who would like to postpone or avoid conception for various reasons that seem to them good. However, emotion is not the basis on which this matter should be decided. To be quite frank from the beginning. I can find no reason for approving the use of contraceptives. My reasons for this view will be stated unemotionally and plainly — with all due regard for the right of others to disagree. All that I ask is that they give me an equal right to be heard.

I am not going to deny that certain ends that are good in themselves could be achieved by the use of artificial contraceptives. The protection of the health of a potential mother, for whom another pregnancy may be fatal, is an excellent end. The avoidance of overpopulation of the earth seems to me to be a very good end. Doubtless there are many others that are similarly good. To my mind, however, it is not merely a question of achieving a good result. I do not think that a good end can justify a bad means. It is not that I refuse to consider the end to which an action is directed — that is very important. But I do not think that you can take an action that is already bad and make it good by setting up some laudable goal to which it is further directed. To feed the poor is a very good thing, but you may not murder someone in order to get the food. Our problem, then, centers on whether artificial contraception is an approvable action in itself.

Fundamentally there is only one philosophical argument (that I know) against the use of artificial contraceptives, but it may be developed in two forms. The first stresses the idea that contraception is an unreasonable interference in the course of a natural activity. The second form of the argument emphasizes the peculiar character of sexual procreation as a common, or joint, activity that is directed to a common end. In both forms the argument appears to me to be convincing.

Contraception is the use of some sort of physical device, or some sort of drug, which prevents or minimizes the possibility of biological conception yet permits a man and a woman to engage in sexual intercourse. Let us not call celibacy contraception; that sort of thing only confuses the issue. To take care of peope who are worried about celibacy (oddly, it is usually the same people who are also concerned about overpopulation), may I simply stipulate that not all human beings have an individual obligation to beget children? There are various reasons why the general duty to ensure the continuity of the human race would not be applicable in given cases. That is not our problem here.

Nor do I think that contraception means abstention from the act of sexual union. Advocates of some sort of contraception are not arguing for greater abstention from intercourse. To have the situation of contraception, as I am using the term, there must be engagement in the sexual act plus the employment of some positive physical means that is calculated to prevent biological conception. This is the setting of our problem. Without going into any technical details as to the nature or efficacy of contraceptives: may a married couple use some sort of pill, let us say, that is recommended by a competent physician as a preventive of conception? Notice that I am not restricting the question to Catholics. It is a problem for any married couple. (I take it, of course, that we are not involved in a discussion of extramarital sexuality.)

The act of sexual union should be examined first on the biological level, for it is not an angelic activity but can be performed only by beings with living bodies. Viewed in its entirety it is evidently directed to a definite purpose in the biological nature of things: to bring about the existence of new members of a species. What makes this action possible is a complementary arrangement of organs in the male and female, plus a set of instinctive drives toward the performance of the sexual act. The female organs are not merely genital but include arrangements for the development of the fetus after conception and even for the feeding of the offspring after birth. Even the male human being is provided with nippled breasts (nonfunctional in the present state of affairs, which made St. Augustine wonder as to their purpose). This complicated natural equipment, viewed scientifically, is obviously not provided for the mere entertainment of the adult male and female. When the natural biological process that starts with intercourse reaches its term, a new living member of the species is the resultant. Biologists are not concerned with whether God or nature so designed things, but they know full well why the higher animals have these organs and instincts. Although this process does not invariably carry through to its term, it is not doubted by any life scientist that the functional arrangement of male and female is adapted to one goal, and that a complete and successful functioning of these organs is only accomplished in the situation where a viable offspring is produced.

A partial parallel is found in the biological process of self-nourishment. The intake of food and drink involves the use of a set of organs associated with the mouth; there is a certain pleasure connected with eating. But this is not the whole story. The process of assimilating food continues in the digestive organs and eventually results in a replenishment of the organism as a whole. In its entirety this process is adapted to a discernible purpose. It does not always work successfully, but there is no question as to what a successful process of self-nourishment entails.

In brute animals the basic biological functions are generally the same as in human. There is this important difference: human beings may take thought upon these processes and either aid them or interfere with their course. Thus some men may endeavor to secure the pleasure associated with eating but stop the process of

assimilation before digestion occurs. Other men may try to secure
the pleasure of sexual intercourse but stop this process before
conception is accomplished.

Here we come to the heart of the matter. The dimension of
rationality and freedom in human life introduces a new level of
problematics into human biological functioning. That certain
interferences with natural biological processes may be reasonable,
even advisable, is granted. Hair and fingernails, for instance, tend
to grow long and become impediments to the various activities of
human life. These growths may be cut, with a view to the optimum
functioning of the whole organism. Probably in the vigorous life
of the caveman the fingernails were broken or worn off before
they interfered with manual activity. This removal does not stop
the process of growth and is not unreasonable. The situation is
different, however, in regard to nutrition and reproduction. Interference with these processes involves more than a mere sloughing
off of excess growths.

Now, what makes interference with the process leading to conception unreasonable, and so, immoral? Two things. First, the act
of sexual union is a voluntary action on the part of both participants. This means that the performance or omission of this action
lies within the personal control of both man and woman. (If the
action is not voluntary, it does not fall within the domain of
moral action.) Second, this process of conception is but the beginning of the process of procreation. It is unreasonable to begin a
natural process that is obviously designed to move to a certain
term — and at the same time to frustrate the ongoing development
of that process. Such frustration is a basic offense against the
nature of the agent engaged in the activity.

Notice how different is the case of the natural process of growing fingernails. This is not initiated or carried on voluntarily.
Here, too, the term of the process is not the production of exces-
sively long nails; rather the natural end product seems to be the
provision of some sort of protection for the fingertips. Trimming
the nails does not frustrate the movement of this growth process
but aids in its achievement.

Similarly, let us suppose that a wife requires a surgical operation to remove some obstacle to conception. May she voluntarily and reasonably undergo such an operation? Of course she may, because this is a matter of aiding in the fulfillment of a natural process. On the other hand, suppose a wife decides that she does not wish to conceive any more children. May she voluntarily and reasonably undergo a sterilization operation? She may not, because in this case she is working against the fulfillment of a natural process. But suppose she needs this operation in order to stay alive. She is then morally right in undergoing the operation because death is the greatest frustration of biological processes.

Why do some people desire to have sexual intercourse that will not result in conception? If this question be answered honestly, is it not because they desire the pleasure associated with sexual activity but do not desire the offspring which, in the natural course of events, may result from such activity? This means that pleasure is being made the chief end of the sexual act. I mean "end" not only in the sense of the desired objective but also in the sense of the finish of the action. This seems to me to be a prime example of natural frustration. I am not saying that a given person should not enjoy the natural pleasure of sexual union. What I am saying is this: if he or she voluntarily seeks this pleasure, then he or she should also voluntarily accept the natural resultant of such activity.

A person who thinks that artificial contraception is quite reasonable may say that all this is beside the point. There are too many children being conceived, and this evil result is going to continue unless we approve some effective means of cutting down the number of conceptions. We interfere with nature in other areas of human activity — why can't we do it in the process of conception? Moreover, the act of sexual union is not a mere biological activity in the case of human beings; rather, it is an act of mutual love between two persons in which they fulfill themselves as intelligent beings. Sexuality must be exalted, in the case of human agents, to the level of mutual sharing in a truly human love. If too many children are produced, this higher love between husband and wife is disrupted and married life becomes less valuable. Also, if many more than two children live to maturity in each family, then inevitably the earth will become overpopulated. So, there must

be something unreasonable about advocating uncontrolled conception on the part of all members of the human race. These arguments I have tried to state briefly but fairly.

Looking back over this sort of argument in advocacy of artificial
contraception, I find in it what seems to me to be a basic error.
The raising of a biological activity to the level of rationality
should not, to my mind, entail the destruction of the natural
character of that activity. It is all very well to talk about the idealism of mutual love between married persons, but this should not
be carried to the point of denying the facts of physical life. Human
beings are not pure spirits; they are animated bodies. There is no
point in trying to pretend that men are angels; they are not. And
if they were without bodies, our problems would not arise. Mutual
love between human beings is not simply an affair of the mind.
It was not necessary for the Brownings to marry in order to engage
in a poetic meeting of minds.

Furthermore, one may wonder whether the mutual love between
potential parents who use contraceptives is not necessarily inferior
to the experience of parents who engage in sexual activity without
artificial restraints. Who show the greater love: parents who want
a child, or parents who do not want one? On this theme I should
like to quote a few lines from a book written by two men who do
not condemn (at least in this book) artificial contraception. They
have, however, put their finger on a very significant point.

> Sex-lust lives as a phase in the total conative life of a person,
> and its meaning in his life will depend on whether it is a threat
> to or a partner of the gratification of other interests. To take
> one notable instance, the way in which sex-experience is con-
> nected with the desire for children will greatly affect the mean-
> ing it will have for partners.
>   Indeed, although we shall not discuss the matter here, the
> whole discussion of the desirability of the use of birth-control
> methods needs to be infused with concern for the quality in
> sexual experience and the effect of use or nonuse of the partic-
> ular contraceptive methods on the individual concerned. Fear
> lest conception take place, or anxiety that one is breaking norms
> that one respects by using contraceptives, may destroy possibili-
> ties of value in the sex experience. On the other hand, two
> persons who enter upon intercourse in the hope of becoming
> parents to a child they both desire can enjoy an experience of

union that goes far beyond, and yet is heightened by, the harmony of their mutual responses.[1]

I could have quoted the last sentence out of context, with a view to making it appear that Professors Bertocci and Millard wholly agree with me. This sort of trickery has no place in an honest discussion. I am not trying to win an argument but to explain a point of view. Yet I ask my readers to meditate on their last sentence. Is it not true that "two persons who enter upon intercourse in the hope of becoming parents . . . can enjoy an experience of union that goes far beyond, and yet is heightened by, the harmony of their mutual responses"? I ask you to think why this is so.

This brings us to the second form of the argument against artificial contraception. Precisely what sort of activity is sexual union between two human beings? I am going to suggest that it is strangely different from most other human activities because it cannot be performed by one agent alone. Two agents are required to act in common, jointly, each making a different contribution to the process. The result is not a personal achievement or production by either person taken singly but is precisely a common good. From the viewpoint of its progenitors a new child is one of the most striking examples of such a good.

To realize the significance of an action directed to a common good requires hard thinking. No amount of effort on the part of a man or a woman working alone will conceive a child. Conception is necessarily a joint activity of complementary agents, male and female. The end product is not a good of the individual person of either or both parents. This is why procreation is a much better name for the complete sexual process than reproduction. This cooperative act redounds to the good of the human species (a universal good), rather than to the private good of either parent. In a sense two persons who conceive and raise a child are performing a function in which they transcend their private interests. They do their part, not always with full consciousness of what they are accomplishing to ensure the continuity of the human race and the common welfare of mankind. It is not necessary for parents

[1] P. A. Bertocci and R. M. Millard, *Personality and the Good* (New York: David McKay Co., 1963), pp. 663–664.

fully to understand this except in cases where they contemplate
a modification of the procreative activity which contradicts its very
character. If they endeavor to "control" the act of sexual union
by deliberately making it nonprocreative, they are turning sexuality away from its potential contribution to the common good of
man and making it an instrument of their transitory private
pleasure.

The pleasure associated with sexual activity is wholly an individual and private good. One does not feel the pleasure that is
enjoyed by another person. The assertion has nothing to do with
the fact that one person may contribute to the pleasure of another.
If I enjoy hearing Menuhin playing the violin, he is certainly
contributing to my pleasure. There is even a certain mutuality
here, in that Menuhin's art is fulfilled, reaches its term, in the
enjoyment that he enables other persons to experience. Indeed, one
might well argue that a complete art experience usually involves
at least two persons, one of whom is active in the process of artistic
communication, the other comparatively passive but not inert.
Notice the word "communication." It suggests a sharing in something that is greater than an individual good. There is an aspect
of common goodness to the art experience. But the pleasure associated with this experience is not common; it is a private good. I
simply cannot feel the pleasure of another person.

Apply this to the act of sexual union. It, too, requires communication between two persons. The pleasure derived from it is a
private good for each of the persons involved. There are two
pleasures and not one joint or common pleasure. Unlike the art
experience which has no external product that is common, the
sexual experience does have a really common resultant. The child
is not the offspring of the mother alone, or of the father alone,
but the resultant of their peculiarly intercommunicative, common
activity.

To initiate an activity of this type that is by its very character
directed to a common good is to set in motion a joint human
activity of a very special type. Its peculiar character arises from the
fact that its goal is a new human being. The character is destroyed,
however, when the sexual act is performed for the sake of personal

pleasure alone, in such a way that the common good (the child) cannot result from the activity. Artificial contraception does this: it takes an action that is of its own nature ordered to a common good and turns it away from this common good toward a merely private good. It is not that personal pleasure is an evil thing — not at all. Rather, the point is that an action which has a common good as its goal becomes evil when performed in such a way as to make the attainment of this common good impossible.

In more technical language, now, let us express this, using the terminology of the end-of-the-work (*finis operis*) and the end-of-the-agent (*finis operantis*). The end-of-the-work of the medical art is the good health of the patient; this is the reason why there is such an activity, so that people may be restored to, or maintained in, health. On the other hand, the end-of-the-agent (the physician's private purpose) may be to make a good living for himself through the practice of medicine. Morally, an action is approvable when the end-of-the-work is good and the end-of-the-agent is not in contradiction with this end-of-the-work. Thus a physician who practices his profession for the money that he derives from it is not necessarily a bad physician. But one who practices in order to enjoy the pain of others (a sadist) is necessarily a bad physician. Where the end-of-the-agent is directly in conflict with the end-of-the-work, the resultant action is immoral.

Transfer this precision of terms to our problem. The end-of-the-work of sexual procreation is the existence of a child. A potential parent who engages in this action for the sake of personal pleasure (his end-of-the-agent) is not necessarily a bad parent. He only becomes immoral where he engages in this sexual activity for an end-of-the-agent that runs counter to the end-of-the-work of procreation. Such an end-of-the-agent is intended when the agent deliberately decides to engage in sexual intercourse in such a way as to exclude the possibility of procreation. In this case his personal aim conflicts with the goal of the activity in which he is engaged.

Contraception seems to me to be one of the plainest cases of the abuse of a natural function. It is more than an act of personal self-abuse (which is inherently immoral in any type of ethics); it

is a case of joint abuse of a common activity whose end is frustrated
in the very manner in which the action is accomplished.

Notice that I do not conclude that artificial contraception is
wrong simply for Catholics. I say that it seems to me to be wrong
for all human beings. The question of the religious affiliation of
the potential parent is incidental to the above argument. For a
Mohammedan, an atheist, or a Protestant to use contraceptives is,
to my mind, just as unreasonable as it is for a Catholic — provided
we are viewing this problem on a purely natural basis. The Catholic belongs to an ecclesiastical society that forbids contraception,
but that does not make contraception naturally immoral. His
Church also forbids him to eat meat on most Fridays, but there
is nothing naturally immoral about eating meat on Friday. We
are not dealing with some peculiarity of positive Church law when
we are talking about contraception; we are considering a proposal
that is intended to frustrate a natural process itself.

In contemporary ethical theory there is a standard of judgment
that is very widely accepted, the principle of generalization. It was
used, in one form, in Immanuel Kant's categorical imperative.
I do not think that it is the only standard of ethical judgment,
or even that it is the best, but it has considerable validity when
applied to problems involving interpersonal actions. Let us see
how it would work in regard to the problem of artificial contraception. In its simplest form the rule of generalization requires
that a morally good action be capable of being universalized
without entailing results that are obviously evil. Applied to a
contemplated act of murder, for instance, the principle of generalization would require us to ask: What would be the result if everyone in similar circumstances committed such an action? The answer is that it would be bad, and so this proposed action is bad.

Is artificial contraception good or bad according to such a
standard? Of course, if everyone practiced it all the time, there
would be no future for the human race. However, this degree of
generalization is not what is advocated by supporters of contraception. They suggest that adults should be free to make their own
decisions on the number of children that they will have. What
would happen if no one disapproved of artificial contraception?

This question is not easy to answer. My own answer is admittedly a mere opinion. I think that some potential parents would still want children, but that these would be in the minority. Of those who would like to have children, many would postpone conception from the early years of married life, until they felt that they would be better able to support a family. (Note that children born to parents over, say, thirty-five are less well endowed biologically and that older parents are less able to adapt to the rigors of parenthood than younger parents.) I doubt that the general use of cheap and effective contraceptives would provide enough offspring to maintain the human race in existence. And I think that underpopulation is just as much to be feared as overpopulation. In other words the generalization principle does not confirm the claim that artificial contraception is advisable.

It is not at all suggested that this is a valid argument against contraception. The generalization test is not automatically indicative of morality. I simply ask my readers to ponder the question for themselves: What do you think would happen to the human race if we could all, with complete impunity, avoid the obligations of parenthood while missing none of the personal advantages of married life?

A final word should be said concerning the use of the so-called method of rhythm. This is essentially the avoidance of sexual intercourse in periods when the potential mother is most likely to conceive. It requires considerable intelligence and skill in practice, and, of course, it cannot be claimed to be as effective a control of contraception as artificial contraception. First of all, people who get married and then practice the rhythm technique throughout their married life, so as to avoid having any children, seem to me to be immoral. I am supposing that they are in ordinary health and circumstances. It is simply unreasonable to do this. Married people who can have children should do so. This does not mean that they should have twenty children per family. Catholic moralists are now beginning to suggest that the injunction to "increase and multiply" should be tempered by a reasonable concern for the ability of parents to support and manage their children. I think potential parents should try to determine the number of

children that seems right to them, in their individual circumstances, and make that number their objective. There is no natural
ethical obligation to produce a large family.

Second, for a young couple to use the method of periodic abstinence to space their children according to some intelligent plan
does not seem to me to be immoral or unreasonable. What is the
difference between rhythm and artificial contraception, then? In
the case of rhythm a couple voluntarily abstains from the sexual
act at certain times, with the purpose of avoiding too many, or
too frequent, conceptions. At other times they engage in sexual
union in a wholly natural manner. If both husband and wife agree,
I see no reason for condemning their temporary avoidance of the
marital act. This is an abstention from sexual activity, a negative
decision that in no way disrupts a natural process. To my mind
such abstention is utterly different from initiating the process of
procreation by sexual union, while using some positive means to
interrupt the completion of the process.

If my readers do not understand this difference at this point, I
feel that little more can be said on the matter.

18. *Some Difficulties in Contemporary Ethics**

At the end of his recent book, R. M. Hare remarks:

> When South African believers in white supremacy read this book, will they at once hasten to repeal the past laws and make the blacks their political equals? This is highly unlikely; and in any case they will not read the book. To get people to think morally it is not sufficient to tell them how to do it; it is necessary also to induce in them the wish to do it. And this is not the province of the philosopher. It is more likely that enlightened politicians, journalists, radio commentators, preachers, novelists, and all those who have an influence on public opinion will gradually effect a change for the better — given that events do not overtake them. Perhaps people in areas of racial conflict can be, in the end, brought to think of the resemblances between themselves and members of other races as morally relevant, and of the differences as morally irrelevant. Perhaps, even, they may learn to cultivate their imaginations. But this much can be claimed for philosophy, that it is sometimes easier to bring something about if we understand clearly what it is we are trying to do.[1]

This quotation suggests several problems on which we might meditate, but I should like to concentrate on Hare's central claim: it is not the function of the philosopher to attempt directly to influence public opinion.

Whitehead once asked whether a man is justified in devoting his life to pure mathematics, apparently thinking that this sort of activity is close to being an endless game of solitaire, fascinating to the player but contributing little to mankind and perhaps no lasting compensation to oneself. My version of this question would be: Is a man justified in devoting his life to pure meta-ethics?

On one side of this problem lies the fear of activism, of over-

---

* Paper read to the Missouri Philosophical Association, October, 1965.
[1] *Freedom and Reason* (London: Oxford University Press, 1963), p. 224.

involvement in practical affairs. Doubtless many persons here considered going to Selma and then rejected the proposal for what appeared to be good reasons. Usually the philosopher who goes into politics, or starts writing on current social questions, or becomes the advocate of a special cause, seems to become less and less the philosopher. Impartiality and objectivity of judgment, it may be argued, demand that the philosopher — even the so-called practical one — remain somewhat aloof from participation in the affairs of his community. In other words, the ivory tower serves a purpose.

Nevertheless, I should like to argue that some philosophers who think about ethical problems should try to influence their fellowmen. I have put this so minimally that even Hare would probably agree with me. It is more a question of degree than of absolute disagreement that I would have you consider. It seems to me that philosophers in the Anglo-American tradition have retreated a little too far into the upper regions of their ivory towers — and Latin American and many European philosophers appear to be too much involved in the active life.

At a recent Thomistic Congress in Rome I read a paper on the notion of a finite God, as represented in the writings of some American thinkers who have come under the influence of Whitehead. I thought it might be a useful point of information to show that some quite able people differ from Thomists in their way of understanding the term God. The critical reaction of one Polish Thomist was startling to me but rather typical of several other comments. This man insisted that finite-God theorists are involved in a contradiction because the Constitution of the United States of America upholds an infinite God! Leaving aside the questionable merit of his assertion, let me simply say that it would not occur to me to use a political document to argue a point such as this. Evidently this indicates a difference of philosophical temperament in Europe and the United States.

In any case, this is my first problem: To what extent may, or should, a moral philosopher (an ethicist, ethician, or whatever) become involved in the practical life of his community? Is Hare's position of withdrawal the only valid one?

A second thing that puzzles me is the effort of some ethical thinkers to establish a sort of fixed scale of moral values. Parenthetically I am not sure that all of you know that value theory has recently received much emphasis in some textbooks and ethical studies stemming from Catholic writers. People such as De Finance, Fagothey, Messner, and others have shifted from natural-law language to that of axiology. Where formerly most value theorists in ethics were either idealists in the German-Austrian school or empiricists of the type edited in several works by Ray Lepley, there is now a growing group of realistic axiologists using the language of value to restate and perhaps further develop the kind of traditional ethics which orginated with Aristotle and Thomas Aquinas. I wonder what is gained by such a shift in terminology.

All of us have had the experience of attending philosophy meetings where some fellow presents his treasured scale of values. Let's say he claims that there are three obvious levels: at the bottom are the things that contribute to the physical health and well-being of the individual person; in the middle are the values which mark the mental, cultural, even spiritual perfecting of the person; and at the top are the values of the social community: justice, brotherly love, and so on. I am simply using this simplified scale as an example of the sort of thing that is often done.

The problem, of course, is how to justify such a ranking of values. I can see four ways of attempting this. The first is one of the oldest: one may claim that God has established and conveyed by some sort of revelation to men a set of moral standards. This is what T. E. Hill calls a theological approbative theory[2] and the very name suggests its weakness. If ethics must take its basic scale of values from another discipline, such as a certain type of theology, then it loses its autonomy and its right to be regarded as an independent study. Or one may put this difficulty another way: theological approbation can only be as good as the theology which backs it up, and can be acceptable only on the merits of that theology of which it is an extension.

A second way of validating a scale of values lies in the advocacy

[2] *Contemporary Ethical Theories* (New York: Macmillan, 1950), pp. 97–113.

of some sort of generally shared intuition of key values. Here I am not thinking of ethical intuitionism in the British sense popularized by G. E. Moore; whatever it is that a Britisher intuits in his ethics it is not a universal value — not "goodness" but simply "good." I do refer to the kind of thing found in Max Scheler or Nicolai Hartmann, and in modified form in some types of phenomenology. [3] Briefly, the claim of this intuitive approach to values is that one may come to appreciate a certain ranking of ethical standards by personal meditation on certain facts of inner experience and by some sort of process of distilling what is valuable from the introspective analysis of consciousness. Plato's story about the man emerging from the shadows of the Cave and rising to a personal vision of the Idea of the Good may be the original instance of this theory.

My question about this second approach to value is this: What good does it do to talk at a philosophy meeting about this wonderful intuition? Advocates of such an approach usually insist that it takes long training, many years of effort, and special gifts to achieve this vision of the good and the beautiful. It is hardly the kind of thing to be presented in twenty minutes or even in a one-semester course. If possible at all, this special intuition of values would seem to me to be the privilege of a necessarily small group of people.

The third way of finding a ladder of ethical values is that of the social utilitarian. One may simply take it that the society in which one lives embodies the best available ideals for human living. Plato also thought this way and it is the sometimes irritating procedure of many British writers on ethics. People like Nowell-Smith, Hare, Toulmin, and so on, usually insist that they deal with the logic of ethical discourse and deny special interest in a given moral code. However, examples must be given and positions taken for the sake of explanation and illustration. These illustrations nearly always reveal a sturdy bias toward the ideals of the educated Englishman. [4] Nowell-Smith makes no effort to conceal

---

[3] The second volume of Hartmann's *Ethics,* translated by S. Coit (New York: Macmillan, 1932), presents a complicated theory of moral values.

[4] Cf. Mary Warnock, *Ethics Since 1900* (New York: Macmillan, 1952), pp. 119–140.

his contempt for Hitler; Hare is equally transparent in his references to South African racism. Of course, this is not only true of British analytic writers: most of us who teach or write ethics use examples and points of view drawn from our contemporary society and culture; I do not know what else we could do. But this is rather different from a rather formal effort to rank values on the basis of the way that they are already ranked in popular opinion. The same thing was done by Rosenberg in Nazi Germany with just as much utilitarian logic as by Nowell-Smith in England. If social utilitarianism provides the standards of ethical judgment, then ethics becomes a sophisticated exercise in opinion sampling.

To me this last comment seems to apply also to the fourth approach to value, the experimental, statistical, social-science, investigation of prizing. Interesting work in this field has been done in the United States. I am thinking of studies at Harvard and Chicago to establish preference ratings in the aesthetic response of many subjects to selected paintings.[5] It is possible to develop scales of aesthetic valuations, possibly of moral evaluations, based on the statistical processing of many appraisals of given art objects, or moral activities. Indeed I am much in favor of more of this being done because it provides information about the moral climate of our world. In regard to the problem of censoring allegedly obscene materials, for instance, we have now no other dependable means of discovering the community standards of which the Supreme Court speaks so confidently.

My reaction to this empirical approach to values is not critical of the experimental or statistical method but of the value language itself in such a context. That is to say: one hundred opinions, or one thousand opinions, about an ethical question do not seem to me to become scientific or more reliable merely because they are treated statistically or depicted in elaborate graphs. The multiplication of aesthetic and moral opinions is not changed by calling the resultant a value. And I would say the same thing about recent Catholic efforts to translate a theory of moral ends, goods,

---

[5] Cf. Charles Morris, "Significance, Signification and Painting," in *The Language of Value,* ed. by Ray Lepley (New York: Columbia University Press, 1957), pp. 58–76.

and duties into value language. It is a matter of terminology, not a new approach to ethics.

If we turn, for a moment, to the radically different method of founding an ethics which has, since Kant, been called formalism, we encounter difficulties of another order. Formalistic ethics has not been very popular in this country but Marcus G. Singer has brought it to the forefront of attention.[6] He offers many statements of the generalization principle and associated arguments but his simplest formula is: "What is right (or wrong) for one person must be right (or wrong) for any similar person in similar circumstances" (p. 5). I hope I will not be judged hopelessly old-fashioned and even idealistic if I admit that much of Singer's argument appeals to me. Not that one can deduce a whole ethics from such a principle, without any further appeal to experience — Singer does not claim that and I would not either.

My difficulty with formalism reduces to this: granting that one can do something like what Singer proposes —"to lay the groundwork for a rational and normative system of ethics" (p. 6) — what utility would such a system have? Singer sees it as a means whereby "moral disputes can be rationally settled" (p. 6). But I think that only a small number of people in any era achieve the mental sophistication and impartiality of judgment required to appreciate Singer's high-minded argument. These are not the people most immediately involved in the real moral discussions of our time. (Wouldn't the problem of the use of nuclear weapons be a marvelous instance of the validity of Kant's categorical imperative — but who in public life will listen seriously to such reasoning?) So we are faced here with another version of the problem presented by Hare's position: no matter how logical or scientific an ethics may be, is it worth doing if it must remain the exclusive property of a highly educated elite?

Perhaps it was thinking such as this that stimulated Jean-Paul Sartre to take his odd ethical position. In a way he has done precisely the contrary of what Hare advises. Sartre has abandoned system-building and thrown himself into the maelstrom of moral, social, and political problematics. As might be expected, he finds

6 Cf. his *Generalization in Ethics* (New York: Knopf, 1961).

no ready-made answers for the questions of contemporary man. Instead, he keeps telling us that we must strive to be "authentic." In many books and plays this virtue of authenticity is presented as the kernel of moral endeavor but in the final analysis Sartre's message seems to be: "Do what you can in life and don't think that you can do very much." Sartre has little hope for the future of ethics:

> Either morality is stuff and nonsense or it is a concrete totality which achieves a synthesis of Good and Evil. For Good without Evil is Parmenidean Being, that is, Death, and Evil without Good is pure Nonbeing. To this objective synthesis there corresponds, as a subjective synthesis, the recovery of negative freedom and its integration into absolute freedom or freedom properly so-called. The reader will understand, I hope, that what is involved here is not a Nietzchean "beyond" Good and Evil, but rather a Hegelian *"Aufhebung."* The abstract separation of these two concepts expresses simply the alienation of man. The fact remains that, in the historical situation, this synthesis cannot be achieved. Thus, any Ethic which does not explicitly profess that it is *impossible today* contributes to the bamboozling and alienation of man. The ethical "problem" arises from the fact that Ethics is *for us* inevitable and at the same time impossible.[7]

The precise meaning of this diatribe may be a question open to much discussion. The book *Saint Genet* first appeared in French in 1952, and it seems to be far more revealing of Sartre's ethical nihilism than the more recent *Critique de la raison dialectique* (1960). In the earlier work he rejected systematic ethics in any form and also value theory.

> In an ethic of praxis, the Ego is not distinguishable from its possibilities and projects. It is therefore defined by the complex body of its decisions, which are supported by an original choice, and is revealed only in and by acts. It can be the subject of investigation and evaluation only afterward. As soon as I wonder, *before* the theft, whether *I* should steal, I detach myself from my undertaking, I am no longer at one with it; I separate the maxim of my act from my intuition of myself as if they were two separate realities, and I decide as to their suitability or unsuitability as if it were a matter of a necktie and a shirt. This abstract attitude is called *nobility;* it is ruinous for both the act and the man.[8]

[7] J.-P. Sartre, *Saint Genet* (London: Allen, 1964), p. 186.
[8] *Ibid.*, p. 187.

And then Sartre demolishes axiological procedure by using his principle of ambiguity:

> A value has, in fact, two contradictory exigencies: on the one hand, we must try to incorporate it into being, and, on the other, it requires that we situate it beyond any realization. The moral agent can satisfy this twofold exigency only, so it seems, by giving his life to realize the ethical imperative and by dying as a result of not having achieved his goal. Our social pantheon abounds in exemplary disasters.[9]

In the face of such statements, I wonder how anyone can maintain that there is an ethics of any kind in Sartre. Certainly he offers a critique of human existence, but does he not end with the proposition that life is all sound and fury signifying nothing? Yet the word has gone around that Sartre has something to say on ethical problems and many of our brightest young people are eagerly trying to discover his message.

I think that Sartre personally exemplifies the final problem that I would set before you. Granted that a philosopher can retreat too far into his ivory tower, granted that a rather perfectly developed system of abstract ethics may have little or no meaning for the majority of people — what is the price that one pays for moving to the opposite position of complete involvement in practical living? Is it necessarily such an extreme relativism of outlook that, in the final outcome, one must abandon all effort to describe the good life for man? If so, then I fear that the noble enterprise started in Athens by Plato and Aristotle has ended rather ignominiously in the hands of a little man sitting in front of the Deux Magots Café in Paris.

[9] *Ibid.*, p. 190.

Index

Absolutism, Catholic morality and, xviii
Abstinence, periodic sexual, 206
Abundance, economy of, 191
Abuse, of natural function, 203
Actions, essentially bad, 78; real context of human, 47; types of human, 182
Activism, fear of, 207
Adelmann, Frederick, 57 n
Affectiones theory of will, St. Anselm's, 57 f
Agent, the perplexed, 75 f; reasoning of the moral, 64 f
Albert, St., 59; on role of philosophy, 23; uses Augustine's *pondus* theory, 55
Ambiguity, existentialist, 214
Ambrose, St., 67
Anselm of Canterbury, St., defined justice as rectitude, 122; on justice as rectitude, 126; on original justice, 121; special meaning of *libertas*, 58; theory of two *affectiones*, 6; on two dispositions of will, 57 f
Anthropologists, interest in natural law, 110
Anthropology and human life, 175
Appetites, concupiscible and irascible, in Damascene, 56; non-Augustinian, 54; theory of plural, 56 f; theory of single, 54 ff
Appetition, rational and irrational, 56; theories of, 53 ff
Aquinas, St. Thomas, as not being an authority on modern abortion, 27; on decisions as to means, 86 ff; not definite on practicality of wisdom, 67; distinguishes philosophy from theology, 22; four meanings of *ratio*, 104 f; ignores the *pondus* theory of will, 55; on legal precepts, xx; on moral circumstances, xx f, 114; on

natural law, 103 ff; on the need for theology, 21; on participation in divine law, 100 f; and philosophy, 139; on private possessions, 184 ff; professional theologian, 16; realist view of natural law, 12; on religion as a natural virtue, 73; and situationism, xviii ff; special meaning of *boulesis*, 59; on subordination of sciences, 23; on synderesis, 6; on teleology, 80; theory of wisdom, 67 ff; three distinct appetites in man, 57; two views of justice, 125 f; value of his *Exposition of the Nicomachean Ethics*, 25 f; on virtue of justice, 122
Aristotle, 16, 20, 97, 129, 188, 214; on choice, 49; did not speak of *thelesis*, 57; on the end of man, 181; on five intellectual virtues, 69; on goal-directed activity, 80; hesitation on practical uses of wisdom, 67; naturalism of the *Nicomachean Ethics*, 124; on nature of justice, 126; *Nicomachean Ethics* never censored in thirteenth century, 24; owes nothing to Catholic theology, 24; St. Thomas' expositions of, 21; speculative character of *Nicomachean Ethics*, 5; theory of proof in *Posterior Analytics*, 3 f; treatise on *Physics*, 140; on wisdom in a virtuous life, 71; young people cannot learn ethics, 7
Aristotle's *Nicomachean Ethics*, self-perfectionism in, 52
Asch, S. E., 81 n
Atomic bombing, morality of, 183
Atomism of sense data, 147
Augustine, St., 12, 39, 67, 125 n, 137, 197; on appetitive dispositions, 6; on human appetition, 54 ff; ignorant of Aristotelian ethics, 24; and immutable laws, xv; "love and do what you will," xiv f

215

Socrates, 97, 176
Sophia, in Plato, 67
Space age, morality in the, 170 ff
State, as supreme lawmaker, 132
State of nature, primitive, 96 f, 108
Sterilization, morality of, 199
Stevenson, C. L., 10, 33 *n*
Stoics, natural law of, 12
Stroll, A., 33 *n*
Suarez, Francis, voluntarism, 127
Suitability, as test of goodness, 182
Summa Fratris Alexandri, 59
Summers, R. E., 160 *n*
Supreme goods, theory of two, 61 ff
Surgical operations, morality of, 198 f
Syllogism, cognitive moral and operative moral, 2; cognitive practical and operative practical, 64
Synderesis-principle, 40 f, 142; ("Good should be done, evil avoided"), 9; a special habit, 8; views of Bonaventure and Aquinas, 6

Teleology, ethics and, 181 f; and human life, 52; natural, 143 ff; in recent thought, 80 f
Television, censoring, 169
Tempier, Bishop Etienne, 16 f
Tendencies, human, 53 ff
Ten Hoor, Marten, 154 *n*
Thelesis, in Damascene, 56
Thelesis and *boulesis,* in Thomas Aquinas, 59
Theology and moral philosophy, 15 ff
Thinking machines, and human life, 173
Thomas, St., *see* Aquinas, St. Thomas
Thomism, in America, 178; as a philosophy, 139; and self-perfectionism, 39
Toner, Jules J., xvii *n*
Totalitarianism, restriction of individual under, 159
Toulmin, S. E., 31 *n*, 210
Transcendental good, unspecified, 60
Truman, H. S., decision to bomb Hiroshima, 84

Underpopulation, 205
Understanding, and sensing, 31
Universals, stripped, 110
Usury, relation to right to use, 188 ff
Utilitarianism, ethical judgment in, 36; social, 147

Valenciennes, Dominican Chapter at, 23
Values, Austrian theory of, 32; freedom as absolute, 157; empirical study of, 211; moral, 8; relational theory of, 37 f; Sartre on, 214; a scale of moral, 209 ff; subjective and objective, 46 ff; universality of, 32
Value theory, as approach to freedom, 45; and standards of judgment, 36
Van Doren, Mark, 156 *n*
Van Roey, J. E., 73 *n*
Varro, M. T., opinions on the end of man, 12
Verbeke, Gérard, 59 *n*
Vergil, 170
Virtue, wisdom as a practical, 67 ff
Voluntariness, 181; Aristotle on, 49 f
Voluntarism, legal, 123, 127; St. Thomas rejects legal, 126
Voluntas ut natura, 59 f
Voluntas ut ratio, 59

Warnock, Mary, 30 *n*, 210 *n*
Wars (s), censoring in time of, 160 ff
Wars of the future, 175 f
Weigel, Gustave, 112
Weiss, Paul, 123
White, Morton, 2 *n*
Whitehead, A. N., 207
White supremacy, belief in, 207
Will, Augustinian view of, 54 ff; divine, 56; interpreted differently by Bonaventure and Thomas, 61; justice and God's, 126
Will-act, specification of, 60; Thomistic analysis of, 69 f
Will to end, natural, 59 f
William of Ockham, 17; influence on philosophy and theology, 19; moral extrinsecism, xvi; voluntarism of, 127
Will and intellect, Aquinas on, 60
Will as nature, 59 f
Will of the people, 63
Will as reason, 59
Wisdom, the gift of, 71; of the heart, 73; its place in moral life and ethics, 64 ff; source of justice, 128
Wishing of an end (*boulesis*), 59
Witnesses, contradictions among scientific, 43 f
Wolfson, H. A., 56 *n*, 57 *n*
World citizenship, 172